all
this
wild
hope

sabina laura

Cover design by Luísa Dias
Edited by Alison Malee

ISBN: 9798558846157

longing

we all need
some measure of comfort,

the safety of a cocoon.

but i remind myself
that change is good,

that i cannot spend
my whole life
being a caterpillar,

that courage
wears butterfly wings
and the sky
has never looked
more inviting.

please don't be afraid
when i tell you
about this emptiness
i carry.

i am still so full of love.

i want the smile
with teeth showing.

i want the smile
shaped by honesty.

for my eyes to feel it
until it leaves wrinkles at the corners.

for my heart to feel it
until it smooths out the ache.

the one that breaks into laughter
and doesn't hide itself away.

the one that feels like
finally coming home.

there will always be
the bitter days.

sharp citrus
that stings,
that stains.

but i still bite into the fruit
to test if it's ripe,

i pour sugar over the ache
and pray it will become lemonade,

and i remember,
there will always be
the sweet days, too.

it is not always about
the light at the end of the tunnel.

mostly, it is about
stumbling through the blackness
but still believing
you will reach that light,
eventually.

i pray
that my bones
will not crumble
when i fall
back to earth.

and i pray
that, if they do,
i will not
bury myself
beneath
the wreckage.

i search for joy
in between the rise
and fall of every breath,
and find it. mostly.

remind myself
that it'll be easier
when spring arrives
and everything grows lungs.

i have rain in my eyes
and storms in my heart
but i still find the courage
to greet the sun every morning
and ask it for the same thing:

let me be all light today.

every day, i try
to make self-love
more of an ocean
than a stream.

i admit,
i have forgotten
to always remember
the most beautiful parts.

i have hidden them in pockets when
depression demanded my attention.

i have left them on the table
and not come back for them.

and i know
that just because i have hungry eyes
it does not mean

my belly isn't full enough already.

but gratitude is not always an easy thing
when it's there and sometimes
it does not show up at all.

but it's okay to forget
for a little while,

and when you do, know that
shame does not live there,
nestled in between the trying.

it does not belong.

i used to be
a collection of fault lines
and there was an earthquake
in my mouth.

my voice trembled
and this heart shattered every day
until one day it didn't.

they will label it *disaster*
but they do not know
the strength it takes to break,
the strength it takes to rebuild.

i am always trying
to be more than i am
instead of remembering
that what i am
is more than enough.

love should not need to be
an immaculate garden
that fits their expectations.

let it have thorns and weeds
because we have no need to pretend
we're perfect,

and i would always choose
wild and overgrown
over artificial.

let it be filled
with the sweet scent of honeysuckle,
unstoppable as it grows,

and birds and bees and butterflies
bursting with life.

let there be rain
but never so much it drowns us
and always enough sunshine
for us to grow.

let it always be a safe space
to bury our fears,

and let it be cared for
by untrained (but gentle) hands,

the kind that never give up waiting
for things to bloom.

you are not weak
if you collapse under
the weight at times.

some days
are just heavier
than others.

i wrap my fingers
around hope
and still remember
how to hold it
even after
all this time.

but that's the thing about hope.

even if you let it go
it will find its way back.

weeping
is not weak –

i hold
the weight
of mountains
in these eyes
before
they ever spill
over
into rivers.

i have a heart
full of lullabies
i never knew
how to sing,
and poems stuck
in the back of my throat
or caught
between my teeth.
but tucked away
between splintered ribs
and punctured lungs,
is the thought
that there are still
miracles to come.

i open all the windows
to let the light reach me,

but now i realise,

it is less about
letting the good things in,

and more about encouraging
fear to sneak out
of the back door.

the skyline melts into tomorrow and i become
a shadow, but even when i fade with the light, i
still exist. i wonder if they will notice, or if
they are too busy chasing their own indigo
skies. i try to find my own, but the only indigo
i find is this skin. perhaps i will always be
covered in bruises, and perhaps one day i will
not mind. because although it may seem like i
have disappeared into the night, i am leaving
footprints for those who look closely enough.

i don't want
hope to be just
a whisper.

i want it to be
so loud
that the windows
shatter.

and i want to remember,

it is not always bad
when something breaks.

the scent of rain
lingers long after
the downpour has passed,
and i want a love like that.

one that doesn't fade
even after the storm.

it is both
overwhelming
and beautiful

to be human,

to feel everything
so deeply,

to see the world
rose-tinted
and black and white
all at once.

despite the war
beneath this skin,
i think i could remember
how peace feels
if i try hard enough.

(i am still finding
that there is a home
beneath it, too).

i wake up
with deep bruises resting
beneath heavy eyelids,

but i still open them
no matter how much it hurts.

there are times
when i am too aware
of everything,

(especially
the lost things).

but i will never forget
all the ways
i have been held,

i will never forget
how well some days
have loved me.

i have my head in the clouds,
building castles in the air,
i throw pennies into fountains
and hope they land the right way up,
and whenever the night feels lonely,
i hold dandelion seeds in my palms
and blow wishes into the sky.

but the dreaming
will never be a waste.

when everything becomes too heavy,
it reminds me how to feel weightless.

i will always try
to hold tomorrow
with brave hands
even if the weight of it
almost crushes my bones.

there is not much good
to be said about grief, but
i will say this:

it would not exist
if we did not feel love
the way we do.

i will knock on every door
until one of them invites me in.

i will knock on every door
until one of them tells me
to hang up my coat,
put my feet up,
leave my keys on the table.

i will knock on every door
until one of them asks me
to stay.

i skip hope across the ocean.

it ripples,
as if to prove it's still there.

i skip hope across the ocean

and i know the waves
will bring it back.

i do not need love
to always be
beautiful bold flowers
that the world can see.

mostly,
i need it to be
thick roots
digging down
into the soil,
hidden away
but always there.

unbreakable.

i am
like the moon;

lost
in a sea of darkness
but knowing
i will return
to full.

isn't it beautiful, the living?

how we are always open mouthed
and carrying a song,
weaving promises into tomorrow
like a slow dance.

how we do not always
fall asleep with warm hands
but still hold a prayer for
wide morning smiles.

how we breathe every new day in
and ask it to be kind,
know that at least some of them
will rest in our lungs.

because isn't it beautiful, the living?

(close my eyes, take a deep breath),

even the parts we miss.
even the parts we never had.

i write about love
and ask it to stay.

i write about love
and realise:

if it's real,
it will.

one day,
i will know bravery
so well
that i'll wear it
as a second skin
and it will never feel
out of place.

- to make a home out of courage

sometimes, i see a glimmer of the world i want
to live in, one that doesn't know the meaning
of the word hate.

you see, there is so much light in this world,
but i think we have lost sight of what matters.

because what lives inside us is far more
important than what's on the outside. because
our skeletons look the same and one day, our
graves will, too.

because one hundred years from now, the
world will not know my name, and i will no
longer know the world.

because we are all living and dying with every
breath and forgetting how significant they both
are.

because no matter what god we are praying to
or what corner of the earth we call home, we
are all looking up at the same moon and asking
her for a little more light.

and sometimes, i see a glimmer of the world i
want to live in, one that doesn't know the
meaning of the word hate.

you see, there is so much light in this world,
and i think it will shine even brighter when we
remember what really matters.

some nights,
the memories still find me
in my sleep,

but i have spent too much time
being a graveyard.

in some ways,
i will always be haunted,

but for the most part,
i take comfort in knowing:

the things we have loved
always find a way
to come back to us.

i let the bitterness fall
from my eyes;

it is better than keeping it
inside my heart.

years ago,
i took a breath
and it settled at the bottom
of my lungs,

buried itself with the answers i seek
and the stories i have yet to tell.

but i drag myself into the light
over and over,

keep climbing despite
the growing pains,

always keep one eye on hope,

(and wait for an exhale).

i paint the walls
of my mind
with positivity,
sprinkling light
wherever i can,
and remember
that the ache
is just a sign
of the way things
are healing.

THINGS I AM NOT

i am not / always this war / a place for fear to
live / a burial ground for hope / a garden of
weeds / an apology for any part of myself / the
things i fall back into / the things i cannot keep
hold of / the grief i carry / the darkness within
me / my thoughts / my unfulfilled dreams / just
a memory / a shadow / a ghost / anything less
than i should be.

THINGS I AM

i am / hummingbird wings / strong yet delicate
/ a slow tide / when i want / a tsunami / when i
need / sunset flooded cheeks / blushing warm
with joy / crescent moon lips / that hide no
midnight / in the corners / eyes that hold
galaxies / bones made of stardust / that know /
they are more than a skeleton / of my past self
/ *enough* / *enough* / *enough.*

i will unravel
at the smallest bump in the road
and wonder if they'll understand
the tenderness of limbs searching
for their way home.

maybe they will not see how
we put ourselves back together
even though some pieces
no longer fit,
are missing,
are sharper edged this time.

but we always do.
we always do.
we always do.

learning

i change like the seasons
but i will never apologise
for my winters.

they are the reason
i know how to grow.

i have faith
that wings can grow
from wounds,
that soft feathers will
replace these scars,
that i can teach myself
how to rise
like a phoenix
from the ashes
of what burnt me.

bite your teeth into the day
and do not worry about the wound.

dig your nails in
and do not worry about the dirt.

let every moment
sink into your skin

and every breath
sink into your lungs.

meet hope at every sunrise
and joy at every sunset.

s l o w   d o w n

do. not. miss. a. thing.

for every time
i remember
how it feels
to be drowning,

i remember
how it feels
to be saved.

i used to think
that finding peace meant
everything would fall
silent.

but now i realise
it is more about
falling in love
with the noise;

feeling the calm
even in the chaos.

i am choosing /

to search for joy / in everything / and hold it
close /

to surround my heart / with the things that help
it beat / a little easier /

to stop allowing fear / to be the narrator / of
my story /

to still believe / in miracles / even when they
are not happening to me /

to remember / that even in the dark /
everything is beautiful / it just takes a little
longer / to see it.

i tried retracing my steps
to get back what i lost,
but it only ever taught me one thing:

you must always move forward.

it's okay
if there are days
when you can't leave
your home,
your bed,
or your mind.

it's okay to say
i will try again tomorrow.

- on mental health

you would not place
a dead flower
in the soil,
water it,
show it the sun,
and expect it
to grow.

so why do you do that
with dead relationships?

a promise:

the heaviness in your chest
may not feel weightless,
but it *will* become lighter.

the possibilities
became an orchestra of fear
conducting my life.

i forgot
that every negative outcome
also has a reverse.

now, i am trying
to remember
to just enjoy the music.

pain visits, of course it does,
but it does not live here.

it does not make a home out of me.

today,
i will be braver
than i was yesterday.

tomorrow,
i will be braver
than i am today.

even the smallest steps
bring you a little closer
to where you want to be.

do you see all the things
that are worth saving?

do you see all the things
that *aren't*?

but that's the best thing
about breaking –

when we begin to heal,
we get to choose
which pieces
to leave behind.

i remember that
i cannot be spring all the time,
but autumn has always felt more like
a new beginning to me, anyway.

learning to love myself better
is a work in progress,

but it still looks like such lovely art
when i started with a blank canvas.

healing is bittersweet / like / waking up before
the sun / on a sunday morning / lemon and
sugar pancakes / for breakfast / the scent of
summer rain / after a heatwave / the new
beginning / that follows an ending / sad tears
followed by / the sweetest laughter / times of
darkness / but *so much light.*

do not confuse the two –

i am full of riot,
not war.

there is no road
that leads straight to healing,
no fast lane or easy route.

instead,
there are back roads,
indirect and slow.
there are dead ends
and crossroads,
potholes and roadworks.

but i have atlas eyes
and a compass heart.

i am on my way home.

they tell me
i must learn to be
unbreakable,
but when seeds
fall away from
the wildflower,
she finds another place
to bloom.

i have been
the ocean
and the shore.

the lighthouse
and the storm.

the salt.
the wound.
the gauze.

the ship
and the wreck.

the wave
and the seabed.

the rise.
the fall.
the rest.

always be kind.

after all,
most hearts
are home
to some kind
of pain.

search for joy in everything / ripe blackberries
/ at the edges of country lanes / guitar strings /
watercolour paints / driving into a tangerine
sky / and leaving the past behind / coffee shop
hum / old book smell / all the colours of spring
/ melting the winter frost / daisy chains /
honeybees / between breaths / and the lines of
a poem / build new homes for it / and move
your heart in / whether they're ready for you /
or not / and when you find it / save it for later /
save it for tomorrow / *never* / *let* / *it* / *go*.

it is okay
to dig up your roots
if they are all tangled up
in grief.

i am not saying
we forget the wounds.

some still pull us in
like black holes.

but when i run a fingertip over
the bump of the scar,
i trace constellations.

and when i want
to hide in the dark,

the stars illuminate the sky
to remind me that honesty
is the most important part
of healing.

when the day is unkind,
i become a parachute,
always floating somewhere.

in this way,
i know that falling
will be a soft landing.

the bad things have a habit
of making themselves known.

they shout and scream in your face
until you have no choice but to listen.

the good things, however,
can be harder to find.

they often hide themselves away,
becoming lost as they fall quiet.

until you remember them.
until you choose to search for them.

coax them out of their hiding places
and brush away the cobwebs.

and then, the sound of them
will fill the room.

our lungs felt
entwined
for so long
but every day
i take back
a little more
of this breath.

it belongs only to me.

forgiveness
comes like the rain
but we only
need a little
to help us grow –
too much
will simply
drown us.

when i outgrow myself,
i shed my skin.

let the layers
that no longer serve me
fall away
and find a new beginning
underneath.

but that's the beauty of life:

whenever you need to,
you can start again.

pick the locks
on their closed door.

let yourself in
with gentle hands.

leave footprints
(the good kind).

and weave kindness
into every space.

some
things
must wilt
for better
things
to grow.

sometimes
you must let anger
be water
through your fingers
and teach yourself
to instead hold
only kindness
in your fists.

- anger is for letting go of

it is true
that some things will let you go.

but do not let yourself
settle like dust
in forgotten places.

you are always worth holding.

you have to burn them,

those thoughts
that eat away
at your happiness.

you have to burn them,

so you can rise
like a phoenix
from the ashes.

i will not forget
the places
i no longer belong,
keep them safely
tucked away
in the attic
of my mind,

but i will only
visit
occasionally.

i will not
live there
anymore.

the day
is a hurting thing,
but i let it stay,

and this,
this is how we begin.

let your voice
echo like thunder.
cause hurricanes.
create tidal waves.

let your voice
be a storm
they cannot ignore.

i have turned crash landings
into more than just a wreckage
and always found something to save.

i refuse to keep defining myself
by all the things i've lost.

my heart is dancing
w i l d e r
under the silver moon
and i open my eyes
w i d e r
to let all the light
fall through.

healing looks different some days.

like tears on my pillow
and sad songs on repeat.

but i have spent a lifetime
getting back up,

carrying on
with grazed knees
and scraped palms,

because it is such a brave thing,
to keep believing
that something good
is around the corner,
even though
it may not look the same.

i am finding comfort
in the stillness
that surrounds me,
making peace
with the gentle beating
of my own heart.

because
silence is not always
an emptiness.
silence is not always
something that needs
to be filled.

some days are heavy with sorrow
and god, do they weigh me down,

but always, i rise again.

one of the most important lessons
life has taught me
is how to fill every space
with more of me.

(and oh, how i am still learning).

too many dreams
have fallen from these eyes
and my heart
never wants to let go.

but it wasn't always this way –
i used to believe
that there was nothing
hopeful eyes couldn't reach,
until one day the world
came crashing down around me.

but as i pull dust and debris
from the wreckage,
i remember:

i have been rebuilding
all my life.

one more broken dream
will not defeat me.

never graze your knees
by begging them to stay.

the things that want to leave
will always find a way.

some days,
the prayers are louder.
violent things,
chewed up and spat out.

but on the good days,
my smile
gets caught up
in my eyes.

on the good days,
i reach out
and everything
reaches back.

before you speak,
always remove the sting.

let kindness coat your words
like the sweetest honey.

healing is about
the undoing.

the unlearning
of thought processes.

the unravelling
the pain into
something smaller.

the letting go
of what weighs us down
but still knowing about wholeness.

because the truth is,

you can leave pieces behind
and not miss them.

you can leave pieces behind
and not feel empty.

joy and i do not speak
for weeks at a time.

i often struggle to believe
that there is something beautiful
on the other side of this darkness

(that there is anything at all).

but joy is quiet at times,
more whisper
than wildfire.

a flicker.
a yawning dusk.
a small bird learning to sing.

a slow tide
but an open mouth.

a wind i cannot see,
but how it moves me,
how it finds its way
into everything.

so although
joy and i do not speak
for weeks at a time,

always,
in some small way,
it is there.

unfurl your fingers
one by one,
loosen your grip
on this fear,
and instead,

dig your hands
into the dirt
and feel yourself grow.

healing

the poems
are my lungs;

they breathe life
back into me.

the day will wake you
with so much light
that yesterday will not
cast a shadow,

which is to say,

today is a different story.

you tell me i am home,
and so i plant flowers
and leave a light on.
i write welcome on the doormat,
pop the kettle on,
plump the cushions.
and you do not seem to mind
that sometimes i let the flowers wither
and my eyes adjust to the dark.
and if i forget about
doormats and kettles and cushions,
i know you will not mind.
because i will always remember
to leave at least a window
open for you,
and you are welcome to stay here
however long you like,
if only you don't mind the mess.

i am redefining happiness,
claiming it as mine,
breaking it up into
a thousand smaller
more achievable pieces.

if you ever feel
insignificant,
remember how
you stitched your world
back together
with nothing but
your own hands
and a thread
of hope.

now i know
why things fall apart –

so they can realign
how they were meant to be.

when the ache / is a suffocating thing / i
remind myself / that even on these days / the
sun still rises / and the birds still sing / there
are still favourite songs / and forgotten songs /
breakfasts in bed / and dinner dates /
handwritten letters / love notes / new dreams /
old films / cosy nights in / road trips /
sunflowers / moonflowers / and there is still
poetry / *oh* / *what poetry there is* / *to come*.

these stories we wear –

scars,
stretchmarks,
wrinkles,

are wrongly labelled
as imperfections.

but aren't they such beautiful,
courageous signs
of how we have lived?

do you see
how the morning is ripe with hope?

bite into it.

i can understand laughter in any language
and feel the meaning of a song
without knowing the lyrics,

i know that the love spilling
out of warm eyes
does not need an explanation,

and the hands that keep
reaching for me are wonderful,
even in their quietest moments.

what i am trying to say is that
of course the poetry is glorious,
but the living is where we find it.

his love
feels very much
like gravity
yet
very much
like learning
to fly.

- *the perfect balance*

i have a wildfire heart.

i won't let their rain
extinguish the spark in me,

and i am no longer afraid
of burning bridges.

they show me
what they think
the end of the world looks like,
but i will no longer
p a u s e
just because
they tell me to.

i trace my scars
with a fingertip
and untangle them
into an atlas.

because this is a road
i must walk alone,
but it doesn't have to be lonely.

i only need myself to show me the way.

today,
i am wearing gratitude
like daisies in my hair,

because through it all,
there has always been
some kind of love.

i have spent
a lifetime wanting
to be invisible,
and i am still breaking
into myself
like a pair of new shoes.

finding comfort
within my own skin
is taking so much time,

but i have walked so far
on this path
that it is beginning to feel
like coming home.

but always,
the road stretches out ahead
like a promise
and i cannot help
but chase it.

perhaps
this open road dreaming
almost looks
like running away,

but i swear,
i am just wildly
chasing tomorrow.

the past
is a kaleidoscope of memories
but time alters their hue,

and we cannot paint the future
when we do not know
its colours yet.

all we know for certain is now,

so i let my eyes focus only
on every shade of today,

vibrant
and incredible
and *here.*

when i choose to let it in,
i find that joy fits perfectly
beneath my skin.

and in time,
it will write a new story
on my bones.

what a wonderful thing it is,
to wake up every day
with a heart searching for you
and knowing you are always
within reach.

my world threatens to split open
but it is no longer a sinkhole.
it no longer takes and takes.

these foundations i have built
stay steady, no matter how much
the ground beneath me shakes.

this love,
it has not changed.
it has not aged.

just grown and grown

and grown.

they ask where the words come from
and i tell them that i am a sky
who cannot hold her rain.

they try to tell me
that nothing grows from a flood,
but i do not hear.

i am busy unfolding myself,
like the way the clouds
fill the sky before a storm.

i am made
in equal measures
of grit
and grace,
salt
and smile,
flowers
and fire,
diamonds
and dust,
woman
and wild,
softness
and strength.

some days
i am more hurt
than human

but always
more hope
than hurt.

i hold the day in my mouth,
peach-coloured and dripping honey,
and for once, it does not taste
like an apology.

we have known this love
from the start.

we have known it like
the backs of our hands,

the feel of lips curving
into a smile.

we have known it like
chasing sunsets
into tomorrow,

like staying
despite the dark.

we have known it like

looking for nothing
and finding everything,

even with eyes closed.

even in the quiet, damp,
forgotten places.

and perhaps
the most beautiful part of all,

i think we know this love
like tomorrow.
like the day after that.

like always.

the sun
always comes back,
letting her silhouettes
fall on my skin
as the trees dance
with the light.

all along,
it is as if
she never left.

how incredible our hearts are,
rebuilding time and time again.

she dances
in the moonlight
and doesn't care
whether anybody
is watching,
and when they call her
a lost soul
she will remind them:
she is not lost,
she is free.

forgiveness is
as light as a feather.

this is how
we grow our wings.

this is how
we find our freedom.

every star represents
another reason to stay,
and tonight, the sky is full.

i read
your palm lines
like an atlas
and finally
i have found my way
home.

slowly but surely,
hope creeps in
like the sunlight
that finds its way
even to the deepest parts
of the forest.

it is a slow thing,
but eventually
the pain inside
falls quiet
until
you almost
cannot hear it.

these eyes have known love
from the day they opened.

she is the sun,
painting my world
in shades of autumn,
and i am always
climbing mountains
to reach her light.

but she points me
in the right direction,
showing me how to rise
no matter the season

and i remember
that this heart knew love
long before it knew light.

- mother

an encyclopedia / a completed crossword / a
film camera / a vapour trail /

the tree trunk / the root / the entire garden /

the scent of coffee / engine oil / nectar / freshly
cut grass /

the sound of train tracks / music / full-bellied
laughter / spilling over / into everything.

- things that remind me of my father

one day,
the light will find you
and you will not
have to reach for it.

this mouth
will never again
shape into
an apology
for myself.

the hurting is a temporary thing.

see already how time
is pushing the pain further away?

how at a distance,
it looks smaller, simpler,

as if one day,
it might disappear entirely.

as if one day,
you will look back
at the way you survived
and call it a miracle.

as if one day,
you will realise:

the days don't ache like they used to.

it may be bruised,
but it still holds a softness.

like the winter sky,
like forgotten fruit,
like so many hearts.

your love is like spring;
breathing life back into
forgotten things.

like a moon
that needs time
away from the world,
we are not always full
but, my love,
we are never empty.

when they see
how the dandelions grow
through the cracks
in the gravel,
they call them weeds
and not miracles,
but i have always admired
the way they persist.

the sky is never afraid
when the light goes.

she is nocturnal
like these eyes,
like this heart.

i will
no longer hesitate
at mirrors,
no longer cover
this body in apologies,
no longer feel ashamed
of the space it takes up.

i will spill
over into everything
and feel no guilt.

i have spent
countless nights
falling apart
as this thundercloud heart
carves rivers below my eyes.

but dawn always comes,

breaks open
with a smile,
speaks with soft hands,

becomes a story
when we are brave enough
to ask her to stay.

i am made of flowers,
the kind that always grow back
even after the frost.

no matter
how many storms
pass through it,
this heart is still
a gentle thing.

i hold poems
between my fingertips
at all times,

weave words together
until they look something
like hope.

and i find them
everywhere i look,

but on the worst days,
it is always the words
that find me.

this is not a poem.

this is a soft prayer
(to anyone willing to listen).

this is something to hold onto
when the light fades.

this is setting free the ghosts
that live inside my ribcage.

and, most of all,

this is an exhale
after so long.

despite everything,
my palms
are always open
to the sky
with all this wild hope
beneath my skin.

Thank you for giving
my words a home.

Follow on social media:
@sabinalaurapoetry

Sabina x

Also by Sabina:

Moonflower

A Little Sunshine and A Little Rain: A Poetry Journal

.

Printed in Great Britain
by Amazon

32800363R00098

DARKHAVEN

For Hugh and Audrey

BY

JACKIE LOGAN

Grosvenor House
Publishing Limited

The right of Jackie Logan to be identified as the author of this
work has been asserted by him in accordance with Section 78
of the Copyright, Designs and Patents Act 1988

The book cover picture is copyright to Inmagine Corp LLC

This book is published by
Grosvenor House Publishing Ltd
28-30 High Street, Guildford, Surrey, GU1 3EL.
www.grosvenorhousepublishing.co.uk

A CIP record for this book
is available from the British Library

ISBN 978-1-78148-356-5

Acknowledgements

- With a deep debt of gratitude to Christine Ashby for a wealth of literary insight, erudition and encouragement.
- To Frederick Tweed for constant belief and support.
- To Jack and Nessa Humphries for input and interest, Joan Burns for a helping hand and Carl Stapleton for early work.
- To the staff at Grosvenor House Publishing for professionalism and efficiency.
- And to Peter for all our yesterdays and the beginnings of a sentence.

A community can live in fear of many things – an earthquake or hurricane, an outbreak of disease, an economic recession, or even some seductive serial killer picking off its unwitting residents. The people of Whitehaven lived in fear of few, if any, of these threats to the disruption to their lives. They lived securely in their small seaside town, guarded to the south of the bay by a great stone promontory – the Blah Hole – set high up on the hill above, and by the lighthouse which commanded the black basalt cliffs to the north. They lived uneventfully, the inheritors of the grand Edwardian houses which lined the promenade and of the grander architectural homes which swept up towards the cliffs, built many years ago by the rich doyens of society.

Time of course had brought change and changes in fortune. Some of the grand old houses no longer remained in the hands of the old Whitehaven families. They had been purchased by outsiders – professionals with expendable incomes – in search of peace and quiet, a safe place to raise their children, and an easy commute to their working lives in the city. The newcomers had been drawn too by the allures long forgotten by the outside world, for the seaside town's tourist trade had long since departed for the shores of Spain and Greece and further, in search of more exotic adventure. The once famed coastal walk – running along the shore front and spiralling up the Blackhead cliffs to the lighthouse – was magnificent, if badly neglected by the local council, but it could still be walked. It had not quite yet fallen victim to the tyrannies of Health and Safety. They were fortified by the sea air – fresh and bracing – and the sea itself both calmed and exhilarated the senses, occasioned by the weather. A small coterie of local shops, where they were greeted and enquired about, provided for their weekly needs and there were clubs and societies to be joined for recreation. Entertainment was however limited. The picture house was long since gone and the last remaining hotel, having been converted into a lucrative private nursing home, now housed the elderly and infirm. One public house, the Whitecliff Inn, served as a gathering place for those in need of sustenance, and the many churches, if they chose to attend, sustained the soul. It was a good place to live, a safe place, unthreatened by the outside concerns of the world.

Unthreatened too were the old Whitehaven families. They accepted the newcomers into their circles but not wholly into their society. They were in Whitehaven but they were not of it. Old Whitehaven lived its life, as it always had, perpetuating the past in the present. Landmarks and roads were referred to by their age old names and not by latter day signage. Shops were known by the names of the long dead and the newcomers' rights of home ownership went largely unacknowledged. 'Ah, Miss Turtle's house, ah the McKibbens' house,' they were politely informed on introduction, as their successors would be, after the present occupants had moved away to further their careers or to follow their children, when they moved on and up.

Old Whitehaven, at the turn of the new millennium, lived unashamedly in a past world. They privately enjoyed the moniker disparagingly given to their town, in an unremembered time, by some unremembered wordsmith. They were indeed all 'pianos, pearls, and no washing on the line'. They lived in fear of no natural disaster, no global contrivance and no threat from any outside force. Their fears came only from within – the fear that someday an insider, would not only hang their washing on the line, but would wash their dirty linen in public for all of the outside world to see.

1

Maybelle Mountjoy was unaccustomed to receiving telephone calls on a Sunday afternoon and was displeased that her telephone would ring at any time on a Sunday at all – she was old school Presbyterian. Her home help, as help was called these days, but whom she employed privately, had already departed. Wilma was a capable woman, who performed her duties without intrusion or over familiarity, and was moreover a good, plain cook. Maybelle had enjoyed two tender lamb cutlets, three small new potatoes and a spoonful of garden peas. The mint sauce, freshly made from her garden, had been especially pleasing. When Wilma left, Maybelle was still sitting in the veranda where she liked to take Sunday lunch looking out over the sea. She was now finishing off a small glass desert bowl of sweet rice pudding. She had a good appetite for her age.

In the spring and summer months the veranda was her favourite room in the house – a space enclosed by a panorama of windows from which she could survey the entirety of the bay. She had positioned herself in a corner which trapped the afternoon sun. There she could sit unseen by the walkers who passed along the top cliff path. Today, the Sunday Telegraph lay beside her on a sun chair and although the newspaper was delivered early in the morning, it was left unopened until Church had been attended and Sunday lunch served.

Maybelle Mountjoy was a woman who kept to her routines and who, in her eightieth year, preferred to keep to herself. She had not, however, withdrawn altogether from society. In the summer months she could still be found, on occasion, at the bowling green, observing a tournament whilst taking tea in the pavilion. She no longer played but continued to accept an annual invitation to throw the first bowl of the season on Ladies' Opening Day. She was still called upon to present the Edward Mountjoy Memorial Trophy on prize giving day, following the regatta, and attended some other annual events in the yacht club, of which she was an honorary life member.

It was just as she reached for her reading glasses, on this bright spring Sunday afternoon that the telephone rang. Maybelle considered not answering, but the persistent clanging could not be borne, and with increasing irritation she walked through to the vestibule. To her even greater irritation the caller was Dilys Bishop, whom she disliked. Maybelle considered her an insubstantial woman, a woman who talked for talk's sake and who discussed personal matters seemingly at will. Dilys' children were delivered over and over again in gruesome detail around countless social tables. Her personal battle with the menopause and her interminable treatments were also a constant topic. 'Do stop me if I've told you this before,' was a mere precursor to the story being relayed yet again at length. She was also one of those unfortunates who followed every utterance with an involuntary hooting laugh, no doubt the manifestation of a nervous disposition, but it was nonetheless extremely grating. She was also, Maybelle considered, disdainfully, a 'joiner'.

Dilys had arrived in the town some thirty years before from England, with her Oxford educated husband who had taken up a lectureship at the newly created Polytechnic in Jordanstown, some ten miles away. They had bought the Deacon's House, a fine Victorian property and one of the oldest in Whitehaven, which was more than big enough to accommodate them, their three children, various pets and the lecturer's large library of books.

'Dilys Bishop, the bishop in the Deacon's House', was her favoured form of introduction – a rather weary witticism – followed invariably by a self-congratulatory hoot. Two of the children, who were almost in their majority when they had arrived in Whitehaven, had long since departed, and nothing would be known of their achievements, other than that their adoring mother took every opportunity to regale an oft times captured audience. The third child and referred to fondly as the 'after-thought' was also gone, travelling the tediously well-worn path of the gap year student. The various pets were long since dead, as was the lecturer's experiment with small town life. He had returned to the mainland many years ago, accompanied by neither wife nor child, but with a willowy young student from his American literature class. The despised Juliette, as they had been told, was now the mother of a second family of younger Bishops. Dilys had lost her husband but had kept the Deacon's House and her children kept occasional contact although they rarely visited. She had also kept the

3

lecturer's large library of books, a bitter-sweet act of revenge.

It was not because of the departure of the lecturer, the children, or the pets that Dilys had become a joiner – she had always been inclined towards it. On arrival in Whitehaven she had immediately joined the tennis club and the yacht club and had forced her way onto the parents' committee of the local primary school where the fond after-thought attended. In latter years she had joined the bowling club, the art club, the gardening society and the community association. Over her many years of joining Dilys had been elected to various positions – secretary, treasurer, and vice-president – protesting her inadequacies rather too feebly, Maybelle thought, before accepting office. Until now a presidency had escaped her. How had Whitehaven ever managed to survive without her? It was a question which Dilys on occasion asked herself.

'Hi Maybelle,' the overly cheery voice said down the telephone, 'it's Dilys.'

Maybelle responded with a good afternoon, which now it most decidedly was not. Dilys over familiarly enquired about her health and reminded her that the book club would meet at the Deacon's House the following Friday evening at eight o'clock. Maybelle had never invited Dilys to address her by her Christian name and the taking of this liberty irked. There were few people left in Whitehaven, or on this earth, who were accorded the privilege. She listened without response. Although somewhat advanced in years there was nothing wrong with either her health or her memory.

The book club somewhat new to the town, inspired by Dilys, the self-appointed president. Maybelle had first become aware of its existence when loud and unavoidable posters had appeared around the town. Personal approaches had been made to her, and to the other ladies in her circle, persuading them at length of the merits of joining. Maybelle had not been persuaded, although others had obviously succumbed to Dilys' persistence, the names of who she was now relating down the telephone. She was informed that, amongst others, Lillian Livermore and Marjorie Day would be there as would Mrs Lockhart, her near neighbour, who could surely pick her up and take her home again, if it were difficult for her to get there under her own steam, no less. Saved to last, was the information, delivered in an excitable rising pitch, that the minister's new wife would pop in and how it was a wonderful opportunity for them to get to know her. If that was a further bid to persuade an appearance it was utterly misguided. Maybelle had disapproved of the minister's divorce and had no intention of lending support by befriending his new wife. She kept her thoughts on the matter to herself as Dilys rattled on, dearly hoping that she would at last join them, and adding that, not to worry, the evening was as much a social gathering as anything else.

Maybelle Mountjoy was not worried. Throughout the entire monologue, neither the title nor the author of a book had been uttered. It was not a surprise. She did not need to hazard an even uneducated guess that some work of fiction from the best seller list would be briefly discussed before a rapid descent into gossiping around the promised supper. Her only surprise had been in the dropping of the names of those expected to attend. She would have thought that Norma Lockhart, at least, would have been more discerning.

When finally a breath was drawn on the other end of the telephone Maybelle determined to bring the unwelcome interruption to a close. She thanked Dilys for the invitation, wished them all a pleasant evening but declined, citing a previous engagement. She was just about to replace the receiver when that abhorrent expression was uttered – a prolonging device and a means of introducing the real intention of a conversation. Those three little words were never truly innocent.

'By the way,' Dilys said, 'have you seen the paper yet?'

Maybelle replied that she had not as yet *read* the newspaper, the telephone having disturbed that very intention, and hoped that the irritation in her explanation would register. It appeared that it had not, as Dilys carried on regardless, hooting and screeching, until finally the real intention of the phone call had been delivered. Maybelle replaced the receiver and made her way back to the veranda.

Dilys had revealed that whilst sitting over breakfast she had turned immediately to the book section of the newspaper. It was nothing to do with her being president of the book club – she had always been an avid reader of the book reviews – but now more than ever she needed to keep up with the latest publications. Everyone had different interests and tastes – Mrs This loves her romances, Miss That likes her crime, and Mrs So and So can't do without her Maeve Binchy. It was really never ending although she wasn't complaining. And it was when she got to the latest paperback section that she saw it, right there in front of her on page thirty three – the featured book. She couldn't believe it at first. She didn't believe it now. It was the illustration on the book jacket which had caught her eye, something very familiar about it – the line of the bay, the promenade, the tall Edwardian houses, and then there it was up on the hillside under the bluff, surely it was, her very own Deacon's House. She was right, she was sure, and once she had read the review she knew there could be no mistake. Someone had written a novel set in Whitehaven. Well the town wasn't called Whitehaven, it was called Darkhaven, but there was no doubting it. And the funniest thing, the thing that would interest Maybelle, was the title of the book, 'The Montgomerys of the Mount'. So funny since she was a Mountjoy of The Mount. Wasn't it funny? It couldn't just be a coincidence could it? She had the paper right here beside the phone, would she like her to read the review out to her?

'No thank you,' Maybelle managed to interject, before a further streaming invitation to attend the book club concluded with an extended hoot, during which Maybelle replaced the receiver and returned to the veranda. Having stood for a moment looking out over the bay, she took her chair and turned her attention to the newspaper.

She leafed through the various news items of the week, none of which interested her particularly, and skipped over the society columns, populated with unknown celebrity names. She read an article about an inheritance case concerning one of the stately homes of England, and details of an illegitimate claimant, which was of interest. As always she read the gardening and business supplements which she kept and discarded all the other extras, sorting them into a neat pile for Wilma to dispose of during the week. She sat back in her sun chair and turned to the cryptic crossword. Her afternoon was taken care of.

2

The plane started its descent over the Irish Sea. He had requested a window seat and had hoped for a clear day. He was not disappointed. The coastline was now in view and as the plane banked, preparing for its final descent over Belfast Lough, he strained to see out of the window. Below, the old familiar landmarks were clearly visible – the lighthouse, the cliff face, the bay. It had been a long time.

He took a taxi from the airport, an affordable extravagance. The driver chatted for a while, but he responded unenthusiastically to the homely banter and turned to the window. The morning rush hour was over and they passed quickly into the city and up onto a flyover above the docks – the waterfront below rejuvenated with modern apartment blocks and a leisure complex, declaring recovery and confidence. To the left, impressive glass-sheeted office blocks momentarily screened his view of the city. He caught a glimpse of old Belfast behind them. They drove away from the city, skirting the sea along the motorway – once distinctive boroughs now subsumed by urban sprawl, hemmed by industrial estates and shopping complexes. He was glad when they left it behind for the green of the countryside.

Finally they rounded the bend at the Blah Hole and suddenly the town was there below him, stepped in a rising amphitheatre around the bay. He would like to have asked the driver to stop, had felt an urge to get out and take in the view, but it was a treacherous bend and too dangerous to pull over. Maybe he would walk back later, although that first moment had already been lost. The driver turned down into the town and he directed him over King's Bridge, right at the Recreation Grounds and then asked him to stop. He hadn't forgotten the way.

The lounge bar of the Whitecliff Inn was empty, but then it was just past opening time. He took a stool at the bar and ordered a pint of lager. The barmaid engaged him in some pleasantries about the weather and then disappeared into the public bar, responding to a glass being rattled on the counter. He wasn't the first in then, which at least took the bad look off him. The place had changed. He vaguely remembered it as an old fashioned hotel-like pub with small divided rooms. He was sure there had been a pot-bellied stove in the middle of one of them, but the large lounge was now completely open plan – the polished counter running along most of its length and turning through into the public bar in the back. Progress, he supposed, but it was pleasant enough.

The door opened and an elderly man nodded a cordial good morning and then eased himself onto a stool in the far corner of the bar. His dog, a big old retriever, padded after him across the carpet and lay down contentedly at his feet.

'Large bottle Captain?' the barmaid enquired, as she came through.

'Sad about Tom Donaldson,' he sighed, accepting the bottle of Guinness.

'Aye, it is,' she responded, 'but sure it's a blessing.'

Their reminiscences about Tom were interrupted as the door opened and the Captain was joined by another gentleman. The bar stools began to fill and the sad news was passed on to each new arrival. Most of them had already heard. The men, white-haired and ruddy-faced, were of a similar age and similarly dressed – their tweed jackets, blazers, collars and ties harking back to a more genteel age. As the company grew they retired to the more comfortable green leather seats by the bay window, with their bottles of Guinness and whiskey chasers. They were a congenial group, familiar in each other's company, talking to and over each other. Some listened, nodding in agreement or dispute, as others battled to hold the floor. He ordered another pint.

'Regulars?' he asked, nodding towards the window.

It was a ridiculous question, he knew, as they so obviously were – the barmaid had addressed them all by name, by Mister or Captain, and she was Noreen to them. It had really just been something to say but it had drawn her into an explanation and he learned they were the Thursday morning club, although not really a club, just a group of friends who gathered each week. They were all old Whitehaven people, long retired sea captains and such.

'You're not from around here,' she said, knowingly.

'Just passing through,' he replied.

Her eyebrows raised just enough to let him know that she knew – she knew that no one just passed through Whitehaven.

'Nice bar you have here,' he said, to carry him beyond the knowing look. She supposed it was and no she didn't own it, laughed at the thought, just worked here, longer than she cared to remember. The pub wasn't new she told him when he asked, it had always been in the town, although the old building had been bombed back in the seventies and they'd rebuilt it the way it was now. It had been a terrible thing, but no one had been hurt, and they'd been luckier than a lot of other places. Only the Whitecliff had been bombed and, she remarked, as if nearly almost forgotten, The Royal Hotel. That had been an incendiary device too but it was all a long time ago and thank God it was all over now. She was called away again into the public bar and he watched her setting pints up on the counter, chatting with her customers and going about her business. She had been matter of fact about it – about bombs – neither sensationalizing it nor attempting in any way to unsettle him, an outsider. It was just what had happened, part of their history, and that was how she had related it. It struck him.

The conversation at the window returned to the sad news about Tom and a dispute ensued about his exact age. It was finally settled by one of the gentleman who had survived with him when their ship had been torpedoed and sunk in the war. The story of their survival was recounted. They seemed to have heard it all before but listened again, at times diverting the teller of the story with remembrances of their own. He ordered a whiskey and was offered the local newspaper. He leafed through the news items, the pictures of schoolchildren, the charity and church events and the advertisements. There were a few obituaries, among them notices for

Captain Thomas Donaldson. The funeral was to take place the following Monday at Whitehaven Presbyterian Church. The family had requested donations to the Missions to Seamen in lieu of flowers. He finished his whiskey and put the newspaper in his bag.

The sunlight hit him after the darkness of the bar and he took a moment to get his bearings. Crossing the road he noticed there was a Chinese take-away where he was sure the Silver Strand sweet shop had been. He turned down towards the promenade noticing that McCrellis' chip shop had also disappeared. The promenade seemed unchanged if less well cared for. He leant over the railings, taking in the salty air and the pungent smell of the seaweed, brushing the flecks of rust off his jacket sleeves, as he watched the ferry coming up the lough and ploughing out into open sea. He would book into his guest house soon – the only one left on the promenade among the tall dolly mixture coloured houses. He liked the effect of the brightly painted frontages which he remembered as a dull plaster grey. The home owners at least had pride in their property and town.

3

Maybelle was taking afternoon tea in the veranda, a time honoured pleasure and a tradition so unfortunately lost to the modern world, she believed. Wilma had brought through a selection of pastries, shop bought of course these days where once on a Thursday the warm comforting smell of baking would have filled the house. It hadn't spoiled her enjoyment though – McKee's bakery, she had to admit, was rather good. It was a fine afternoon, the sea was calm and bright, a few people were strolling along the promenade and several walkers were making their way along the shore towards the lighthouse. Out to sea the island of Ailsa Craig rose up out of the water, like a monk's tonsured head, and behind it the coast of Scotland was clearly visible. The Stena line ferry was powering up the lough and out towards it, sending a great wash towards the shore.

Maybelle sipped her tea and took a bite of a rather tempting macaroon. The sun cascading through the windows was warm on her face, and the red geraniums turning their flowers towards it were particularly pretty, their peppery fragrance filling the veranda. She closed her eyes. These were moments of perfect peace and contentment. The doorbell rang. She hoped it wasn't some uninvited caller – intrusion at any time of the day was loathsome but particularly when taking tea. She heard Wilma's voice at the door and closed her eyes again, confident that any intruder would be repelled. Over the years she had become familiar with her ways.

'Post,' Wilma announced, placing it on the tea table beside the cake stand, 'I signed for it.'

Maybelle regarded the unordered package, the padded envelope addressed to her in large black capital letters and followed by a post code. There had been a time when a letter addressed to her simply as Mrs Mountjoy, The Mount, Whitehaven, would have found its way to her, but now a grand old name or house was insufficient. Now you were a number. She opened the securely taped package with difficulty resorting to using the blunt edge of the pastry knife. Eventually the contents were revealed. It was a book. She looked in the envelope for a letter or card, but there was nothing to identify the sender, which she found peculiar. The book cover was immediately, strangely familiar – inky Edwardian houses lining a promenade, behind them a rather menacing dark bluff, an impression of the sea in the foreground. She took off her glasses and looked down towards the bay following the line along the shore front. It was, even as an artist's impression, unmistakable. She recalled the previous Sunday afternoon's telephone conversation with Dilys Bishop and wondered had she sent it. Surely she would have also enclosed a note. She would have wanted her to know, to force a reply, to forge some intimacy. No it wasn't from Dilys. She looked at the book again – the title hanging dark and gothic and bleeding against a blackening sky – The Montgomerys of the Mount.

Maybelle turned the book over in her hands and read the outline.

One fine spring afternoon a package is delivered to The Mount, home of the Montgomerys, a grand old Ulster family. Inside the package is a book. As Marguerite Montgomery, supposedly the only member of the family still alive begins to read, she realises that she is reading the history of her family. Dark and long held secrets are exposed, forcing her to confront a past which she would rather forget and bringing to her the realisation that someone else out there must also remember.

'A delicious tale of love and betrayal, of life and death and all that comes between. Unputdownable.' The Sunday Express.

'Unputdownable.' Maybelle winced. She detested this predilection for the made-up word. The Queen's English, she believed, was more than sufficient and had always been good enough for her in both the spoken and the written word. Reading had once been a source of great pleasure for her. As a girl she had read copiously, absorbing herself in the literary classics, combing through the lives of great historical figures, travelling through ancient civilizations and far off lands. She rarely read now – the habit of her younger life given over to other activities and concerns – but she would never have entertained a paperback novel, and certainly not the one now in her hand, with its lure of salacious intrigue. It was only that the book was so obviously intended for her that caused her to turn to the first chapter. She replaced her glasses and began to read.

He stood alone up on the height, his back to the great black rock, caught in its long dark shadow, protected from view and from harm. He turned his face out towards the sea and looked down on the bay, surveying the coastline, from the tall Edwardian houses lining the promenade, and along the shorefront to the dark forbidding cliffs and the lighthouse. Black clouds were tumbling up over the horizon, blackening the sea and rolling a shadow over the rooftops of the town. He pulled his collar tight around his neck and shivered. A storm was coming. He turned onto the road and started down the hill into Darkhaven.

Maybelle stopped. It was not to her taste – overdramatic and unsubtle in its intention. She turned beyond the first pages to the second chapter, *Marguerite*, unhopeful that it would improve.

Whentheyoungerwomenin MargueriteMontgomery's circle openly conversed about childbirth – even Lord forbid the details of their own labours – the menopause, or hormone replacement therapy, her mouth tightened into a disapproving thin red slit. She considered such exchanges to be the height of vulgarity and a sad reflection on the modern world that such things were inescapable, not only in the media, but even in her own company. Some fifty years before she had endured a long and difficult labour of her own, the details of which she had never felt the need to share, and at the end of which she had been delivered of a living child. The child was the result of a short-lived marriage to Frederick Montgomery, the only son and heir of the Montgomery family, scions of the Ulster linen industry and the wealthiest family in Darkhaven. It was an experience, Marguerite had determined, as she sank back clammy and exhausted into the feather pillows of the marital bed, which would not be repeated.

It had come as something of a surprise to Darkhaven when the engagement notice of Frederick George Montgomery and Marguerite McBride appeared in the newspapers on Saturday the 30th of August 1952. Only the previous weekend Freddy had lifted the Commodore's Cup at the regatta and at the after party in the yacht club, jovial, and surrounded by friends and hovering beauties, there had been no mention of any impending announcement. He had sailed all summer and it had never been mentioned to his friends. Nor had his parents, George and Adele Montgomery, personally informed any in their circle.

The news was sniffed at over breakfast in the grand houses of Darkhaven. In drawing rooms attempts were made to determine Marguerite's exact place in the family tree of the McBrides. She had invariably been introduced as a niece, on the rare occasions on which she had been presented in their company, but it was thought by some that she was in fact a cousin, once or twice removed, from the direct line of descent. It had also, however, been rumoured that she was not so far removed as the McBride's would have them believe. No one could quite remember how or why she had come to live amongst them. Until now she had not attracted their worthy attention and they deliberated as to how she had attracted the eye of young Freddy Montgomery. No one could recollect ever having seen them together, although the occasions on which he had escorted their own daughters to various social events were now bitterly recalled. They had held quiet hopes of an illustrious union with the Montgomery family and their hopes had now been crushed by an unworthy opponent. They shook their heads and tut-tutted in a chorus of disapproval. Marguerite McBride was simply not good enough for them and certainly not good enough for the Montgomerys.

By lunchtime word had spread around the community as walks were taken, purchases were made in the local shops, and bowling matches were played. By evening the engagement had become a topic of conversation in the members' bar of the yacht club and the speculation and conjecture, which passed around the smoky room with the whiskey and the gin and tonics, had turned to assertions of authority. It had been had on good authority, although the authority remained unidentified, that one of the Dixon twins, whom Freddy had been seen about with all summer, was heartbroken. It was a certainty that the wedding would take place within the month and thoughts as to why were whispered into ears. There could surely be only one reason for the marriage and Freddy must have bowed to family pressure to do the honourable thing.

Seated at a window table with the other yacht club officer's wives, Mrs Doreen Everly, who lived next door to the McBrides on the promenade, needed little persuasion to share her thoughts on the news.

'What can I say about Marguerite?' she rolled her eyes to the ceiling and leant forward into the company.

You were lucky to get a word out of her if you passed her on the steps, so unlike her aunt Ella whom you could hardly get away from. They could believe her that you avoided watering your planters when Ella was about. Marguerite was much more like her uncle Jack. He was – now what was the word for it – aloof that was it – well he was an accountant. She was just like him, and in more *ways than one Doreen intimated, raising a just perceptible pencilled eyebrow. Marguerite worked, she knew, because she saw her leaving the house early in the morning and returning at tea time.*

'What is it that she does?' Mrs Everly mused, sipping her gin and tonic and inhaling deeply on her cigarette holder.

Now she remembered something that Ella McBride had been so very pleased to tell her some time ago, which might explain something about the engagement. The officers' wives drew in closer in anticipation. She wished she had paid more attention at the time but was quite sure she'd been told that Marguerite had taken up a position as a bookkeeper, and they'd never believe where. She leaned back in her seat and brought her drink to her lips.

'With,' she said, drawing on her cigarette and savouring the moment, 'with the Montgomerys' linen company.'

Of course according to Ella she had been recommended by none other than George Montgomery himself. Ella had been very pleased indeed, she now remembered, to tell her that. Well, she had thought nothing of it then, another boast, but she must have met Freddy in the Montgomery offices. There could be no other explanation. Marguerite did not socialise and there were certainly no young gentlemen calling at her door to take her out.

And how Ella McBride must be rubbing her hands now, and how she would have to be even more particularly avoided. Just imagine if she had to listen to her bragging about the wedding plans. It really would be too much to bear. As with all social climbers Ella was a terrible snob, although what she had to be giving herself airs about was quite beyond her. And what Freddy Montgomery could possibly see in Marguerite she also had no idea. Apart from everything else she wasn't much to look at. She was quite plain, mousey in fact, and that hair hanging down around her face she was sure had never been styled. And as for style, she was also sadly lacking where that was concerned – dowdy is how she would describe it, old-fashioned for a young girl. How had she possibly attracted him, as if of course she didn't know? Still, it was entirely beyond belief.

With her opinions about Marguerite temporarily exhausted – for it was a subject that she would return to frequently and at any given opportunity in the coming months – Mrs Everly opened her cigarette case and indicated to her husband at the bar counter that her drink was in need of replenishment. The officers' wives agreed wholeheartedly with everything Doreen had said and took the opportunity to offer up some opinions and remembrances of their own, until together they reached an unshakeable conclusion. Freddy Montgomery could have had his pick of Darkhaven's very available crop and he had not, they concurred, picked a peach.

Having delivered a gin and tonic to his wife's table and enquired if any of the other ladies were in need of a tincture, Eric Everly returned to his own company. Amongst the groups of men standing at the bar counter, in a haze of cigarette smoke, the engagement had also been commented upon. The gathered husbands knew little or nothing of Marguerite McBride's looks or style, but they all knew Freddy. Freddy was a fine young man, a sport, a character, and it had to be said a bit of a dare-devil. They laughed as some of his fabled exploits were recounted by the club treasurer, Mr Pink. The time a for-sale sign had been pinned to Captain Donaldson's yacht, after Freddy had beaten him in the regatta, and all those enquiries he'd had to fend off. And the time he'd lifted Arnold Dixon's lobster pots and put whiskey bottles in them filled with tea, like something out of 'Whisky Galore'. What a great laugh that had given them. They all had a story to tell – do you remember the time he did this or he did that.

'You'd think he was dead the way we're talking about him,' someone said.

'He might as well be now,' Eric Everly shouted out over the chatter.

They roared and chinked their glasses together, cheering in agreement, and stealing glimpses at their wives. There would be no more of it now – no more high-jinks from Freddy, not now that he was caught. He was about to sign his life away and the thought of it brought on a quiet moment of reflection amongst them – memories of their own youth and the freedom they had enjoyed, before they too had signed it away in the marriage register.

'So who is this Marguerite girl?' someone wanted to know.

'Isn't she Jack McBride's niece,' Mr Pink surmised, 'Jack McBride from the promenade?'

'Niece my foot,' Eric Everly blared out rather too loudly, loosened with whiskey, 'she's not his niece at all,' he slurped on his drink and wiped at his moustache, 'she's Jack McBride's bastard.'

He caught his wife's glare across the hushed room and turned to his company whispering that he'd only said what everyone already knew. Some of the men nodded and the hush abated as all wondered how Jack McBride had got away with it. At the ladies' table, Doreen Everly, although discomfited by her husband's propensity to coarseness in drink, took the opportunity to confirm what everyone already knew. Bitterness momentarily turned to sympathy for Ella McBride, for having to bring the illegitimate Marguerite into her home, and great sympathy was expressed for George and Adele Montgomery who no doubt had little choice but to accept the marriage. But, for one person there was no sympathy – there was no sympathy whatsoever for Marguerite.

Maybelle Mountjoy took off her glasses and closed the book. It had not improved. It had not improved at all.

4

ilys Bishop waved her book club ladies out of the driveway, closed the outer door of the Deacon's House, and went through to the lounge. She slipped off her shoes, settled down on the sofa and rewarded herself with a glass of white wine. She couldn't help congratulating herself on the success of the evening. It had not just been a success, it had been a triumph. Indeed, rather than trying to persuade everyone to stay a little longer, she had wondered if they would ever leave. And it had all been down her hard work and attention to detail. If she didn't find books for her club and instigate the discussion she feared it would never start – goodness, if she didn't keep things interesting and moving along, who would? Tonight, however, there had been a transformation. The discussion had been positively animated, and for that she could thank her own endeavours and a certain mysterious gentleman author.

This evening's book, 'The Montgomerys of the Mount', had been an astonishing find and she'd hoped it would guarantee a new level of interest – members had inexplicably been falling away since the book club had started. As a stalwart of the town's societies she had experienced the inevitable malaise which affected members when there was a lack of energetic leadership, but as book club president, she had determined to galvanize her ladies. Resolute, she had spent most of the previous Sunday afternoon on the telephone telling her group about the review in the newspaper and urging them to try to buy the book. Quite carried away she had even telephoned Maybelle Mountjoy, who although was not a member, had been invited to join them on many occasions. Maybelle had seemed equally intrigued but unfortunately had a conflicting engagement.

Dilys poured another glass of wine, just to finish the bottle, and remembered back to the first time she had been introduced to Maybelle Mountjoy at the yacht club, many years ago.

'Ah, the Deacon's House,' she had said.

Mrs Mountjoy, for they were not then on first name terms, knew the house well and Dilys had invited her to call at any time to the Deacon's house, now occupied by a Bishop – her little joke. Somehow this had never happened. Well, she might not have been able to organize that, but no one could ever accuse her of not having organized her ladies.

Experience having taught her not to leave anything to chance she had formed a plan. On the Monday morning she'd jumped into the car and within forty minutes was proceeding purposefully up Royal Avenue in Belfast. On entering Waterstone's she hadn't even had to browse or ask for assistance – 'The Montgomerys of the Mount' was prominently displayed at the entry to the shop. The cumulative effect of row upon row of book covers, depicting Whitehaven, had almost overwhelmed her and she had had to prevent herself from pointing out her own house to the other customers and to the young man on the till. The book paid for, she returned to the car park, not so much as glancing at a clothes shop or a shoe shop, and was back in Whitehaven in less than two hours.

The book reviewer had been right, it was unputdown-able. Sitting at the kitchen table she had barely touched her coffee and had had to stop herself reading – she had things to do. By one o'clock she had run the last batch of papers through the photocopier in the Community Centre, paid for them, and called into the Candy Box to buy a newspaper. She had taken the opportunity to show the book to the proprietor and had advised him to order it in, certain that it would fly off the shelves. Interested, Mr Bell had made a note of it.

Having returned home Dilys skipped lunch and by two o'clock the first two chapters of 'The Montgomerys of the Mount' had been separated into neatly addressed envelopes, with a note of explanation, and placed on the front seat of her car. By mid-afternoon Dilys was home again and very satisfied with a job well done. There could be no excuses from any of her members about not having been able to buy the book – they all now had pages to work on and for once should turn up prepared and ready to discuss. During the week she had searched the internet for the author hoping to discover more about him. The review site had proved disappointing – a repeat of the biographical information on the inside cover of the book – he was in his fifties, was based in London, and had worked in the hospitality industry for many years before writing his debut novel. She had hoped to discover a link to Whitehaven or a clue to his real identity. What a coup to have been able to reveal it to her members? Although disappointed in that, Dilys' plan had proved successful, and for the first time since the inaugural meeting of the book club everyone had arrived, apart from Maybelle Mountjoy who had again chosen not to join them. In the circumstances that had come as something of a relief. As she'd read the book, Dilys had realised that Maybelle's presence would prove awkward and curtailing. It had worked out very well indeed that she hadn't made an appearance.

On arrival on Friday evening the ladies were shown through to the lounge, the supper contributions taken to the kitchen, and a welcoming glass of wine dispensed. There was the usual small talk, but the preamble, which Dilys usually had to call strongly to order, was short lived. There was an air of anticipation which she let hang for a moment before assuming her place in front of the imposing marble fireplace. With all attention now focused on her, Dilys slowly raised the book from her knee and panned her outstretched arms around the circle. She had been correct in her assumption that they would not have made the effort to acquire it and now, actually here in front of them, it provoked an audible and collective intake of breath. Passing from hand to hand around the circle, the accuracy of the illustrated cover drew a deal of comment, and comments in particular from Lillian Livermore who, along with Norma Lockhart, was the most senior Whitehaven resident present. As Dilys well knew once Lillian got started she was difficult to stop, and book now in hand, the past custodians of each house along the promenade were named, and their family history recounted. It was exactly what Dilys had hoped to avoid. She was all too acquainted with old Whitehaven when they got together and with their lengthy excursions into the past – into a world from which all others were excluded. But, Lillian was off.

'The Everlys lived there,' she indicated, pointing the house out on the book cover, 'and next door were the McBraids and then the Dixons and the McKibbens, and remember their eldest son Walter, he went off as a missionary to Africa and died of malaria.'

Norma Lockhart was sure that Walter was the youngest son, but it was malaria.

'And that house on the end with the turret,' Lillian continued, 'that was the Mountjoy's house before they built the Mount.'

Dilys was momentarily interested, 'I didn't know they ever lived on the promenade,' she admitted.

'How would *you* know Dilys,' Lillian dismissed, 'I wonder who lives there now?'

'Well at least we all know who lives here,' Dilys declared, retrieving the book from Lillian and pointing to the illustration of her own house.

Getting the proceedings back on track Dilys suggested a reading. The minister's new wife had forgotten her photocopy – not an encouraging sign – but Mrs Day, the town's librarian, offered to share, and everyone else had thankfully remembered theirs. They were lucky to have Mrs Day, an OBE, and the only member Dilys considered, other than herself of course, really able to offer any proper literary criticism. If there were no objections, Dilys suggested she would read the first chapter aloud, and after a sip of wine and a considered clearing of the throat, she commenced, 'The Montgomerys of the Mount', Chapter One.'

It was a short chapter, a setting of location and scenic description and they concluded that the man, alone up on the height, was obviously standing at the Blah Hole. Mrs Day alluded to the sense of foreboding suggested by the language – the black rocks, the darkening sea, the isolated man walking alone through the town, and the coming storm.

'Do you feel the sense of isolation and foreboding?' Mrs Day asked.

Her question hung unanswered in the air, and, realising that the wine glasses needed refilled, Dilys excused herself and went to the kitchen for replenishments. In her absence the ladies re-read through the first pages of *Marguerite*, deciding that they would like to finish the rest of the chapter for themselves – that was if Dilys didn't mind. Of course she didn't mind, goodness, she was happy to be spared. The room fell into silence disturbed only by the soft ruffle of paper being turned through the remainder of the second chapter of 'The Montgomerys of the Mount'.

In one drawing room, on the promenade in Darkhaven, there was no need for conjecture or speculation of any kind about Marguerite. As she proudly pasted the engagement notice into her album – alongside the births, deaths and marriages of the family – Ella McBride smiled a little more than contentedly at her good fortune. Unlike the many good authorities in the town she knew exactly how Marguerite had arrived into her home, and although inwardly unconvinced as to the why, outwardly accepted her husband's explanation of a youthful indiscretion on the part of his cousin Arthur. Having not been blessed with a child of her own, albeit it a sadness, she had felt no need to compensate by raising that of another. But, with Arthur rather conveniently dead in the war, she secretly thought, and no other branch of the family willing to take responsibility, she had submitted to her husband's wishes. Jack was not an unassertive man and his lack of social ambition had been a constant irritation over the years, however, he had been unusually firm in the matter. When the eight year old Marguerite arrived into her home, she put all thoughts of the child's origins from her mind.

And so she became Aunt Ella to her husband's Uncle Jack and set about the daily business of caring for a newly found niece. She fed and clothed her, enrolled her in the local elementary school, took her to church on Sundays, and determined to turn Marguerite into a young lady fit for Darkhaven society – a society from which she had always been excluded. She might sit with the ladies at church events or take tea with them in the bowling club pavilion, but she was never invited into their homes or to their card parties or drinks evenings. She might live in Darkhaven but she was not of it and had never been accepted into the circles to which she aspired.

Ella invested her frustrated hopes in Marguerite and turned to her aunt Ruby's 'Complete Etiquette Book for Young Ladies' which had been the cornerstone of her own education. She laid the cutlery out on the dining table and taught Marguerite which knives and forks and spoons were used for which courses. Over dinner the girl's table manners were corrected and refined. Afternoons were devoted to deportment – Marguerite walking up and down the parlour with a book balanced on her head – and lessons on how to enter and leave a room and how to sit on a chair, knees and feet together.

Vowels were corrected at every opportunity and she had sent her to Mrs Stephens for elocution classes, in the hope that the last traces of a Belfast accent would be extinguished. That had barely lasted a summer, Marguerite's tears finally stirring Jack to admonish her to leave the girl be.

Aunt Ella, however, was not wholly deterred, and taught her niece to play the piano, to sew and knit and crochet – the skills required in a young lady. In all of this though, she felt that Marguerite did it only to appease her, returning as soon as possible to some solitary pursuit. Marguerite she found was a shy, remote child. She did not seek company, preferring to sit quietly with a book, and did not join the other children on the beach or ever ask to bring a friend home from school. She received few invitations and would have accepted none if Ella hadn't accepted them for her. Her awkwardness in company had never been resolved. When forced to attend some social event in the town, she was quietly polite, then mute. If anyone came to the house she disappeared into her bedroom. She seemed to have spent her girlhood in that room or in Darkhaven library – the only place apart from school to which she went willingly. Ella had to admit that Marguerite had been a clever child. Her report cards were always excellent and in all of her subjects she was top of her class, but to Ella it was unnatural, and in her particular ambitions for her she remained a disappointment.

When it came to a time of thinking about Marguerite's future Aunt Ella was at a loss. She entertained no hopes of a husband for her – any attempt at putting an eligible young man in her path was immediately seen through for what it was – and she was certain that she would find no husband on her own. For a time she had held out hopes of young Walter McKibben, from two doors along, who appeared to carry a torch for her. He would wait for them on the steps after church and amble home alongside Marguerite making tongue-tied attempts at conversation. Once he had called to the door, as stiff as his brylcreemed hair – a desperate foray into fashion for Walter – in a misconceived attempt to impress. Marguerite had rejected his invitation to a walk along the shore as stiffly as his hardened helmet of hair. And once Ella had invited the lovelorn young man for afternoon tea and had had to entertain him when Marguerite adamantly refused to come downstairs. When she'd heard that Walter had died in Africa she could still see those huge sad eyes staring at her over the cup and saucer, like an owl looking out of an ivy bush. Poor Walter. She was convinced he had been driven into missionary work by a broken heart and that that, as much as the malaria, had killed him. Jack had ridiculed the notion and told her not to make a fool of herself by putting such a thing around the town.

'Let the girl be,' he had growled but it had suited her to be able to talk about Marguerite's tragic romance when the Darkhaven ladies were confiding their own daughters' prospects to each other. And what did Jack McBride know about women anyway? All women, no matter how much they might deny it, needed to know they had been loved.

Aunt Ella's hopes had disappeared into the grave with Walter and it would never have occurred to her that Marguerite harboured any hopes of her own. She was completely unaware that behind those impenetrable dark grey eyes was concealed a deep desire, for her niece imagined herself at University, and beyond, a life of study and scholarly contemplation. It was a cherished dream that would never be mentioned or fulfilled, for another course had been contrived, and dependent on her aunt and uncle, Marguerite acquiesced, keeping her dreams to herself.

It was time, Aunt Ella had decided, that her husband relieve her of some of the burden of what to do about Marguerite, as with marriage unlikely, suitable employment must be found. She was persistent in this and felt she would scream if told to 'let the girl be.' Her campaign began in the morning when she pricked him as fiercely as she pricked the breakfast sausages. After dinner she read job notices to him from the newspaper and later assaulted his ear on the pillow. She pursued him around the house at the weekend driving him out through the door. To her surprise he offered a solution which she might have thought of herself. He wasn't suggesting that Marguerite follow in his footsteps into accountancy, but bookkeeping was an acceptable occupation for a young woman, and perhaps he could secure her a position with his company. After reminding him again on the fourth day, on his way out the door to work, he returned in the evening with the news that he had spoken to Mr Montgomery and that a place would be found for Marguerite. He hoped Ella was damned well happy now and that he would be left in peace. She was both happy and relieved, never imagining that her persistence would eventually lead to the fulfilment of everything, and more, than she had ever dreamed of.

Less happy was Marguerite but she accepted the decision about her future placidly with no outward sign of resentment. Two weeks later she boarded the early morning train with her Uncle Jack, on her way to the city, to be trained as a bookkeeper in the accountancy offices of the Montgomery's Ulster Linen Company. In her third week Marguerite was introduced to Mr George Montgomery, as she and Uncle Jack encountered him on the steps on the way into work.

'Very pleased you've joined us,' he said, doffing his hat and reaching out his hand, 'and I hope everything's going well.'

She took the hand of the tall auburn-haired gentleman, shyly meeting the bright hazel eyes regarding her, and quite truthfully replied that it was. As the junior in the office she didn't attract much attention, and, after several rebuffs to friendly invitations to shared lunches, she was left alone. She spent her lunch hour browsing in the book shops on the Dublin Road, or walked up past Queen's University to the Botanic Gardens. She liked to sit there watching the students rushing back and forth, enviously imagining which great subjects they were studying. She had never lived in a house with a garden. Her grandmother had kept potted geraniums on the windowsill of the kitchen house near the docks in Belfast where she had spent her first years. Red geraniums would always remind her of the grandmother she had loved – a large jolly lady who had smelled of fish, and whose bed she had shared. Other memories of her early childhood were unsure. She had only a vague memory of her mother but had never known her father. She did recall a well-dressed gentleman visiting her grandmother's house when she was maybe five or six years old. She'd been dressed up in her Sunday best when it wasn't a Sunday and been sent out to play in the backyard. The man, a shadowy image, had watched her through the window. She was never

sure if he was the same man who had come and taken her
away when her grandmother died – she was never sure if
he had been Uncle Jack.

Dilys Bishop sat in front of the fireplace, drumming her fingers noiselessly on her leg, waiting impatiently for the book club ladies to get to the last page. It really would have been so much easier if she had read it aloud rather than bowing to the majority – then they could all have kept up. Lillian had lifted her husband's glasses by mistake and the bifocals were making her dizzy. Mrs Day and the minister's new wife were reading at different speeds on their shared pages and Norma Lockhart appeared to be re-reading passages, her face stern in concentration. Only Mrs Hanley junior and Miss Lydon were reading at an acceptable pace. It really was taking them an age and it wasn't as if the book was exactly taxing in a literary sense. She would have to wait until they were finished and then patiently explain not only the story, but the writer's intent and the devices used to convey it. Having once taken a short course in creative writing, at which, although she would never say so, she had excelled, she considered herself well qualified to do so. She wished she had kept at it. If she had, she could have published a book of her own by now. Her course tutor had certainly praised her work.

'Description Dilys,' he had said, 'is your forte.'

The ladies sitting in her living room were not unlike those that she had fictionally described in one of her stories. Norma Lockhart – as neat as a pin, perfectly coordinated in muted tones, her short hair softly tinted – defied her almost eighty years. Lillian Livermore, another near octogenarian, presented quite a different picture. As plump and round faced as Norma was thin, she wore her long grey hair pinned up in an unruly bun, wisps escaping from the clasps and falling around her ears and neck. Lillian favoured colour – a multi-patterned scarf trailing down her shoulders over a loud and uncoordinated blouse.

The telephone rang interrupting Dilys' descriptive train of thought. As heads lifted the minister's new wife, in flurry of apology, fished the offending mobile phone out of her handbag, knocking her shared pages onto the floor. Apologising again, she excused herself from the room – it was her husband. Marjorie Day picked the pages up from the carpet and arranged them back into order as the others rubbed their eyes and stretched a little.

'You see Norma, I told you it was malaria,' Lillian said, 'I knew Walter McKibben died of malaria.'

'I didn't disagree with you Lillian,' Norma responded, 'not about that anyway,' she said quietly, raising her eyes to Miss Lydon who nodded and smiled.

'Just imagine Walter being in a book and just when I was talking about him,' Lillian continued, 'and Doreen Everly, who would credit it, Doreen Everly in a book. Wouldn't she just have loved that?'

'I doubt it,' Norma responded, 'it's not exactly a very flattering portrayal.'

'Well I think the writer's got her down to a tee,' Lillian countered, 'just like her.'

'That's what I mean,' Norma said, as Lillian stared at her in confusion.

The minister's new wife reappeared.

'Is everything alright Jane?' Dilys asked, noticing the serious look on her face.

Everything was fine it was just that her husband had come home from visiting Mrs Donaldson and had wondered where she was. He had forgotten about the book club.

'He's very conscientious,' Dilys commented, 'to be visiting at this time of night.'

'Captain Donaldson died on Wednesday,' Norma informed her, 'haven't you heard?'

Dilys had not heard the news, but was forced to sit and listen as Lillian began to recount the story of the Captain's very long life. Becoming increasingly impatient she intervened to bring the proceedings back to order, urging the ladies back to their pages with the promise of supper once they had finished. Quite hungry by now, glasses back on and heads lowered, they continued more purposefully from where they had left off.

It was sometime in the middle of Marguerite's second year that George Montgomery's gleaming black Bentley pulled up alongside her on York Street. There had been an unexpected downpour and, soaked and chilled, she was hurrying towards the railway station. He wound down the window and asked if she was going to Darkhaven. Taken by surprise she couldn't think of an excuse, and reluctantly manoeuvred, knees together, onto the car seat. She was practised at avoiding company and to be so closely confined was excruciating, particularly with Mr Montgomery – outside of his world of sophisticated assurance she felt painfully self-conscious and inadequate. She dreaded how long the journey home would take.

'Who would have expected this rain?' he said.

She nodded and agreed, fixing her eyes on the windscreen, the wipers slapping as the car moved off.

She couldn't think of anything to say, had nothing to say, and was glad when he started to talk about work. Had she really been with them for two years already? Did she know that her Uncle Jack had been with the company for nearly thirty years and had started off with his father? Of course she must know about the New York account and it couldn't be in safer hands than Jack's, too important a venture to be looked after by anyone else.

'Just imagine all those rich Americans sleeping on Montgomery linen sheets or dining off our table cloths,' he said, 'the Rockefellers, or maybe even a film star or two, or why not President Truman himself?'

'President Truman's not going to run again,' she stated, 'it's likely to be General Eisenhower.'

He looked at her in amazement and she had amazed herself by saying it.

'I didn't think young ladies were interested in politics,' he said.

'I'm not really,' she replied shyly, 'I just like to read. I read a lot about different things.'

'My son must be about the same age as you but he's not interested in reading,' George Montgomery raised his eyes.

The journey passed more quickly than she could have imagined but it was still a relief when he pulled up on the promenade and she ran quickly up the steps, grateful that Aunt Ella hadn't seen him helping her out of his car – that would have brought forth questions and an obsequious veneration of the grand Montgomery family, with whom her aunt was embarrassingly impressed. Marguerite changed out of her damp clothes and sat by the bedroom window looking out over the grey overcast sea. He was not as formidable as she'd imagined but she wished she hadn't embarrassed herself by mentioning Eisenhower. What had possessed her to say it and what must he think of her? She would not have believed that when George Montgomery drove off home towards The Mount that he had been very impressed by the serious and intelligent young Marguerite McBride.

It happened again some weeks after that. He pulled up alongside her on the street, not far from the office, and drove her home. He talked as before about America and the growing sales which she had seen in her account books, but not at length.

'You were right,' he said, 'about Eisenhower,' but she didn't respond and he didn't pursue it.

He was quieter than before, as if he had something on his mind, and she didn't try to fill the silences. In the days after she was careful, looking out for his car, an excuse at the ready if he stopped. Within the week however she was to learn what was weighing so heavily on his mind and she learnt it from George Montgomery himself.

Mrs Hanley junior turned her page and let out a long deep yawn, causing the other ladies to lift their heads and shift in their chairs.

'Any sign of supper yet?' Dilys heard her whisper to Miss Lydon, who thumbed through the rest of the pages counting them silently.

'Not for a while,' she whispered back.

'What was that?' Lillian asked, taking off her glasses and rubbing the reddened indents on her nose.

'I was just saying about supper,' Mrs Hanley junior ventured.

'My apple tart would need to go into the oven to heat through,' Lillian suggested.

'Ladies, ladies,' Dilys clapped her hands in encouragement, 'just a little more to go and we're coming to the best bit.'

Peckish, but resigned, they lowered their heads and continued on.

The morning started as any other and moved uneventfully towards lunchtime. At two minutes to one Marguerite closed her ledger and took her handbag and lunchbox out of the desk drawer. The office was already quiet, the others as usual having slipped away a few minutes early. Her eye caught a shadow at the partition window.

'*I was hoping I might find you here,*' George Montgomery *smiled, stepping into the office.*

Marguerite felt a wave of heat rising from her neck and averted her eyes. In the blur of words coming out of his mouth she found herself complying with what he was requesting of her. No, she wasn't particularly in a hurry home. Of course she could spare him a moment of her time. Yes, she would come to his office after work.

'*A quarter-past five then,*' *he said,* '*there's a business matter I'd like to discuss with you.*'

Marguerite's afternoon was not spent in a concentration of work but in a race of thought towards the appointed hour. What business matter could Mr Montgomery possibly have to discuss with her? Perhaps she'd made some dreadful mistake which had affected the accounts and she was to be let go. Of course, in deference to Uncle Jack, he'd feel he should tell her himself. Or maybe she was to be given a promotion or maybe, the thought shivered up her back, it wasn't about work at all. It had seemingly been by chance that he'd come across her and driven her home but what if he'd realised she was avoiding him and meant to force an encounter. Surely it couldn't be that? What man, let alone a sophisticated gentleman like Mr Montgomery, would give her a second look, not that she even wanted a first one.

At ten-past five, alone in the office, Marguerite put on her coat and started slowly up the stairs, now believing that she'd imagined it all. She would knock on his door and he would ask what she wanted, horrified to find a junior employee in his office. What could she possibly say? As she reached the top of the stairs George Montgomery came out onto the landing, coat over his arm and hat in hand. She had imagined it, he was leaving to go home, and she tried to retreat unseen to the stairway.

'Exactly on time,' he smiled down the hall, 'I hope you don't mind, but I'd prefer to talk about this away from the office. Shall we?' he motioned her down the stairs and out of the building to his car. As he drove into the hotel car park Marguerite began to drown in fear of her thoughts.

'This way,' he took her by the arm.

He walked her out of the car park and across the road, shielding her from the traffic, until they reached the gates of the Botanic Gardens, 'I believe you like to come here,' he said.

They walked together through the gardens in the evening sunshine and he kept his hand at her elbow, gently directing her from path to path and around the rose garden, until they reached the bandstand. He took off his hat, placing it on the seat between them, unbuttoned his overcoat and fingering at his shirt collar, turned to her.

'The matter which I want to talk to you about,' he said, 'is I suppose, what you might call a proposition.'

Marguerite dropped her head towards her tightly clasped hands, eyes fixed on his polished leather Balmoral shoes. Now it would come she thought. He'd been clever, bringing her to the gardens, trying to catch her off guard before he propositioned her and led her back to a room in the hotel. She wouldn't let it happen. She would get up and walk away and she didn't care if she lost her job, she would keep her dignity.

'It's about my son,' he said, as she raised her eyes to look at him.

At her nervous request George Montgomery had left her in the Botanic Gardens to think about his extraordinary proposition. She had thought of nothing else as she walked to the station, or as the other passengers in the compartment closed their eyes and gave in to the slumbering sway of the train from Belfast to Darkhaven. As Aunt Ella brought her dinner out of the oven, complaining that it was ruined with her being so late, she picked at it and offered no explanation.

'What's wrong with that girl Jack?' she heard her say, as she left the kitchen, 'why didn't she tell you she was going to be late? If she'd told you I'd have kept the gravy in the pot.'

'Let the girl be,' Uncle Jack growled, as the dishes crashed into the sink.

In the quiet of her bedroom Marguerite could think and she tried against all reason to make sense of Mr Montgomery's proposal.

'*I believe you are a seriously-minded young woman and I don't wish to offend you,*' *he'd said, while nonetheless describing the reality of her circumstances – she could never aspire to the life of wealth and position inhabited by the Montgomerys. And somehow he had managed to suggest that the possibility of such a life might appeal. He had not talked much about his son, confiding only that he had embarked on a wholly unsuitable relationship of which no details had been given. He believed that Freddy needed a sensible, trustworthy young woman in his life and he would like to arrange for him to call on her.*

'*Please at least consider it,*' *he'd asked, as he left her,* '*and what may or may not come of it, I'm sure I can trust you to keep this between ourselves.*'

Mr Montgomery had made it all sound so straightforward, so business-like, but now, lying alone in bed it seemed utterly ridiculous. Why on earth would Freddy Montgomery call on her? She had seen him in the town, and from her bedroom window on the yacht club slipway, always surrounded by a crowd. He could have his pick of Darkhaven and he would never pick her. And anyhow, she didn't want to be picked, had never entertained the thought of marriage. But, to be Mrs Montgomery, that was a different proposition. She turned and turned on the bed. It was now more utterly ridiculous than before. Sleep would not come.

She threw off the blanket and opened the bedroom curtains to a bright full moon, the black sea under it catching the light in a rippling silver shawl. She leaned out of the window into perfect calm, hugging herself in the chill of the night air, and looked out across the bay towards the lighthouse. On the top cliff path, flooded in cold moonlight, the great white house, The Mount, commanded Darkhaven. In bed, shivering, she pulled the blankets around her, searching for warmth, until sleep finally came.

'So what time shall I expect you home tonight?' Aunt Ella enquired, scraping the barely touched fried egg from Marguerite's plate into the bin, 'that's if it's not too much trouble for you to let me know.'

'Let me be,' Marguerite snarled, scraping her chair back from the table.

'Well, what a thing to say,' Ella's voice trailed after her as the kitchen door slammed back against the wall, 'I hope you're happy now Jack,' she gritted, 'she gets that from you. And what have I done to deserve it, only put meals on the table and keep them hot in the oven when no one gives a blind bit of notice about telling me if they'll be late. I don't know why I bother, I really don't. There's no appreciation in this house at all. Well, don't you have anything to say and believe me if you say let the girl be I'll.. . .'

Marguerite blustered back through the doorway. 'I won't eat soft fried eggs,' she shouted, 'I like hard fried eggs, from now on make me hard fried eggs.'

The kitchen door slammed shut and the rattle of the front door closing behind her echoed down the hall. Aunt Ella slumped down onto her chair.

'Well, I hope you're not going to stand for her talking to me like that Jack,' she trembled, 'and after everything I've done for her. Lord knows I've tried and no one in this world can say I haven't. I've done everything for her and this is the thanks I get,' she whimpered, wiping her eyes with her apron. 'You need to have a word with that *girl Jack,' she sniffed, 'so help me you better have a word with miss high and mighty.'*

Jack McBride put down his knife and fork, took a last mouthful of tea, and sighing deeply departed for the train station with the promise having been wrung out of him that he would talk to Marguerite. His walk to the station each morning was generally undisturbed and perfectly timed – two minutes along the promenade to the turn onto Marine Parade, two minutes to the Silver Strand and through the gates of the railway station, a minute along the platform to the kiosk to buy his morning newspaper before he boarded the train, seldom more than three minutes later. Order informed the habits of his life. He desired it in his work and in the running of his household – without order he believed there was chaos.

The normal course of his morning had, however, been entirely and unexpectedly disrupted. He walked distractedly to the train station thinking of what he might say. He had no wish to involve himself in an upset between two women – such a thing was quite beyond him – but there had never been such an outburst in the house before. Turning onto Marine Parade he contemplated on how to restore the peace. He knew Marguerite had been a disappointment to his wife and had rarely interfered in her attempts to mould her into the young lady she would have wanted her own daughter to be. But, he couldn't think too badly of Ella in all of this – her heart, if sometimes misguided, had mostly been in the right place. He would explain to Marguerite that Ella did things with the best of intentions, and ask her to make it up with her aunt. As he neared the Silver Strand the train pulled into the station, clouding the footbridge in a screeching blast of smoke and steam. He quickened his step through the station gates as the last of the passengers stepped quickly onto the train. The guard held open a compartment door, ushering him in, and he took a seat as the occupants moved up to make room. Across from him a woman smiled, and through a gash of bright red lipstick, said good morning. He doffed his hat and reached into his coat pocket for the newspaper. He realized, for the first time that he could ever remember, that he hadn't had time to buy one, and sat uncomfortably as the woman engaged him in conversation all the way from Darkhaven to York Street Station in Belfast.

He looked for Marguerite at the terminus but couldn't see her in the crowd. As he began his twenty seven minute walk to work she was nowhere to be seen on the road ahead. At three minutes to nine Jack McBride walked through the doors of the Montgomery building and climbed the stairs to the first floor. On the way to his office he noticed that Marguerite was already working at her desk in the bookkeeping department as the others were hanging up their coats and chattering with each other. She might be a disappointment to Ella in many ways, and the morning's unpleasantness would have to be confronted whether he wanted to do it or not, but he couldn't criticise Marguerite's diligence or the meticulousness of her work. In that she was a credit to him. He would have a quiet word with her in the lunch hour or find a time in the afternoon. It would keep until then.

Lunchtime came and went. At three o'clock he thought to walk along the corridor and seek her out but he had an appointment with Mr Montgomery at half-past the hour. He would wait. As the minutes ticked away he gathered up his ledgers and took the stairs to the third floor. As he reached the landing the office door opened and Mr Montgomery walked out into the hallway with a young girl. Realising it was Marguerite he stood back into the shadow of the stairwell. He watched as George Montgomery took her hand in both of his and leant towards her.

'Thank you Marguerite,' he heard, 'I'm most grateful to you.'

Jack McBride retreated down onto the second floor, waiting there for Marguerite to clear the stairs. What had she been doing up there – unthinkable for a junior member of staff – and why was Mr Montgomery grateful to her? He couldn't comprehend it but everything today had taken on a disorderly turn. He kept his appointment, forcing himself to concentrate as they discussed the month's figures. On leaving the office he was again complimented on his management of the New York account, and told to keep up the good work.

'I meant to ask,' Mr Montgomery said, 'your niece, Marguerite isn't it, still getting on well with us I hope?'

Jack McBride thanked him for asking and replied that she was.

'Good,' he said, 'very good. A fine young woman I hear.'

For the first time in living memory Jack McBride missed the twenty-to-six train home to Darkhaven. He couldn't turn his mind away from what he had witnessed upstairs or why Mr Montgomery had asked about Marguerite when he had just been talking to her. The figures which he needed to check turned unusually complicated, the papers on his desk seemingly out of order. He stayed on to finish his work, leaving the office at half-past five, and boarded the train forty minutes later than usual. In the train compartment he rested his head back on the antimacassar and wondered what would greet him at home. After last night Ella would now be angry that he was late for dinner and after this morning's tirade she and Marguerite may have had words. By now she would know that he had failed to speak to her. Ella would affect a silence with him and keep it up until bedtime and for days beyond. Perhaps, he thought, closing his eyes and trying to put it off, he should be thankful at least for that.

He woke up as the train shuddered to a halt and wearily followed the clanking feet up over the iron footbridge and down the other side.

'Friday's come early this week,' Miss Hattrick raised her eyes from behind the counter of the Silver Strand.

'I'm sorry?'

'It's only Wednesday Mr McBride' she explained, 'you usually call in on a Friday night.'

It was true. On Friday nights without fail he came in to buy his wife her weekend treats.

'Same as usual anyway?' she asked, weighing out a quarter each of barley sugar, lemon bonbons and Riley's toffees from the jars on the shelf, and lifting out a bar of Fry's Chocolate Cream and Turkish Delight from the glass display case under the counter. He paid her, put the bags into his pockets and went out of the shop, the doorbell jangling behind him.

He walked down onto the promenade, the sea in front of him marooned in stillness, not a breath in the air. He walked across to the railings and stood for a while, looking at the boats moored motionless out in the bay.

At the yacht club some children were playing on the end of the slipway, jumping in and out of the shallow tide, laughing and happy, immune to the cold sea water. Their mother appeared and shouted that it was time to go home. The children ignored her and jumped in again. He turned from the railings and walked across to the house, loth to go in.

Jack McBride closed the front door behind him and hung his hat and coat up on the hallstand. The clock began to strike the hour and over the chime he heard the natter of women's voices coming from the kitchen. Someone must have called he thought. Ordinarily he would have been displeased but tonight he was glad of it and put his foot on the stair. He would escape to the quiet of the bedroom.

'Is that you Jack?' Ella shouted out, 'we're in here.'

He came reluctantly down the hallway and pushed open the kitchen door. Ella and Marguerite looked up and smiled, a pile of magazines spread out between them on the table.

'Marguerite wants to buy a new dress,' his wife beamed, 'and we're looking at different styles.'

He stood and watched as they returned to flipping and earmarking pages, Ella offering advice and Marguerite making some suggestions of her own. He sat down at the table, as they turned from dresses to shoes to hats, opened the previous evening's Belfast Telegraph and re-read the news.

'Goodness me your dinner Jack,' Ella gasped, 'I'd clean forgotten all about you.'

She brought his plate out of the oven, prodding it with a fork, telling him that it wasn't too dried up at all. If he wanted anything else there was a pot of rice pudding on the stove and she would make him a cup of tea later. The ladies gathered up their magazines and set off for the parlour.

'I don't know what you said to her Jack,' his wife whispered as she made for the door, 'but whatever it was it's certainly worked.'

Jack McBride pushed a potato over the dry congealed gravy on his plate. It was not what he was used to, but would settle for it, comforted that order had been restored. In the incoming days he was to discover, however, that the old order of things had changed. The natural rhythm of his household, its patterns and routines, would be given over to the impenetrable intimacies between women, with their shared knowledge of dresses and shoes and hair, and their whispered secrets. He was not resentful of it. He was grateful to be left alone.

The following weekend Aunt Ella zipped Marguerite into one of her new outfits, having finally given in an attempt to persuade her into something. She had wanted her to wear the poodle-skirted yellow dress with the black polka dots but Marguerite favoured the straighter line of the turquoise chemise dress.

'Quite lovely,' Ella praised, although unconvinced that Marguerite's tall thin figure would not be better served by a flattering flounce.

Marguerite, looking in the mirror, was also unconvinced and again suggested that she change into her usual blouse and skirt. Aunt Ella would not hear of it.

'A young man,' she declared, 'especially a Montgomery man, expects a lady to dress with style'.

Sitting at the dressing table, as Aunt Ella clucked and plucked – pinning up her hair, powdering her face and persuading her to coat her lips with lipstick – she decided not to go. When he called her aunt could go downstairs and say she had taken ill. It wouldn't be a lie. She had started to feel quite nauseous.

'I'll do no such thing,' Ella responded in exasperation, 'you were brought up with better manners than that and I won't have you let us down.'

Marguerite forced her eyes to the mirror. Whoever it was looking at her she knew it wasn't her.

'Something borrowed,' Aunt Ella laughingly hinted, taking off her strand of pearls and clasping them around her niece's neck, 'and something new,' she slipped Marguerite's feet into the newly bought court shoes and then held out the white cotton gloves, smoothing them up over her wrists.

'Well I never, a true picture,' she said, kissing Marguerite on the cheek that had been turned away from her.

Ella went to the bedroom door and shouted downstairs, 'Jack, Jack, yoo hoo, Jack.'

'Well, what do you think?' she asked, gesturing towards Marguerite as he appeared in the doorway.

'Very nice,' he muttered, retreating from the room.

'Nice indeed,' Ella disparaged, 'he has no idea about these things. You look perfectly lovely my dear, quite the young lady.'

Aunt Ella positioned herself at the bedroom window, 'He's here,' she cried out, ducking back as the shimmering blue sports car drove along the promenade and stopped in front of the house. She ushered Marguerite out onto the landing, rushing back and retrieving the forgotten handbag from the bed.

'Remember which knives and forks to use,' she pleaded on the second flight, 'start from the outside in.'

Yes, she would remember. 'And let the waiter pull your chair out, don't do it yourself,' she implored on the first floor landing. She wouldn't. 'And don't open your own napkin.....'

'Let the waiter do it, I know,' Marguerite bit, as they reached the hall.

The door knocked.

'Don't come with me,' Marguerite instructed, 'I'll answer the door myself.'

Too excited to be put out Aunt Ella went into the parlour, peeking out from behind the curtain to take a look at him, and hoping that today of all days Doreen Everly might be watering her planters. In that she was disappointed, but not in the handsome, expensively-suited and polished young man, standing on her step with his bouquet. Marguerite caught a glimpse of herself in the hallstand mirror. It would have to do. She took a breath and opened the door. He was taller than she'd realised but, hardly able to look at him, his features under the sleek auburn hair remained a blur. Soft colours were what she would remember filling the doorway – the light cream of his linen suit, the sun streaming in behind him, and roses, yellow roses.

'Miss McBride, Marguerite,' he said, holding out the bouquet to her and standing aside, 'shall we?'

Finally, after what had felt like an age, pages were rested on knees and Dilys, having forgotten about supper, leant forward into the circle ready to expound her theory on the 'Montgomerys of the Mount'. It was all so utterly obvious that no one could deny it and she was ready and willing to put her case to the test. Just as she was about to speak Mrs Day returned to her theme of isolation. Of course Dilys could see that Marguerite was also an outsider but this was just the type of thing she had an issue with. It had been typical of the lecturer, as she had taken to referring to her husband since the divorce. Yes, the lecturer had been inclined to form opinions on a character and weave the tiniest and most unlikely shreds of evidence into some great enthralling hypothesis which the author might not have intended at all. She listened impatiently as Mrs Day warmed to her theme. What had brought about Marguerite's isolation – some inner flaw or some outer force – that was the question? Dilys sighed inwardly and looked around the circle, the tightened brows confirming that they were not enthralled, they were utterly lost. In the interests of enlightenment she interjected.

'But surely the big question Mrs Day,' Dilys said, holding her hands out towards the group, 'is not what, it's who. Who is Marguerite Montgomery?'

Mrs Day thankfully concurred, nodding enthusiastically, that it was indeed a most important question. Who was she and what had made her who she was? Realising that the point had been entirely missed Dilys firmly took control, as she had had to do on so many occasions, and returned to her own question, posing it this time in such a way that there could be no confusion.

'Not who is the character in the book,' she emphasised, 'who is the character in reality, who in Whitehaven is Marguerite?'

With Mrs Day lost for words and the company she noted with satisfaction, genuinely in thrall, she expounded her theory, drawing on the evidence paragraph by paragraph. When she had finished she sat back and drained her wine glass, entirely satisfied as to the veracity of her exposition, and suggested further discussion over supper. At the prospect of supper everyone breathed a sigh of relief.

In the kitchen, Norma Lockhart and the minister's new wife were washing up the supper plates and acquainting themselves with each other. Jane was enjoying living by the sea and was taking advantage of the wonderful walks along the shore and up to the lighthouse. She had been amazed to discover the Blackhead path – truly one of the country's best kept secrets and a place that could hold its own with any natural attraction in the world, she believed.

'Is it true the council's trying to close it?' she asked.

'It seems so,' Mrs Lockhart said, 'but the town won't stand for it.'

'Have you always lived in Whitehaven?' Jane enquired.

'Born and bred,' Norma replied, rinsing the plates under the tap.

'Then you must know what Dilys was talking about because I got a little bit lost,' Jane shook her head, 'I mean the book is about this Montgomery family but Dilys was going on about the Mountjoys. Are they a real Whitehaven family?'

'Indeed they were, I mean are,' Norma corrected, 'and actually their house is called The Mount.'

'I see,' Jane nodded, 'so the house at least really exists.'

'You'll have seen it on one of your walks, you can't have missed it,' Norma told her, describing the first architectural home ever to have been built in Whitehaven.

'Ah, the one on the top cliff path,' Jane recognised, 'the huge white house with the flat roof and the long veranda.'

'That's it,' Norma confirmed, 'and if you walk up the front avenue, right to the top, it's the one with the tower and the stained glass windows.'

'So, that's The Mount then, but do you think Dilys is right about the Montgomerys really being the Mountjoys?'

'I think Dilys has rather fanciful ideas,' Norma stated.

'I thought the theory about the names was stretching it a little,' Jane concurred, 'I mean Marguerite, Maybelle, Montgomery, Mountjoy, just because they all start with 'm' doesn't necessarily mean anything does it?'

'I wouldn't think so,' Norma said, handing Jane a drying cloth and turning to her own thoughts about it.

She really wished that Lillian hadn't got caught up into the whole name business by mentioning that Maybelle had been a McBraid before she'd married Teddy Mountjoy and that had started it all off again – Freddy and Teddy and McBraid and McBride. There'd been no stopping Lillian then and her revelation that Maybelle Mountjoy had once worked as bookkeeper had only encouraged Dilys to probe further, her inquisition turning to Teddy Mountjoy and in particular to the manner of his death.

'Well of course everybody had their own ideas about it at the time,' Lillian gushed, 'and even after the inquest there were still questions about.....'

'Lillian, let's go and do the washing up,' Norma had suggested, in an attempt to shut her up, but in full flow she would not be moved and Jane had offered to help.

Now with the dishes washed and dried they sat down at the kitchen table and finished their wine.

'I wonder why Dilys is so interested in the Mountjoys,' Jane said.

'Dear knows,' Norma sighed, turning the stem of the glass around in her fingers.

And whatever the interest, from whomever, Maybelle Mountjoy deserved to be left in peace. Too much tragedy had been suffered in that family and it didn't need to be picked over again.

'It's getting late,' Norma said, 'we better go back through.'

Dilys looked up from her book and ushered them across the room, informing them that they had missed quite a bit of story. They had missed Marguerite and Freddy's courtship and the wedding, but she wasn't going to go back on it. She continued reading as they slipped back into their seats.

Doctor Dunbar, the town's general practitioner, attended the overnight delivery. He had delivered a generation of Darkhaven's offspring and Marguerite, despite her newly found social status was firmly instructed, as every woman was, to stop that screaming and get on with it. With a final muffled groan and push the slithery child was handed to the midwife, much to the relief of Marguerite and to the doctor, who had an appointment to keep with a hotly tipped racehorse at the Lisnalinchy races. After an appropriate time – during which the infant was washed and wrapped, the bed linen changed and Marguerite made presentable – the expectant father was invited into the bedroom where calm and order had been restored. What Freddy Montgomery's true thoughts were on that early June morning, as he looked down into the crib where the next generation of Montgomerys lay swaddled and whimpering, will never be known. It was the first and the last time that he would look upon his child. Many stories, theories, real and imagined details, would emerge in the aftermath of the tragedy which was about to unfold, and would weave their way into a patchwork of remembered certainties.

It was Tess O'Brien, the housekeeper, who eventually opened the door. She had been expecting the private nurse, hired to look after Mrs Montgomery in the incoming weeks, and was taken aback to find the grim faced Constable McCullough on the doorstep. He enquired if Mrs Montgomery was at home and asked if he could come in. Tess explained that she was indisposed and couldn't be disturbed – perhaps he could come back later when Mr Montgomery had returned. Looking into the Constable's eyes she knew that something was wrong, terribly wrong. He removed his cap, and head bowed, came into the house. Tess didn't quite know what to do. She shared her dilemma with him and he shared with her the sad reason for his visit. It was a shock, he knew, and with them not even over the last tragedy. He reached out and took her arm to steady her. No, she couldn't tell Mrs Montgomery, she just couldn't. No, she didn't know of anyone to call. Constable McCullough followed her slowly up the staircase. She announced him at the bedroom door and closed it behind him.

He found Tess later in the kitchen with the nurse, who had finally arrived. He had broken the dreadful news as gently as he could and Mrs Montgomery had been remarkably brave. She hadn't cried or screamed or fainted. The grief, he was sure, would come later when it had sunk in. He didn't have time for a cup of tea as he still had a lot to attend to. Tess escorted him to the front door and as he started to crunch down the driveway on his bicycle he remembered that she had been crying.

Norma Lockhart was waiting impatiently in the car for Lillian, still deep in conversation with Dilys on the doorstep of the Deacon's House. Dilys, she suspected, had discovered an ally for her nonsense and would know how to cultivate her. If Lillian didn't come soon she would sound the horn – it would be rude, but it was almost midnight.

'Don't worry, I won't forget. I'll get my son to pick me up a copy in Belfast tomorrow,' Lillian shouted back across the forecourt as she finally got into the car.

It was only a short drive home but irritatingly Lillian talked and talked, affecting her concentration – she wasn't used to driving at night. She was irritated too that Lillian had taken up the gauntlet, reiterating Dilys' theory which she felt compelled to counter as it flooded forth.

'I just can't see that you don't get it Norma,' Lillian said in exasperation, 'that you don't see the similarities.'

'For heaven's sake it's fiction,' she snapped, bringing the car to a sudden halt outside Lillian's house and jolting them both towards the windscreen.

'Tell me that after you've read the book,' Lillian retorted, getting out of the car, 'I'll get David to bring you a copy too,' she said, slamming the door.

Pulling into her own driveway, down below The Mount, Norma noticed that Maybelle Mountjoy's bedroom light was still on. It was the sort of thing you noticed when you'd lived in close proximity for so many years and was unusual. Norma went uneasily through her door, hoping that nothing was wrong.

In The Mount, Maybelle was propped up in bed on the pillows, her eyes closed but far from sleep. Her mind was too full of the past, of memories stirred up from over half a century ago. And it was a simple thing which had stirred her most – as simple as yellow roses. They had not been roses, how ridiculous that would have been – a romantic fantasy born of an author's imagination. They were pink and white carnations and Teddy had handed them to her with practised ease. She had never received flowers before, and embarrassed, had left them on the hallstand as he retreated down the steps and opened the door of his car for her. They had driven along the Antrim coast, meandering around the limestone cliffs, through the small seaside towns and villages, and had stopped for lunch in the Londonderry Arms Hotel in Carnlough. She had rarely dined in a hotel and never on her own with a young man. He was as assured as she was self-conscious, attracting attention with ease and ordering with confidence, effortlessly engaging in conversation with the other diners. Her small rehearsed attempts at conversation had been exhausted almost by the time they had driven out of Whitehaven and she was grateful to escape from the awkward silences in the car.

On the way home he compared the hotel to the other establishments he and his family frequented. She had nothing to compare it to. He talked of his travels on the Continent – in France and Italy and other places – and she shyly asked him about the Louvre and the Uffizi. He laughed at that and said he'd managed to miss them. She laughed too, taken with his honesty, and he had turned his dancing green hazel eyes to hers, and for the first time really looked at her. The journey home passed more quickly than she could have imagined and she thanked him as he helped her out of the car and walked her to the door.

She ran quickly up the stairs, ignoring her aunt calling from the parlour, and from the bedroom window, half hidden by the curtain, watched him drive across to the yacht club. As he got out, a group of jostling friends surrounded him and propelled him down the slipway. A girl, one of the Dixon twins, stripped off Teddy's jacket and he jumped into a punt, standing up and rocking it from side to side in the water. The laughing twin reached out her hand and he caught her in his arms as she stepped in beside him. He rowed away out towards his yacht, the Elizabeth Ann, as the others launched into the water and pushed off after him.

Her aunt came into the bedroom, carrying the carnations and a vase, making a fuss of arranging them on the dressing table. She hadn't wanted to answer the questions about where he had taken her, what they had talked about, or if she had remembered her manners. She had given annoyingly undetailed replies, waiting for the only question which she knew her aunt really wanted to ask.

'And will he be calling again?'

'He's asked me to go to the pictures,' she said, as her aunt threw her hands up in delight and as she avoided the arms coming towards her. In the days before their date she spent her lunch hours, as she often did, in Belfast City Library. 'A bit of a change for you,' the assistant said, stamping out her books,' I wouldn't have put you down as interested in sailing.'

Maybelle Mountjoy opened her eyes. She didn't want to think about the past. She had left it where it needed to be left but someone was obviously unable to. She could think of no one who could have written this book. The author's name meant nothing – no doubt a pseudonym. The people who knew her were all too old to write a book, or dead. But someone knew her – someone knew her life. This was no mere coincidence. She put her glasses back on and turned the page, loth but compelled. A name from the past leapt out at her. She stiffened in the bed, a cold wave carrying her back into a dark sea of drowning memories. So, was this what it was all about?

5

As a young girl of fifteen, Theresa O'Brien had come up from the country, like many young girls, to work the summer season as a chambermaid in The Royal Hotel. She had been a pretty young thing then, with thick dark hair, dark eyes and a rosy complexion, somewhat typical of her distant rural county. It was an excited, if slightly apprehensive Tess who boarded the early morning bus in Fivemiletown headed for the Antrim coast. She had never been out of Tyrone before, had never spent a night away from home, and had never seen the sea. It was the beginning of her young life's adventure – the result of the first stirrings of a determination in her character which had been consolidated into months of resolve. Her mother had been against it. She couldn't spare her. Who would help with the children? Who would help with housework? She was too young, and God only knows what might happen to a good Catholic girl up there with all those black-hearted Protestants. Tess refused be put off. She pleaded and reasoned and reasoned and pleaded. Her sister Deirdre could take on her chores and didn't they know lots of girls her age who had gone to work in the hotels and nothing had happened to them? Hadn't her *mother's own sister worked up there for a while? She appealed to her father who said it was up to her mother, but she knew he was taken with the idea of the money coming home, and she knew that he knew how to spend it. Between them Mrs O'Brien was steadily worn down, more than she already was in life, and eventually gave in. Theresa could do what she liked she said – repeating her world weary mantra – they could all do what they liked, for who the hell ever did anything for her?*

And so Tess got her way and got off the bus in Darkhaven, in the spring of 1948, with her one borrowed suitcase. Along with the determination which had brought her to the town, a lively, cheerful character accompanied her out of the bus depot and up over the railway foot bridge to the Royal Hotel to begin her working life. She wasn't afraid of hard work. Although the other girls complained of the long hours of bed making, cleaning and laundry, with only one day off a week, Tess had no such complaints. This was, so far, the best time of her young life, released from the much greater burdens of home. Her days in Darkhaven may also be filled with work, but in a way they were her own.

Tess was immediately popular with the English tourists who flocked to the seaside town in the summer to enjoy the spectacular cliff paths and promenade walks, to travel the Antrim Coast in Devenny's gleaming fleet of Irish tour buses, and to quick-step around the ballroom at the Saturday night dances. She did well on tips from the English gentlemen, who couldn't resist a pretty face, and from their wives who appreciated the fixing of a loose button or a cold towel for an afternoon headache. A dutiful daughter she sent most of her wages home to support the ever growing O'Brien family, if her father didn't get a hold of the money first, but her tips she kept for herself. With the extra money she bought her first ever own dress and, daringly, a little make-up. She and Marie, her room-mate and new best friend, practised with it in their quarters, copying the look of the film stars in the tourists' discarded magazines. They dreamed of the handsome film stars in America and fixed each other's hair in the mirror – she a more dark-haired Dorothy Lamour to Marie's red-haired Rita Hayworth.

After work on Saturday nights, hair and make-up done, they scurried out through the kitchen and around the side of the hotel, stopping to admire the ladies in their finery through the widows of the ballroom, and then on to the picture house for the late night show. They swung arm in arm up the road, past the local boys who waited outside the cinema to flirt with the hotel girls, turning their heads with a look and a laugh as the boys stood there with their two arms the same length, working up the courage to ask them out. At night in bed they talked about the film, if they liked it or not, and who they would marry – Cary Grant or Robert Taylor – and which boy they would go out with if they were asked, and which one they most definitely would not.

'I'd rather be shot than poisoned,' Marie said, sending them into giggles as they described the boys whose names they didn't know. They each had their dreams but Tess never allowed them to distract her from work, and unlike some of the girls, was never told off for dawdling or daydreaming. At the end of the season, with the

tourists gone, Tess and Marie hugged each other at the bus station and promised to meet up the following summer in the Royal Hotel.

In her second summer season Tess' diligence was rewarded. One of the girls had received a letter summoning her home and Tess was trained as a Silver Service waitress in her place. It was a great promotion. She spent her days and evenings in the red-flocked dining room under the watchful eye of Mr McCaw, the head waiter, dispensing portions of beef, chicken and fish and eventually mastered the peas. Rarely known for compliments, Mr McCaw nodded occasional approval in her direction. By the middle of the season, silver serving spoons firmly under command, Tess was stationed at the best tables in the dining room – those reserved for the grand Darkhaven families, who dined regularly throughout the year in The Royal Hotel.

It was here that she first came to the attention of the Montgomery family, whose arrival in the hotel was met with an organized flurry of activity. George and Adele Montgomery were greeted always by Mr McAllister, the hotel manager, who personally took their coats, showed them through to the lounge, and oversaw the serving of drinks and delivery of the menu. Mr McCaw came through to take their order, complimenting them on their choices, whatever they chose being particularly good that day. When he seated them in the dining room, all eyes were drawn to admire the beautiful Adele, hoping that those blue-velvet eyes would turn to look at them. They would sit quietly, the Montgomerys, he expensively and she exquisitely attired, acknowledging the other diners with a nod or a good evening and enquiring from time to time about each other's dishes – the dishes served attentively, as she had been strictly instructed, by Tess O'Brien. As Tess would come to learn, however, Mr Montgomery often dined alone. She was always disappointed when he was unaccompanied by his wife, the Elizabeth Taylor of Darkhaven, but never with the very generous half-crown, left under the rim of the side plate for her when she cleared away.

Towards the end of the season Mr Montgomery was joined at his table by a young gentleman whom Tess hadn't seen before. As she approached, balancing the platter on her arm, his hand was being shaken furiously by another diner. She stood back from the table and waited to serve.

'Very well done Freddy,' the man congratulated, 'about time Tom Donaldson was put in his place. Great race, great race, didn't think you'd get past him, he didn't see you coming.'

The man was thanked several times but carried on excitedly. Everyone was delighted to see Freddy home, they'd missed him and the sailing hadn't been the same without him. He hoped he wouldn't be going off travelling again – some young girl at the bottom of it no doubt. There was laughter and a denial. There would be no more adventures now, the man was sure.

'Your father will be putting you to work now Freddy. He'll be turning you into a business man before you know it.'

The corners of George Montgomery's mouth forced themselves up into a half smile and his son raised his eyes and said nothing as the diner finally relinquished his hand and crossed the room to his own table.

'It is something we have to talk about,' George Montgomery insisted.

'*Please not tonight,*' Freddy pleaded, '*can't we just celebrate tonight, can't we talk about it tomorrow?*'

'*It's always tomorrow,*' Mr Montgomery sighed, unfolding his napkin, '*and this can't wait for ever.*'

Freddy gave his solemn promise that they would talk in the morning as Tess, relieved that the food hadn't gone cold, moved forward to the table and began to serve. As she spooned the last of the carrots onto Freddy Montgomery's plate he turned his eyes up to her and smiled, his lips parting in a thank you.

'*You're welcome Sir,*' she said, the colour rising in her cheeks as she turned away towards the kitchen. He was like his father, she had noticed – the same strong jaw and nose, the cleft of the chin, the scattering of dark freckles across his face and the deep auburn hair. But it was the eyes – eyes that Marie would say you could fall into. When Tess woke in the morning she was sure she had dreamt of those dancing green hazel eyes, the eyes that had looked up at her.

When George Montgomery woke in the morning he dressed, breakfasted and took the newspaper through to his sitting room. When the door knocked he looked up expectantly from his desk. It was not Freddy. It was the housekeeper, asking for a moment of his time. Mrs Green had been a constant in his life since childhood, overseeing the running of domestic arrangements for his father and then for him. She kept him abreast of matters, consulted him as needed and didn't disturb him lightly. This morning she wearily informed him that a problem, which had been disrupting the household since the beginning of the summer, had again returned. The maid appeared to have disappeared in the night, there was no doubt about it – bag and baggage she was gone. Mrs

Green despaired of these young girls today, there just wasn't work or appreciation in them and this was now the second to flit in as many months, without so much as a by your leave. She wasn't complaining, but with young Mr Freddy having come home at the beginning of the summer, there was a lot of extra work. She just couldn't take it on herself, not with other – she had hesitated and looked at him – with other things to contend with. He knew what she contended with and was deeply grateful for it. They only ever referred to it obliquely and he was grateful for that too. Mrs Green had devised a term for it many years ago and it had slipped into their exchanges, easing their embarrassment when referring to Adele. He would come home and ask how things had been.

'A good day,' she would say to his relief, 'changeable weather,' she would say, to his resigned disappointment.

Mrs Green had never disappointed him but now she was considering her position, 'I'm no spring chicken,' she said, 'and maybe it's time for me to go.'

He was genuinely appalled, professed that he couldn't do without her, and promised to attend to the matter personally. It was in this worrying domestic circumstance that George Montgomery placed a telephone call to the Royal Hotel and asked to speak to Mr McAllister. He was specific in his request and although it was an inconvenience to the hotel manager, he could not say no to Mr Montgomery. The following day Theresa O'Brien presented herself at the back door of The Mount.

Mrs Green looked her up and down and brought her through to the kitchen, introducing her to Mr Milligan, the gardener, who turned around from the sink drying his hands on a towel.

'Call me Jim,' he smiled at Tess, 'call me Jim,' he said again.

Tess sat down at the table with Mrs Green and the duties that would be required of her – the living arrangements and the remuneration – were explained. She would start at six o'clock in the morning, finish when she was told, and Monday would be her day off. There was to be no slacking, no back talk and no complaining.

'The devil finds work for idle hands,' Mrs Green pronounced, pursing her lips and giving Tess a hard stare across the table.

The gentlemen of the house were to be addressed as 'sir' and, if she encountered Mrs Montgomery, she would address her as that, but Mrs Green herself attended to the mistress.

'But you can call me Jim,' the gardener reminded her, taking his pipe and tobacco out of his waistcoat pocket, as Mrs Green continued.

Tess may have come recommended by the master of the house, but she was to keep to her place, and not to be getting above herself.

'And don't be getting any ideas about young Mr Montgomery,' she stated as Tess blushed, 'there's been quite enough of that sort of thing lately,' she said out of the side of her mouth to Call Me Jim, who raised his eyes at her forthrightness. Padding the tobacco down into the bowl of his pipe, he struck a match and lit it, sucking, as the sweet fruity smell drifted across the table.

'Aye and then there's changeable weather,' he said, exhaling.

'You can leave the weather to me,' Mrs Green said sharply, catching his eye.

'Aye, that we can,' he nodded, stepping out of the back door into the garden, 'that we surely can.'

Having informed Tess as to how she liked things done and without any great hopes, Mrs Green instructed her to return a week on Monday, it having been agreed that she would work out her notice in the Royal Hotel. And so Theresa O'Brien did not return to her distant home county or family at the end of her second season but remained, for better or for worse, in Darkhaven.

For the first time in her young seventeen years Tess slept alone in a bedroom of her own – a small room on the ground floor at the back of the house. Mrs Green had done her best in the time, complaining to Call Me Jim as he repainted the walls and carried in extra pieces of furniture that it had been perfectly good before.

'For the life of me I don't understand why Mr Montgomery's insisting on all this fuss for a girl yet to prove her worth,' she moaned.

As much as Mrs Green was put out, Tess was thrilled. She had never had a dressing table before and sat delightedly on the little stool, regarding her face in the mirror. She folded her clothes neatly into the chest of drawers, hung her best dress up in the wardrobe, and arranged and re-arranged her few personal possessions around the room. The musical jewellery box which her father had given her one afternoon, when he'd come home from the pub the worse for wear, was placed on the dressing table. She opened it, the tiny ballerina shuddering back and forth, unable to turn as the music played. The little painted china donkey with its turf baskets, which a silly local boy had given to her, was finally settled on the window sill. The window looked out onto the back garden and over the top cliff path to the sea. Tess knelt *for a moment on the chair, watching the last few walkers down on the shore. She had become more used to the sea and the sound of it, but was still unsure of the water.*

'Scaredy cat, scaredy cat,' Marie would chant at her, throwing off her shoes and ankle socks and running to paddle in the cold tide. It did scare her when Marie hoisted her skirt and jumped over the small waves breaking on the sand until her knees disappeared under the water. She was always relieved when Marie came out and hadn't been pulled under by some unimaginable monster lurking below.

Tess pulled the curtains against the last of the evening light and tried on the light-blue uniform which Mrs Green had left folded on the bed. The blouse was a good fit but the skirt was a little loose without the apron tied tightly around her waist.

'Waste not, want not,' Mrs Green had said, telling her that she would get no new uniform of her own until she had earned it.

Lying in bed, Tess looked around her room, unable to settle with the strangeness of it all. Tomorrow she would ask Mrs Green if she could stick her pictures on the walls and eventually fell asleep, deciding which wall was for Rita Hayworth and which was for Dorothy Lamour.

Maybelle had not slept well, fitfully at best, which was unusual. For many years sleep had been undisturbed and restorative – at least since Edwina. The first light was filtering through the curtains, throwing shadows around the room. She turned her head away from it. She always knew when she had dreamt about Teddy. It would come to her in that moment between half sleep and waking. She closed her eyes and let the dream come back to her. It was always the same and had recurred infrequently, but nonetheless vividly, for over half a century.

She was on the Blackhead path walking towards the boathouse. Her step felt light, free in the cool morning air. She was wearing a turquoise dress which had been a favourite when she was young. She was young. The sea was turquoise too, a deep surreal blue-green turquoise, as silky as her dress but strangely translucent, like some far off Aegean Sea. There was a yacht on the horizon – its sails full and pregnant in the breeze although the air was still. It was sailing towards her from a long way off and suddenly it was there in the sea in front of her, so close that she could have reached out and touched its gleaming white hull. She could see every detail of it – the shine of the varnish and the slats on the deck, the weave and twists of the coils of rope – but she couldn't read the name on the prow. The letters were all there, large clear golden letters, but she couldn't make sense of them. She said the letters over and over again, spelling them out, trying to make the word. Then the boat was gone. She had to remember the letters. She had to take the letters to the boathouse. There was something in the boathouse that would give her the name. It wasn't far away but, although she was walking and walking, she wasn't getting any closer to it. And then Teddy was walking along the path towards her in his sailing whites, crisp as the air, his thick auburn hair blowing back from his face – his young handsome face. He was smiling at her, his eyes as bright as the sea. She reached her arms out to him, but it wasn't Teddy, it was his father, it was George Mountjoy and he was saying something to her, 'Only you know Maybelle, only you know.' She couldn't remember what she knew. And then he was in the sea, sinking down into the sea. She tried to call out to him but no words would come and then she saw that it wasn't George, it was Teddy. Teddy was sinking down and down and all the time smiling but he wasn't smiling at her. There was someone else, a shadow on the bank behind her – he was smiling at the shadow.

'She doesn't know,' a girl's voice laughed, 'she doesn't know.'

And then something was knocking, softly, and then louder in the light.

'Mrs Mountjoy.' That wasn't the name she had to find. That was her name. It came again, more loudly and urgently, 'Mrs Mountjoy!'

Wilma was standing by her bed, 'Are you alright?' she asked, concerned, 'it's just that it's almost half-past nine.'

'I'm fine. I woke earlier. I must have fallen asleep again.'

As Wilma went downstairs to put the kettle on, Maybelle eased herself up on the pillows, clammy and exhausted.

Waiting for Mrs Mountjoy to come down, Wilma made herself a cup of tea. She'd had a bit of a shock this morning – not how she liked to start the day. An uneasy feeling had come over her almost as soon as she'd let herself in through the door. She couldn't explain it but, rather than looking for Mrs M in the usual places, she'd gone straight upstairs. She'd half expected to find her dead in bed and it wouldn't have been the first time it had happened with one of her elderly ladies. She had no fear of a dead body but was relieved to find that Mrs Mountjoy had simply overslept. That, in itself, was unheard of, but less alarming to her than the alternative. She had a soft for her employer even if it hadn't quite started out like that. In the beginning Wilma had found her rather aloof but there were no back doors about Mrs M, you knew where you stood, and she respected that. Over the years, she liked to think, they'd not only come to respect each other but grown fond.

'Wilma,' Maybelle said, appearing in the kitchen doorway, 'would you mind changing my bedclothes today, I had such a bad night's sleep and a nice fresh bed might just make all the difference.' Although it wasn't laundry day Wilma was too relieved to mind.

'I'll make you a cup of tea first.'

'That would be lovely,' Maybelle smiled, 'I'll take it out to the greenhouse. I want to work out there this morning.'

Wilma went back up the bedroom – the coldest room in a cold house. She'd never understood why Mrs Mountjoy was so sparing with the central heating, preferring to wrap herself up or fill a hot water bottle. It wasn't as if she couldn't afford it but it was one of her little ways. She opened the widows, letting in the warmer outside air, and stripped the bed, pulling off the eiderdown and blankets down to the sheets – there were no duvets in The Mount. She brought the clean sheets and pillowcases out of the dressing room cupboard holding them up to her face, breathing in the soapy smell of the cool crisp linen. No one had bed linen like Mrs M. You couldn't get sheets like that anymore, or if you could, you couldn't afford to buy them. She changed the bed quickly, smoothed it down, and tidied up a little, not that there was much to do. On the bedside table she noticed a book and picked it up to have a look. She was surprised to recognize the title. This was the book that everyone in the town was talking about, at least according to her daughter-in-law. Rachael was reading it and it was supposedly all about Whitehaven and people in the old days – people she thought Wilma might know.

'Thanks very much,' she'd scolded, 'I'm not that old.'

Wilma went over to the window and looked down into the garden. Mrs Mountjoy was pottering in the greenhouse and would likely be there for a while. She sat down on the chair, ran the duster over the marble top of the occasional table, opened the book at the marker, and began to read.

Within a fortnight Tess had fallen easily into the domestic routine of The Mount. She cleaned, dusted, vacuumed, set the fires as required and helped with the laundry. Once a week she polished the silver and the brasses on the front door, looking around proudly to the avenue – proud to be seen as an employee of the household. She served breakfast in the morning room, where Mr Montgomery ate alone – his son not being an early riser, and his wife taking a tray in her bedroom, which Mrs Green took up well after breakfast time. Lunchtime was quiet, with Mr Montgomery gone to the office during the week and young Mr Montgomery usually out. In the evenings the family very occasionally dined together. The weekend brought little change in the routine of the house. On Saturdays Mr Montgomery took lunch in his sitting room and in the evening went out to dine in the Royal Hotel. On Sunday mornings he went to church and sat down to dinner in the dining room at one o'clock, rarely joined by his son and never by his wife.

Adele Montgomery was something of a mystery to Tess – she rarely saw her. Once, lured by the echo of music, she had stood unseen at the dining room door and watched her playing the piano, rooted by a vision of loveliness as her head lifted and swayed with the melody under her fingertips. And once, having been sent to clean the veranda she'd found Mrs Montgomery sitting there leafing through a magazine. The mistress of the house had got up and, eyes lowered to the floor, had retreated upstairs. The Montgomerys' life in The Mount was theirs and it was not her place to question. She had her own life within the household.

Tess took her meals in the kitchen with Mrs Green and Call Me Jim. She enjoyed sitting at the table with them at lunch and tea time. Call Me Jim told funny stories about everyone in the town and Mrs Green would laugh but then hush him up.

'There but for the grace of God Jim,' she reminded, when he started on, 'there but for the grace of God.'

'Aye Susie, you're right there, you're right there by half,' he would say, before starting up again.

Mrs Green talked about the town's suppliers – Haveron's butcher's shop and the quality of the meat, the fish in season in Hilditch's fishmonger's, and the best potatoes to be bought at Foster's greengrocers. After lunch and a second mug of tea Call Me Jim would go back out to the garden and Mrs Green would sit back in the easy chair in the corner and take her forty winks. Tess would sit on for a while in the warm steamy kitchen, keeping an eye on the pot of stock bones bubbling on the stove, before getting up and quietly washing up the lunch plates.

Mrs Green did all the cooking, and as Tess helped to peel the vegetables, she watched and learned about the different cuts of meat and types of fish and sauces which she had never heard of before. Thursday was the busiest *day in the kitchen and Tess' favourite. On baking day Mrs Green started early, laying out her bowls and tins and scales on the table, and bringing the flour and sugar and slabs of butter from the pantry. The smell of baking followed Tess all over the house, and she would come in and out of the kitchen to see the soda and potato bread being turned on the griddle, the sponge cakes, buns and biscuits coming out of the oven. She liked to get back to the kitchen to wash up the icing bowls and get a lick of the soft sweet sugar. Eventually Mrs Green trusted her to decorate the cakes with the glace cherries and place the angelica into little leaves. Call Me Jim hovered around the kitchen on baking day too and in the end Mrs Green would give in and the warm soda bread was cut. They ate it with jam, the butter oozing down their chins. They were allowed an iced bun each but the cakes were not to be cut and woe betide them if they so much as looked at a macaroon – Mr Montgomery's favourite and saved for him.*

'Susie, I've died and gone to heaven,' Call Me Jim would say, when he'd finished off his bun.

'Get away with you,' she'd tut, putting him out the door but smiling and enjoying the compliment.

Young Mr Montgomery sometimes appeared in the kitchen on Thursdays too, drawn by the irresistible smell, and would beg a slice of cake. He too would be shooed away and his fingers slapped as he reached for something on the cooling stands. He would twirl Mrs Green around and escape with a bun or two, giving Tess a wink.

Tess worked hard, attending to her duties as diligently as she had done in the Royal Hotel. It surprised her how much work it took to take care of one family – compared

*to the size of her own, and to the hundreds of tourists she
had looked after. She had no complaints about her work
but sometimes missed the bustle and companionship of
the hotel. Apart from the kitchen the house was so
strangely quiet, empty, and at times she almost felt
lonely. There was no outlet for her natural liveliness and
there was no Marie to share her thoughts and dreams
with. In the big lonely rooms the suppression of these
outward traits turned inward to imagination. As she
waxed and polished the hallway floors she was no longer
a maid, no longer Theresa O'Brien, she was a passenger
on an ocean voyage, on one of the great cruise liners she
had seen in the pictures – she was Bette Davis.*

*'Oh Jerry,' she ached to her reflection as she polished
the long gilt framed mirror at the top of the staircase,
'don't let's ask for the moon when we have the stars.'*

*She and Marie had cried at the end of the old film
when it was shown the picture house and had talked
about it before they went to sleep – about how Bette
Davis could have given up the man she loved.*

*'I would never give up a man I loved,' Marie said, 'not
for anything, not for all the tea in China.'*

*As Tess swept her duster down the staircase bannister
she looked down into the eyes of the handsome man
waiting to sweep her away. As she dusted the Chinese
vases in the drawing room, with their silk glad emperors
and beautiful long faced ladies, she was a captive princess
waiting for her prince to come. Even in fear of discovery
she would sit on the piano stool in the dining room,
running her fingers silently along the keys, a grand lady
playing for invisible spellbound guests. She would strike
a pose in front of the full-length portrait above the
mantelpiece – Adele Montgomery staring off into the*

77

distance, her hand laid above her breast, her finger toying with a rope of pearls. Once she had turned to see Mr Montgomery standing in the doorway watching her, a quizzical look on his face, and had fled in hot embarrassment. But, as the months passed so too did her feelings of loneliness, and she began to enjoy the peace and quiet, the chimes of the clocks, the smell of wax, lavender polish and cut flowers, and she came to love the house which in her imagination she allowed to be her own.

On her day off, if she wanted company, she called for Marie at the Royal Hotel. Marie had also stayed in Darkhaven, having secured a permanent position. She had a boyfriend now, was madly in love, and didn't want to leave the town. They went up to the room they had shared and chattered excitedly, Marie throwing herself down on the bed in a dream about the divine Sean Brannigan – his eyes, his hair, his strong arm – confiding coyly that he was a good kisser. When she could get a word in Tess talked about the Montgomerys, hotly denying any interest in the handsome young Freddy, getting into a huff until Marie finally gave it up. They got ready to go out, just as they used to, fixing each other's hair and make-up before swinging out of the hotel and into the town. They walked along the promenade and up the rise to the Golden Dawn Café for tea and cake, or sat in the bandstand and watched the boats out in the bay. At tea time they treated themselves to a fish supper from McCrellis' chip shop, sitting in if the weather was bad or on a promenade bench if it was fine, munching on the crispy batter and sucking the soft fat chips, licking the vinegary grease off their fingers.

'*I've died and gone to heaven,*' Tess said, swooning off the bench.

'*I've died and gone to heaven too,*' Marie said, pulling her up by the arm and laughing her deep earthy laugh.

On the way back to the hotel they went into the Silver Strand to buy a quarter of chewing nuts or pear drops and Tess would buy clove rock for Mrs Green, who loved it, although it tasted like medicine. Sometimes, when they'd saved up, they caught the train to Larne to browse in Woolworths or window shop on Main Street, admiring the dresses and shoes.

On Saturday nights Marie and Sean went dancing in the Rinkha ballroom and sometimes Tess went with them. They caught the last bus and jumped off at the stop, a couple of miles away in Islandmagee, and never worried about how they would get home. Sean was good at getting them a lift or they walked home in a crowd, back along the dark country roads, the boys jumping out from behind the trees and trying to scare them. Marie and Sean danced all night, swinging round the ballroom as the soaring saxophones and trumpets of Tommy Strahan's band kept their feet in time around the floor. Tess stood by the wall and watched them in the swirl, trying not to look at the boys in a huddle on the other side of the room, dreading that one would walk across the floor and ask her to dance and dreading that one would not. She was often asked and it was impolite to refuse, but made sure she was on the way to the powder room when ladies' choice was called. Marie had caught her out with that before, forcing her across the empty floor to ask Sean's friend, Pat Devlin, to dance.

'*Don't you know he's sweet on you,*' Marie said, prodding her along, '*didn't he give you that little china* donkey?' She had danced with him that once, as Marie made eyes at her over Sean's shoulder, and had fled to the safety of the powder room.

'I'd rather be shot than poisoned,' she said to Marie.

Tess stopped going to the Rinkha for a time after that, but gave in over Marie's birthday, and promises that 'you know who' would not be mentioned. Marie had looked so beautiful that night, the full skirt of her new dress tightly belted around her slim waist, the soft green complimenting her strawberry-blond hair. Pinned below her shoulder, catching sparkles in the light, Marie couldn't stop touching the star-burst brooch, her present from Sean – given she said with a declaration of love.

'Not that he said it in so many words,' she whispered to Tess, before he came to sweep her off in his arms. 'Of course I do,' was what he'd said, when she'd asked him if he loved her.

An hour later, with the dance floor cleared as Mr Hawkins sprinkled it with powder, Marie was giving out – it got her temper up when Sean went outside with the other boys to drink, leaving her there like a wallflower.

'I'll show him,' she said, looking around the ballroom for someone else to dance with.

It was then that Tess noticed that the brooch was gone. They looked everywhere in the darkened room, asking the dancers to watch out for it and begging its return if it was found. They searched in all the places Marie had been and in desperation in the places she was sure she hadn't been. What if they couldn't find it? What if someone found it and didn't give it back? She hoped Sean wouldn't come back in. She wished she was dead.

Marie ran to the powder room, inconsolable, her eyes pricking with tears. She pushed Tess away from her.

What did she know? What had she ever been given, only a stupid, cheap bloody donkey, from Pat bloody Devlin?

'Who cares if that gets lost?' she brayed, weeping and hugging the wash basin.

The door opened and as Tess lifted her eyes from the floor a girl held out her hand, the brooch cradled in her palm. Marie ran to her, hugging and thanking her, unwilling to let her go.

'I'm just glad I found it,' the girl said, trying to extract herself from Marie's embrace, 'I have to get back, my boyfriend's waiting for me.'

'What's your name?' Marie called after her as she went out through the door.

'Norma,' she shouted back, 'Norma Mercer.'

'God bless you Norma,' Marie made the sign of the cross, and pinned the brooch back on her dress, as the familiar strains of the song flowed into room.

'Do do do do do dup rip da do, wha aaah ah, take away the breath of flowers it would surely be a sin,' Marie started to sing, 'it's our song,' she screamed, abandoning Tess and going in search of Sean.

It was as Tess came out of the powder room that she saw him on the dance floor. A space had cleared around him as he twirled a girl away and back into his arms. The girl pressed into him, her head on his shoulder, and he leant into her ear holding her close and singing, 'Is it a sin to love you so, to hold you close.' Tess stood over at the wall, her eyes following Freddy Montgomery around the dance floor, as the band played the last songs of the night. The crowd spilled out through the dancehall doors and gathered into smaller groups, some squeezing into cars, some deciding to walk home. She recognized his sports car immediately and saw him in the huddle of young men standing around admiring it. He was drinking from a bottle and passing it around.

'That's the real McCoy,' *one of them said, wiping his mouth with the back of his hand and passing it on.*

Tess stood back as Marie went and pulled Sean away, she giving off to him, he protesting that he'd hardly even got a mouthful. They turned onto the road for the walk home. At Cameron's corner the sports coupe roared past them up over the hill, the girl sitting beside Freddy, her arm around his shoulder.

'That car can move,' *one of the boys said.*

'Buy a car like that and I'll marry you,' *Marie hinted to Sean, who rolled his eyes as the boys whooped and whistled and pushed him towards her.*

'Aye, if I win the pools,' *he said, as she took his hand.*

They walked on into town and scattered for home. Tess walked up the avenue and through the front gates of The Mount, scared to take the top path and go through the back garden alone in the dark. Freddy Montgomery's car, she noticed, was not in the driveway. She followed the wall of the house around to the back and let herself in, going quietly to her room. She went to the window, moved the little china donkey off the sill, and pulled the curtains. Marie had annoyed her about that, but that was Marie when she was upset, and at least Pat Devlin hadn't come near her all night – he must have got the message. Getting into bed Tess decided that she would go dancing in the Rinkha more often and tried to fall asleep if only the song would let her. Round and round it went again.

'Though you take away my heart dear, there's a beating still within, I'll keep loving you forever, for it's no sin.'

Wilma lifted her head from the book and looked out the window. Mrs Mountjoy was still in the greenhouse. She looked at her watch and turned the page.

At the beginning of her first full summer at The Mount, Tess was provided with a new uniform – a sign of approval. Mrs Green appreciated her attention to work and found it refreshing that a young girl was both interested and quick to learn. She began to teach Tess how to cook and bake, instructed her about the local suppliers and tradesmen, and explained a little about the household accounts. Towards the end of the summer, and coming into autumn, their working relationship first turned to friendship.

It was jam making time again. The gooseberries and blackcurrants from the garden had already been picked, jammed, jarred and labelled, and stored on the pantry shelves – it was time for the blackberries. Mrs Green knew all the secret spots that no one else could find and had been keeping an eye on her walk to work for the ripening berries. In the morning she and Tess set off along the top cliff path with their baskets, carrying walking sticks to hook the thorny briars. They picked the fruit along the path and climbed over fences and into fields, searching out the hidden bushes. By the time the last basket was filled Tess' hands were scraped red and raw by the thorns. They cut down the Golden Stairs and onto the shore, walking back wearily, their arms throbbing with the heavy load. When they rounded the bend at the old Port Davey slipway Mrs Green gave a puff of relief and pushed open her garden gate with her hip.

Tess had never been in Seaview Cottage before. Mrs Green opened the door into a small cosy room – the flower patterned curtains matching the rosebuds on the wallpaper, crockery and knickknacks displayed on a dresser, a treadle sewing machine in the corner. In the tiny kitchen Mrs Green boiled the kettle, made Tess soak her hands in the basin, and then dabbed the scratches with methylated spirits as she screamed with the pain.

'What doesn't hurt doesn't heal,' Mrs Green said, catching her hands and dabbing again, telling her to stand at peace.

As Mrs Green made a cup of tea Tess recovered in an armchair in the living room. Resting her feet on the warm hearth she looked up at the photographs on the mantelpiece. Above them on the chimney breast, the King, resplendent in his uniform, looked out across the room. Her father, she knew, would have something to say about that. The tea was brought through and poured and Mrs Green caught Tess' eye wandering again to the mantelpiece.

'My husband,' she said, lifting down the photograph and handing it to Tess who regarded the stern dark eyes staring out at her above a rigid black moustache, as Mrs Green started to reminisce. Billy wasn't from Darkhaven. He'd worked as the head gardener on a distant country estate and she still sometimes couldn't believe that they'd ever met.

'But the Lord works in mysterious ways,' she said, 'God brought me to the Montgomerys and they brought Billy to me.'

Mrs Green had started working for the family when she fourteen – the year that George Montgomery was born. They'd lived on the promenade then and it had been hard work but she'd been luckier than most girls in those days – George's father, Frederick, was a good and fair man to work for and Mrs Montgomery was a lady. She'd died when George was two years old and it had almost broken their hearts.

'I was only a slip of girl then really,' she said, 'but I stayed on to look after George and his father and I've stayed on all these years.'

She'd been nearly forty when Frederick Montgomery had started to build the Mount. He'd wanted an Italian garden, had somehow heard of Billy, and had persuaded him to come and work for him.

'Keep that man well fed,' she'd been instructed every morning, before the Montgomery men headed off from the promenade to the office. And every lunch time she'd made up a picnic, walked along the shore and up through the fields to the building site, and called him away from his digging and shovelling and pegs and string.

'That's how it all started,' Mrs Green confided, taking the picture from Tess, 'and before I knew it he'd asked me to marry him and of course I said yes and then Mr Montgomery let us move in here.' Billy had lived to see the garden built but not to see it mature.

'He was only forty six when he died,' she sighed, 'and he was as strong as an ox, but TB got a hold of him and well, that was that.'

They finished their tea and Mrs Green turned her cup upside down on the saucer, turning it round and round, letting the last drops drain away from the leaves.

'Money and a stranger at the door,' she said, peering into the cup.

Money was always good but a stranger could be good news or bad. At first Tess couldn't see the little three-legged pot with the coins piled in it, or the stick man holding out his fist and knocking on a door of tea leaves, *but when the images formed she swivelled her own cup and laughing handed it to Mrs Green.*

'Well I never,' she declared, 'a boat on the sea and a sailor sailing towards you.'

'I can see it,' Tess cried, 'I can see it.'

'Oh, and another man, holding his hands up against a storm,' she said. Tess took the cups through to the kitchen, looking again for the boat and the sailor on the sea, before she rinsed out the leaves. Out of the kitchen window she saw that the doors of the boathouse were open. Freddy Montgomery was inside working on his yacht.

Mrs Green was well rested and they gathered up their baskets of berries ready for the walk back. Freddy Montgomery saw them coming out of the garden gate and called out to them to wait. He took Mrs Green's baskets and they strolled back together, Tess walking behind, the two in front chatting easily and familiarly. At the bottom of the hill they stopped for Mrs Green to take a breath before the climb and Tess walked on ahead.

'We've got a good one there,' she heard him say, as she walked on keeping her eyes steadily on the road.

In the kitchen the baskets were set on the drainer and Mrs Green took off her coat and went upstairs to check on Mrs Montgomery. Tess filled the colander with berries and held it under the tap, shaking it gently, letting the water run through. Freddy Montgomery came up behind her, reached out his hand out to take a berry and before she knew what she had done, she had slapped it. The shock of it made her drop the colander into the sink. He laughed and reached again, popped a juicy fat berry in his mouth, and sucking on it, retreated from the kitchen.

Tess became a frequent visitor to Seaview cottage. In the evenings they pulled the armchairs up closer to the fire and shuddered when great gusts of wind blattered the windows and the sea roared onto the rocks. Mrs Green worried about Tess walking home in the dark, but she always said she wasn't afraid and never agreed to stay. They talked about their day – what had been done in the house and what needed to be done tomorrow. Sometimes Mrs Green brought out her scrapbook, put it on their knees and turned through the pages. Tess knew her father would have something to say about it, but she liked looking at the pictures of the Royal family and most especially of Princess Elizabeth and the handsome Prince Philip. Once, she asked about the empty pages – the brown rectangles of glue left behind where pictures had been pasted.

'That's where the other King used to be,' Mrs Green told her, explaining all about Mrs Simpson and the abdication. 'You can't turn a sow's ear into a silk purse,' she said, and the King should never have got involved with her. He should have stuck to his own kind, for marrying up or down never ended well.

Often Tess talked about her friend Marie, about their days off and their nights dancing in the Rinkha ballroom.

'I wish I had a dress like hers,' she sighed, describing the birthday dress which Marie had danced in. In the spring, Mrs Green said, they would go to Miss Rea's and choose a pattern and material for a new dress.

'It won't take me long to make it once I've got you measured up,' she promised.

The morning which had begun with a feeling of uneasiness for Wilma was ending in a sense of déjà vu. She'd recognized the house as she'd read about it – the vases, the piano, and the portrait above the fireplace. She knew she was sitting in that house now and it intrigued her, but another emotion had taken hold of her. She'd been carried back on a wave of nostalgia to the places and shops of her childhood. Memories of the Silver Strand came flooding back, as warm as the hot Sunpat peanuts that Miss Hattrick had scooped into a waxy bag for her. She'd had the patience of a saint, Miss Hattrick, waiting an age for her to choose from the penny box or the half penny box, her whole world depending on the choice between a black jack or a fruit salad or a sailor's bootlace liquorice. She remembered McCrellis' chip shop and her father bringing home fish suppers wrapped in newspaper for a Friday night treat. And she remembered her parent's stories of how they'd met at a dance in the Rinkha ballroom. It was something that Wilma had always regretted – that the ballroom had closed long before she was old enough to go. She'd had disco but she'd always loved her father's big band records and the romance of it all. She looked at her watch, sat on at the table and turned the page.

It was just after Tess' new dress had been made in the spring that she first encountered changeable weather. After lunch Mrs Green had gone out to visit her sister and she'd gone to her room to try on her dress again. It had taken her an age to choose the material in Mrs Rea's shop, so many bales of fabric had been opened out on the long wooden counter. She had wanted green, like Marie's, but finally Miss Rea had draped the white cotton with the red rambling roses around her and said it was perfect for her colouring and Mrs Green had agreed.

Tess swirled the full skirt of the dress around her hips and pulled the broad belt tighter through the buckle, holding in her waist and looking at herself in the mirror. She couldn't wait to go dancing in the Rinkha on Saturday night for Marie to see her dress. A noise startled her, the thud vibrating across the ceiling. She quickly changed back into her uniform and went out into the vestibule to the foot of the stairs. She heard a howl, a hard crack and the sound of smashing glass. Nervously she went up and stood on the landing. When she heard the scream she turned the doorknob of Adele Montgomery's bedroom and stepped tentatively inside.

The marble-topped occasional table under the window had been overturned, its gold legs up in the air. Mrs Montgomery was slumped at the dressing table – one of the mirror panels shattered, shards of glass scattered around the perfume bottles and brushes and china bowls. Her hand was bleeding, droplets of blood running down her fingers and onto the floor. Tess went to the bathroom for a basin and eased Adele's hand into the warm water, holding the facecloth firmly over the cut. It wasn't deep but she was trembling with the shock of it, and then, in a shuddering choke, it all came out.

'He doesn't love me,' she moaned, her eyes wide and glassy, 'he never loved me. And don't think I wouldn't have left him,' her voice began to rise, 'I would have and I still could. I could leave him tomorrow if I wanted to.'

Adele jumped up, pulling her hand out of the basin, 'I will leave him,' she shouted, as Tess followed after her into the dressing room.

In a fury of energy clothes were pulled from hangers and flung onto the floor, as the blood ran down Adele's arm, and as she railed against her husband. She didn't want or need him and this time she would show him.

'I'm so tired of it all,' she sank to her knees, burying her face in an armful of clothes.

Tess knew she had exhausted herself, gently eased her up off the floor, and guided her back into the bedroom.

'But I need to pack,' she whimpered.

'We'll pack tomorrow,' Tess assured, sitting her down at the dressing table and washing the blood from her face and arms.

'The others loved me and wanted to marry me' she sniffled, 'but he never loved me.'

Tess lifted the hairbrush, picked a piece of glass out of it, and started to brush Adele Montgomery's hair, 'There now,' Tess soothed, 'there now.'

'I was beautiful then,' Adele drew in a sob of breath.

'You are beautiful,' Tess said quietly, 'just like Elizabeth Taylor.'

Mrs Montgomery let out a small strangled laugh, opened her dressing table drawer and brought out a glass and a bottle of gin. She poured a measure and brought it unsteadily to her lips, her eyes never leaving Tess'. Tess didn't try to take it away from her or tell her that she shouldn't have it. If there was one thing Tess knew about, she knew about the drink. She knew, that after the rages and the tearing and the self- pity, there would be exhaustion and calm. She knew that you agreed and soothed until there was sleep. Adele Montgomery took another sip and set the glass down.

Tess helped her into bed and in minutes she was in a deep, breath-heavy sleep. There was work to do. She brushed up the broken glass, righted the heavy table, and hung all the clothes back up on the rails, sorting the bloodied ones into a pile for the laundry. Everything was back in order, only the broken mirror panel reflecting a sign of what had occurred. She stepped out of the room, stopped, went back and put the gin bottle back into the dressing table drawer. Once she had poured her father's whiskey down the sink, after he had fallen out of his rage into unconsciousness. He'd remembered when he'd woken – dry mouthed and rough – that he hadn't finished the bottle and she had never done it again. She knew that as much was remembered in drink as was forgotten, and she knew not to come between a drinker and their drink. That she understood, and she understood more now about Mrs Montgomery and her changeable weather.

When Mrs Green came back and found the clothes steeping in the laundry sink, Tess told her what had happened – Mrs Montgomery had cut her hand but it wasn't deep and she'd managed to get the bleeding to stop.

'Accidents will happen,' Mrs Green said, and told Tess not to worry. She would look in on her shortly.

Tess did not tell Mrs Green about anything that had been said or that Mrs Montgomery drank gin in her bedroom in the afternoon.

It was nearly eleven o'clock. Wilma closed the book, placed it back on the bedside table, and making a mental note of the page number she'd finished on took the bed linen down to the laundry room. She immediately sensed that she wasn't alone. It didn't unnerve her. It was a sense with which she was both familiar and comfortable. For such a practical woman Wilma had a surprisingly unearthly side – a belief in the cards and the reading of palms and the tea leaves. She believed in the other world and in the ghosts who inhabited it. Her shadow of a friend had been in the laundry room with her before and had followed her around the house as she cleaned and dusted. She hadn't known her in this life but now she knew her name. Her name was Tess.

However, she had also read about someone whom she had known in this life. Back in the sixties her grandmother had regularly visited two elderly sisters and she'd always begged be taken along, knowing that the iced buns and the secret drawer were waiting. She would eat her bun slowly as they talked and drank their tea, taking little darting licks of the icing when they weren't watching because she knew it was rude to lick, and always saving the sticky cherry on the top until last. She would wait and wait until her grandmother's cup was turned over and the leaves read, until finally she was told to go to the writing desk. She knew where to find the button to open the secret drawer but was always thrilled to find the bag of sweets. She never went home without them.

Mrs Green's was the first dead body she'd ever seen and even as a child she'd known, before she went into the house that morning, that something was different. She'd sneaked up the stairs behind her grandmother and the other ladies, pulling herself up on her tiptoes to see what they were looking at in the long box at the bottom of the bed.

'She looks just like herself,' her grandmother said, but she didn't think it looked like Mrs Green at all, her face pulled all tight and smooth and waxy. She'd reached out her hand to touch her, had been seen, and taken out the room.

'No place for a child,' someone said, 'it'll be giving her nightmares.'

Outside on the landing her grandmother had explained that Mrs Green was dead but there was nothing to be scared of – it was only her body in the coffin and the Mrs Green she knew was in heaven with the angels. She wasn't scared. She'd already known that Mrs Green was dead and when she went downstairs and found her sweets in the secret drawer she knew an angel had left them there for her.

Until today Wilma had forgotten all about Mrs Green. She'd never known that she had once been the housekeeper in The Mount, but it had to be her – the tea leaves had given it away. She loaded the sheets into the washing machine, ready for tomorrow's wash, and went out to see if Mrs Mountjoy wanted anything in particular for lunch. She wasn't in the greenhouse but she saw her then at the bottom of the garden almost hidden between the hedge and the apple tree. A man had stopped at the gate on the top path and was staring intently up at the house. For a moment Wilma thought he would open the gate and come in. He didn't. He lit a cigarette and stood there smoking it. He couldn't see Mrs Mountjoy, but Wilma could see that she was watching him, and her eyes didn't leave him and she didn't move, not a twitch, until he walked on.

6

He rose early and came quietly down the stairs from the top of the guest house. He could hear the scrape of bacon being pushed around the pan in the kitchen, and although the smell was tempting, popped his head through the door and informed Mrs Rogan that he didn't require breakfast this morning.

'Just as well it's not for you then,' she said, turning back to the cooker.

The sun was up, a shimmering orb hovering over the Copeland Islands out on the horizon. The promenade was deserted – curtains still drawn along its length. He walked along the front to the Blackhead path and stopped for a moment looking across towards the lighthouse, high up on the cliffs above. He closed his eyes letting his senses drift. He had always struggled to describe this feeling. It was to do with sound and smell and air – the last moment of a summer's evening when the sun was slipping away and the smell of newly mown grass still lingered with the birdsong – the soothing soft crunch of the sea on rocks and gulls shrieking and swooping in salt seaweed air. It was when everything combined to bring a moment of perfect peace, when the soul embraced a simple moment of joy. It was now and he gave himself up to it as his thoughts shrank away to a small inconsequence – he could have picked them up and thrown them like a pebble into the sea. The dull whirr of an engine brought him back. He opened his eyes and watched the small boat puttering towards the lobster pot buoys. The boatman waved towards him as he turned and walked on.

He reached the bend at the old Port Davey slipway. Off the path the boathouse was just visible amongst a tangle of bracken and briar. He trampled his way through it, scratched and swearing. He could easily have kicked through the rotting doors but behind the broken planks could see there was nothing inside. He tramped his way back to the path trying to place Seaview Cottage. He had no memory of living there but had been told that he had. Only the foundations remained and around them pieces of rubble strewn in the undergrowth. He sat down on a bench and smoked a cigarette and then another. The tide was ebbing gently back from the shore and away from the Wren's Eggs. It comforted him that these two huge prehistoric rocks – left behind by an ancient glacier – remained permanently stranded on the shore. He had climbed them as a boy, scrambling up their smooth slippery sides.

'I'm the king of the castle. I'm the king of the castle,' he used to sing to himself when he made it to the top. The shore had been his play place, his escape from the boarding house room he'd shared with his mother – he remembered living there.

He walked down across the strip of sand, meeting the tumble of black-green boulders exposed by the retreating tide. Clumsy, without his nimble child's feet, he slipped and stumbled over them getting his feet wet in the rock pools. He remembered searching them for blood suckers to squash his fingers in and prising yellow-bellied limpets off the stones. He struggled on, the call of the castle echoing around him. He reached the Wren's Eggs and had a mad thought to attempt it – to re-conquer his boyhood Everest – but he wasn't as fearless now as he had been then.

He made his way back up onto the path and walked on around the bend, past the foot of the steeply rising Golden Stairs and on past Sunshine House – the solitary dwelling at this end of the bay. The caves, when he reached them, were as deep and dark as he remembered. His mother had filled them full of horrors, threatening, when he was naughty, to hand him over to the mad old schoolmaster who lived there. He'd promised to be good, knowing that the wild-eyed troll of his imagination was lurking under the bridge waiting to drag him away. In his dreams he'd been there, laid down in the schoolmaster's bedchamber on top of the other children's bones. He stood now on the bridge between the caves and looked under it, his deep-rooted childhood fear not quite assuaged, but there was nothing there, only the long drop into the sea below. He lingered uneasily, trying to identify the cavity in the side of the cave wall where well over a century ago the old schoolmaster had actually lived. He thought he had made it out but wasn't sure.

He heard a dog bark and turned to see the morning walkers dotted along the path behind him in a loosely knotted string. He moved on, through the dark damp tunnel cut through the cliff, and came out the other side. He began the long climb up to the lighthouse and found himself counting the steps – a habit formed over the years to persuade his lungs to carry his legs. Somewhere between ninety and a hundred he stopped counting and retrieved his breath on the stretches of path between them. He reached the wall of the lighthouse and followed its curve until it met the top cliff path. He stopped and smoked a cigarette then started back along the path, keeping his eyes down, careful of the slippery packed earth beneath his feet and of the overgrown briars catching at his legs. As he neared the town his footing improved and briar and thorn gave way to a neatly trimmed hedge. He couldn't see over it into the garden but could see the house high up above it – The Mount. He walked along to the garden gate and stopped, looking up over the terraces to the patio and veranda. He lit a cigarette and smoked it, taking his time, taking it all in. A fair-haired woman came out of the house and looked at him suspiciously. He grew uncomfortable and walked away.

By the time he came down off the top path the town was well awake. He could hear the sing-song chorus of children's voices drifting out from the primary school playground and walked across the bottom of the avenue to the railings. He had attended the school for a couple of years before he'd been taken away to England. He watched the children for a while – a few running around the playground, others huddled in groups against the classroom wall, playing games he thought on their mobile phones. He remembered the girls skipping or playing clapping games and hours of chase and catch. He remembered running the field between two lines of chanting boys, trying to breach the British Bulldog wall on the other side. He'd been small but agile and able to side step the bigger boys and get through, the grass burnt knees and bruises a hero's battle scars. They wouldn't be allowed to play that game today – too rough, too dangerous, too ringing the alarm bells of Health and Safety.

The bell rang calling the children in. He crossed the road, walked down past the War Memorial and up onto King's Bridge, stepping off the pavement to accommodate a group of girls pushing their babies in a charge of buggies. They didn't acknowledge his manners and although it would have been refreshing, he hadn't really expected it. Life had changed, even in Whitehaven.

He went into the shop to buy a newspaper. At the bookstand two ladies were engaged in conversation and he couldn't help but overhear.

'Norma you must buy a copy immediately they'll all be gone by teatime.'

'Dilys, I already have it. Lillian brought me a copy a few days ago.'

'And have you finished it?'

'I've just started it.'

'Honestly Norma, how can you put it down?'

Dilys reached for a copy from the book stand, leafed through the pages, and pointing to the title of the chapter mouthed the word, 'Frederica.'

'What about it?' Norma asked.

'What about it?' Dilys hooted, before she set forth.

Frederica was an only daughter and her father was Freddy. And Maybelle had an only daughter, Edwina, and her father was Teddy, or Edward to be precise.

'And what's your point Dilys?'

'Well apart from the coincidence of the names, the Frederica character is quite wayward, rather scandalous really.'

'What's that supposed to mean?'

'Oh come on Norma, you're Whitehaven born and bred, you must know all about Edwina Mountjoy and her life, you must know if Edwina and Frederica are one and the same?'

'I haven't read the blasted book and even if I had I know nothing of the sort.'

'When you've read it you'll see that I'm right.'

'I don't have time for this nonsense,' Norma bristled, and walked away.

The dark-haired, large-hipped Dilys then turned her attention to him, handing him the book and recommending that he buy it.

'It's about us, well not about us personally,' she screeched 'but about Whitehaven.'

He flicked randomly between the covers until his thumb stopped – *George*. He smiled to himself and scanned through the chapter.

7

George Montgomery went to the dining room and poured a whiskey – a rare and unusual act. Although he could pass himself socially, or on the completion of a business deal, he was by nature abstemious. He disliked the effect of not being in control. This morning, however, his infuriating son had failed to keep an appointment, his promise of the previous evening when they had dined together in the Royal Hotel, all too easily broken. He expected appointments to be kept, and to time, and no one in his world dared to keep him waiting. Only Adele abused the unspoken rule but he had long since given up where her transgressions were concerned. He had not yet quite given up on Freddy, and although he'd been giving in to him for far too long, had been prepared to reason with him about his future. Now, having been circumvented, he intended to lay down the law – his father had taken him into the business when he was barely seventeen and at twenty years old his own son would do what he was told or suffer the consequences. He finished the whiskey and poured another.

He knew he wasn't entirely blameless. Freddy's year away from home, wandering around the Continent, had been as much his fault as anyone's. He'd arrived home *unexpectedly one afternoon to find mother and son huddled together in the dining room, the table strewn with papers.*

'Freddy's going to build his own yacht,' Adele had trilled.

Freddy had excitedly showed him his drawings, as neatly drafted as a blueprint, and had talked in great technical detail. He had to admit he'd been surprised and impressed, but he'd had to ask the question.

'And how is this to be financed?' he'd enquired.

Freddy proposed that his grandfather's yacht, the Elizabeth Ann, could be sold and the revenue put towards building a new boat. It had made perfect sense to his son, who believed it would be a good investment, but for him it was out of the question.

'What do you want that old boat for George, you don't even sail, you're scared of the water,' Adele had sneered.

That was true but he couldn't let go of something which his father had built and cherished and named after the mother he had never known. Adele had become upset, turning to the drinks cabinet, shouting and accusing him of being an old stick in the mud and kill joy. Freddy had talked to him quietly then – he had a plan to go to England and maybe Europe for a few months, to visit some boat building yards and get more experience of craft and design. After that, if he agreed to him going, they could talk about it again.

'I suppose you'll scupper that idea too,' Adele had snapped.

To their surprise, he'd found himself not only agreeing to the idea but encouraging it. For the first time he had begun to see something in his son – perhaps even the seeds of a businessman – and caught up with the thought he'd offered to finance the trip. Adele had thrown her arms around him, jumping and squealing with delight, and his son had shaken him warmly by the hand. Freddy's several months away had turned into a year, with money being regularly sent to various destinations, until finally he had demanded that he come home. On his return there had been no talk of yacht building, no talk of any future plan. His son, abetted by Adele, had outwitted him and he wouldn't let it happen again. Freddy would join the company now and that would be that.

George Montgomery turned the glass in his hand and raised it to his wife, her singular beauty captured above the mantelpiece in an innocent wistful pose. His father had commissioned the portrait as a wedding gift and it had delighted him, as he had once been delighted by Adele. It was still a fine painting – a picture of youthful promise – her face serene and caught in the light streaming in from the window which framed her pose. There was no hint of darkness in the eyes looking off into the bucolic scene beyond, or of the torments that he would suffer from those slightly smiling lips. He stood looking at her, as she had once been, his anger giving way to melancholy reflection.

It was not just Adele's beauty which had attracted him, just as it had drawn many others helplessly towards her. Something had set her apart from the few other women he had courted – a vivacity and energy, an irrepressible and fearless spirit. He had never encountered anyone quite like her, the opposite side of his much more serious coin – a bright shining crown to be won. He was not the only man of means to have pursued Adele but he had wooed her relentlessly, competitively, and would not be denied the prize. He might have been ten years older than her but he believed that she had loved him. She had told him so. She had told him more easily than he had been able to express his love for her. He had sought no advice about his choice of bride and none had been offered.

'As long as you're sure of her,' his father had remarked, and he'd seen no intention of a warning in it.

Taking another drink of whiskey his father's familiar voice, deep and gravelled by cigarettes, came back to him – 'Are you sure of her.' Had he seen something in Adele, some hidden trait that he, consumed with passion, had failed to see? 'Are you sure of her?' Twenty years ago, at the beginning of a new decade which had started with such excitement and promise, he had been sure.

In March of 1930 he and his father had moved into The Mount – the house an impressive monument to Frederick Montgomery's success – and he, newly promoted to Chairman of the Board of the company, had been consumed with work. In April he attended a dinner in Belfast City Hall – an annual gathering of leading manufacturers, bankers, city councillors and accompanying wives and companions. He had forgone the invitation to bring a lady guest, although there were several who would have willingly accompanied him. During the lengthy speeches his eye was drawn to the vivacious young woman holding the table next to his in thrall, with her animated chatter, wit and easy laughter. She had caught him looking at her and had held his gaze, drawing him irredeemably into her blue velvet-eyes. He'd asked to be introduced, had danced with her, and in the succeeding weeks began to court her. In June he proposed and to his delight Adele accepted.

They married in August and honeymooned in Paris. Adele's energy was boundless and he followed after her on her adventures through the streets and boulevards, amused at her childlike surprise and joy. As she ran from place to place Parisian heads turned to admire her radiant beauty. He enjoyed the envy in their foreign eyes, proud that she was his. In restaurants she mesmerised waiters and diners, with a turn of those velvet eyes and her giddy schoolgirl French, delivered unselfconsciously and with laughter. She failed in her attempts to make him try.

'Georges, je t'adore,' she purred, reaching her hand over the table to stroke his cheek and teasing his leg under it with her toe, as the diners smiled at them and whispered to each other. They knew about love the Parisians, recognising it when they saw it, and comfortable in its reflection. They went to the Folies Bergere and he became uncomfortable, sitting there in the dark with his young wife, watching the semi-clad dancers on the stage. He wanted to leave but she wheedled and cajoled and then puffed that he was an old stick in the mud. He gave in, sitting there stiffly at her side, and removed her caressing hand from his thigh. The rebuff changed her mood. She refused to speak to him on the way back to the hotel, turning her face away from him, and she turned away from him in bed.

The next morning he made it up to her and swept her off to the fashion houses of Paris where he indulged her and denied her nothing. When they returned to the hotel, laden with boxes, she was feverish with excitement, twirling in the mirror and parading in front of him in her gowns and finery. She struck a pose at the window, looking out over the rooftops of Paris, the white pearl skin of her neck exposed. He would clasp that neck with pearls he told himself, pearls fit for a goddess, but not yet.

'Vous etes une vedette madam,' she said across the room, 'vous etes une vedette, comme Claudette Colbert.' He looked at her in confusion. The couturier had said it, she explained, crossing the floor and leaping, dress hoisted, unto the bed.

'Je suis une film star, je suis Claudette Colbert, non?' his goddess growled, dancing up and down on the bed, swirling the long skirt of the dress up around her thighs. And then she had thrown herself on him and he was Georges again.

In the third week of the honeymoon he surprised her with a trip to Monte Carlo. She was thrilled but teased him remorselessly about his meticulous plans – the route he'd traced carefully on the map, places of interest to see, overnight hotel stops. Adele just wanted to get into the car and go wherever the road took them. She huffed when he stuck to his plan. On the second afternoon, motoring through the countryside, she threw the map and his lists of paper out of the window, hooting the horn, as he walked back to retrieve them. A car drove past, stopped up ahead on the roadside, and he watched as a man came mistakenly to his wife's assistance. Adele got out of their car, chattering and gesticulating, and then accepted the arm of the dark-haired young man as he guided her towards his vehicle. Looking back at him she pretended to get in and as he walked back up the road the car roared off, his wife laughing and waving and after it. He drove on darkly as she tried to bring him out of his mood, snuggling into him, chiding him in her small child's voice for his seriousness.

In the bright reflection of the Mediterranean light and the in attentiveness of his young wife the irritations of the drive south were mostly forgotten. In Monte Carlo they rose early and strolled in the sunshine along the waterfront and through the cooler shadows of the narrow back streets. They climbed the steep winding road to the pink Grimaldi Palace and he took photographs of Adele looking down on the harbour and the villa lined bay below. She posed easily and seductively turning her body towards him, lifting her leg and squeezing her knee into her thigh. She asked a passer-by to photograph them together and he reluctantly gave up the camera, shouting back instructions, as she pulled him towards her and draped his arm around her shoulder. For a long time he had carried that photograph in his wallet. He didn't know where it was now.

They lunched in the sea front restaurants and in the afternoons returned to the cool marble interior of the Hotel de Paris for coffee, or sat outside under the umbrella shaded tables eating ice cream or sorbet, which she spooned from her bowl into his mouth. In the evenings they dressed for dinner and dined in the opulence of the Louis XV restaurant, stealing glances at the other diners and listening to the strange cadences of the old houses of Europe and of the rich Americans. He knew that eyes were also being drawn to the beauty of his wife. After dinner they walked through the palm tree lined gardens to the casino, familiar faces from the hotel joining them at the roulette tables. He didn't play, but was happy for Adele to glow in the adoration and cheers of society when she gathered in some small wins.

On their last night he waited on the balcony of their suite, the evening air a little too warm for his dinner jacket, his black bow tie tight at his neck. Adele changed again and again unable to decide what to wear. He grew impatient, his hand constantly going to the jewellery case in his pocket. He had intended to give it to her on their first night in Monte Carlo but in his irritation had withheld it. Now it was time.

'Close your eyes,' she called from inside the room.

He sensed her then on the balcony, the sweetness of her perfume drawing in on his breath. When he opened his eyes his breath stopped, as she twirled in front of him, the firm contours of her body sculpted in sea-blue silk, her shoulders and back exposed in the long open v of the dress. He slipped the jewellery case from his pocket and clasped his mother's pearls around her neck. In the soft shadow of the lowering Mediterranean sun he kissed her neck and shoulder, and turning her in his arms he kissed away her surprised delight softly with his lips.

'I have another surprise for you,' he said at breakfast the next morning.

'Where is it?' she squealed, patting down his pockets, 'where is it?'

He unfolded the sheet of paper and spread it out on the table, his finger tracing the route of the Monaco Grand Prix as he explained about the race, the cars and the drivers. Before they left for Paris he was going to drive her around the route. Of course it wouldn't the same as the actual race but the bends would be amazing. Adele sipped her coffee and yawned.

'I have such a headache,' she moaned, 'I'm going to lie down.'

Disappointed he went alone, memorising every stretch and bend and gear change to tell his father about. When he arrived back at the hotel Adele wasn't there.

'Madam has gone out,' the concierge was able to tell him.

He supposed that her headache must have lifted and, having come to know her a little, imagined she had gone shopping. He went to look for her but couldn't find her in any of the shops. He walked along the sea front thinking she might want to take in a last view of the Mediterranean before they left. He saw her sitting at a café table, throwing her head back with laughter, as her young dark-haired companion amused her. The man saw him and indicated his presence to her with his dark eyes. Adele turned and smiled.

'This is Etienne,' she said, as he approached the table, 'remember, he stopped in his car, wherever it was.'

He did remember,

'I met him quite by chance just after you left,' she offered, 'quelle surprise,' she laughed.

'Quelle surprise,' the young man echoed, as they looked at each other and laughed again.

'We need to go,' he pronounced, taking Adele by the elbow and bringing her protesting to her feet.

'Au revoir Claudette,' her friend said, taking her hand and bringing it to his lips.

'A joke George, just a little joke,' she trilled, meeting the blaze in his eyes.

They walked back to the hotel in silence and he had their luggage brought down and loaded into the car.

'Feeling better?' he asked coldly, as she got into the car beside him.

She slammed the door closed, and tying her long silk scarf around her neck, looked away.

'It's unputdownable, isn't it?' Dilys interrupted him, peering over his arm to the opened page.

He smiled and shrugged his shoulders.

'Even if you're not a local,' she continued, 'it's still a good read.'

He smiled again.

'You're not a local, are you?' she asked.

He knew her type. She would happily mind his and everyone else's business before she minded her own.

'No,' he confirmed, and replacing the book back on the stand, turned and made for the door.

8

The long morning's walk had not only worked up his memories but his thirst. He headed down to the railway station and across the tracks to the Whitecliff Inn. He was more than ready for a long cold beer, a smoke, and quiet time to think. There was something about the smell of a pub early in the day, the odour of stale cigarettes and beer, which helped to concentrate his mind. He'd read somewhere that smell was the sense most strongly associated with memory and was the last one to leave you. He believed it, that on his deathbed he wouldn't recall images or sounds or tastes, but the smell of his childhood. The smell of it was around him now – the whiff of disinfectant drifting out from the open door of the gent's toilet. The flowery aroma wasn't as pungent as the smell which had come from his mother's mop bucket as he'd followed her around the old bar, a smell that had lingered on her in bed at night.

There was only one other customer in the lounge, sitting in the corner with his dog, as he had been on the first day when he'd arrived in the town. He took a stool at the other end of the bar and opened his newspaper out on the counter. The Captain was a man who drew the eye and he glanced over at him, careful not to be seen observing him. He was good at that. A shock of thick white hair topped a still strongly defined and tanned face, although the ice blue eyes had lost a little intensity with the years. He must have been impossibly handsome in his youth – swashbuckling movies and a particular British matinee idol came to mind but he couldn't recall the name of the actor. It would probably come in the middle of the night when it had kept him from sleep.

His arrival in the bar had obviously interrupted a conversation, and having served him his pint, Noreen lifted the Captain's glass from the counter and pressed it up under the optic until the last drop of Bushmills whiskey had trickled into the glass.

'So, you've heard about it then?' Noreen said, holding up a book.

'Unfortunately my wife's reading it,' he admitted.

'But is he allowed to use real names Captain?' she asked.

'I suppose if the people are dead,' he reckoned, watering his whiskey from the jug.

'Well, in what I've read so far I've come across Mrs Everly from the promenade and she's dead sure enough,' Noreen said.

'Doreen Everly, the less said about that woman the better,' the Captain grimaced.

'And old Mrs Green, do you remember her?'

'Now she was a fine woman,' he nodded.

'But they've both been dead for a long time and Captain Donaldson only died this week, so the writer must have put his name in before he died,' Noreen posed.

'I don't know,' the Captain shook his head, 'but I hope you're not going to find my name in there or I might be on the way out too.'

'You're a long way from dead Captain,' Noreen assured, as he raised his glass to her.

'Life in the old dog yet,' he said, 'isn't that right Skipper, life in both of us yet.'

The dog shifted on the floor, stirred from sleep by the sound of his name.

'But then,' Noreen continued, 'there are the real names and others that seem to be made up, so it's hard to know who's really who, if you know what I mean?'

'I do, but I think I'll leave that and the book to my wife,' the Captain asserted.

'But don't you wonder who the author is?' she persisted, 'everyone's talking about it but no one seems to know the name. Do you think he's from here?'

'I don't have any thoughts on it at all,' the Captain sighed, mouthing to her and pointing down the bar.

'Sorry about that,' Noreen apologised, lifting his empty pint glass from the counter, 'you should have shouted up. We were talking about a book that's been written about Whitehaven, sorry.'

He pushed the change across the counter to pay for the pint.

'It's paid for,' she said, nodding her head up the bar towards the Captain.

He smiled and raised his glass to him in acknowledgement, knowing he'd been caught – the buying of a drink a means of drawing him in. He folded up his newspaper and moved up the bar, although wary. At a bar counter, particularly in these parts, a life story could be drawn out of you between the first and second pint.

'I saw you along the shore this morning,' the Captain said, pulling out the barstool for him, 'did you go all the way up to the lighthouse?'

'I did,' he replied, rubbing his thighs, still tight from the climb.

The Captain didn't go as far as the lighthouse these days but most mornings to the caves and back. 'We're not as young as we use to be, are we Skipper?' he said, as the dog lifted its head and nuzzled into his foot.

As the Captain relayed the history of the Blackhead Path, of Sunshine House and the lighthouse, they fell into buying rounds.

'I'm Bob by the way,' the Captain finally introduced.

'Nice to meet you,' he said, and excusing himself went to the gent's.

He returned to another pint of beer waiting on the counter and the Captain talked about his life at sea, the shipping lines he had worked for and the vessels which had been under his command. He sailed with him around the Far East to the Middle East and to the Americas. When they reached Buenos Ares he decided to jump ship, and draining the last mouthful from his glass got to his feet. The Captain tried to order another round but he refused and refused again.

'Another time,' he suggested, lifting his newspaper and scooping up his change.

'Before you go you might like to sign this,' the Captain said, indicating to Noreen to pass him something from behind the bar.

He stiffened and then relaxed as a clipboard was set down on the counter in front of him. As he scanned the top page the Captain explained that the local council was trying to close the Blackhead Path to the public.

'Scared of rock falls you see,' he explained, 'scared of being bloody well sued if someone gets hurt. Any other council in the world would invest in it,' he raged, 'but here they'd rather spend our money on idiotic schemes that nobody wants.'

'Can they really close it?' he asked, dumbfounded.

'That's what this is about,' Noreen said, pointing him to the petition and handing him a pen, 'we've got hundreds of signatures already.' He signed, and again refusing another drink, made his way a little unsteadily out of the door.

The Captain, with his company having departed, was also thinking about heading home. He sipped on the last of his Bushmills and grew thoughtful with it. There was something about that man that he couldn't quite put his finger on – a look about him that was vaguely familiar. And there was something about the type of him, and he'd encountered every type of drinker in his time – those who told you their life story on the first drink and those who spilled it out on the last, others who no amount of drink would loosen, and some who knew when to stop before they divulged too much of themselves. The man had told him nothing about himself, not even his name. He put on his glasses, running his eye down the sheet to the last signature on the page – an illegible scrawl. One word had been written as an address, it might have been London.

'He's been in a few times,' Noreen informed him, 'English I'd say from his accent.'

The beer delivery truck rattled past the window and turned into the car park. He asked for another whiskey before she went off to count in the order and returned to his thoughts. Noreen was right about the accent but he was sure that he'd detected a trace of something underneath it – the little tell-tale flattening of the vowels which always gave it away. If that man wasn't from Northern Ireland then he'd been brought up by somebody who was. Finishing his drink the Captain determined to put his mind to it.

He walked home with Skipper and around the side of the house to the back door. Unusually Betty wasn't in the kitchen – a pot of potatoes left sitting on the cooker, cabbage sliced on a chopping board on the worktop.

'I'm in the living room,' he heard her call out and walked along the hallway to the door.

'Is it that time already?' she said, lifting her book up from her knee, 'sorry I got distracted.'

Grateful that she hadn't realised how late he was, he retreated.

'Bob,' she stopped him, 'remember Teddy Mountjoy, what was his mother's name?'

'Adelaide.'

'That's it,' she nodded, 'I knew that but I couldn't get Adele out of my head. What do you remember about her?'

'Like what?' he asked.

'Anything,' she encouraged.

'She was a very good looking woman, a beauty really,' he replied.

'Apart from that Bob,' she looked over her glasses at him.

'Well, there was something not quite right about her,' he continued.

'In what way do you mean?' she questioned.

'I don't know, I suppose she was a bit neurotic.'

'Interesting,' she said, 'very interesting.'

'Is it,' he said unconvinced, 'I don't know why you'd be interested in that?'

'I have my reasons,' she said.

'Don't tell me. I suppose it's something to do with that bloody book you're reading.'

'Now Bob, language,' she chided.

He turned from the doorway and started back to the kitchen.

'Bob,' she called him back, 'do you remember a girl from the Royal Hotel?'

'The Royal Hotel,' he snorted in disbelief.

'Well, we went there often enough,' she retorted, 'and this girl would have been there in the early fifties I suppose.'

'This is getting too much now,' he complained, 'that's fifty years ago.'

'Oh well, I thought you prided yourself on your memory,' she shrugged, 'I thought there was nothing you didn't know about this town and its past, away at sea for most of it or not.'

'What girl?' he pacified, feeling a row coming on.

'Her name was Tess or Theresa, Theresa O'Brien, and she might have left the hotel to go and work for the Mountjoys.'

'I really have no idea.'

'But you were friendly with the Mountjoys weren't you,' she went on, 'don't you remember her there?'

'I was friendly with the Mountjoys, Betty, but not with the hired help,' he snarled.

'Sorry I asked!' she turned back to her book.

He walked down the hall to the kitchen.

'I'll be there in a minute,' she shouted, and following her called instructions he turned the hot plate on under the potatoes.

In the living room, Betty McCrae leant back into the cushions on her chair, determined to finish the chapter.

At the end of August George Montgomery brought his young wife home to The Mount to be greeted by two surprises. The first was unveiled before they sat down to dinner.

'You had no idea George,' Adele squealed, hugging onto his father, 'or how we had to sneak about to get it painted without you knowing.'

Over dinner they admired Adele's likeness above the fireplace and she then chattered incessantly about Paris. He managed to tell his father a little about his drive around Monaco until his wife demanded that he go in search of the wine which had been brought home from France. On his return to the dining room the second surprise was waiting.

'I've signed the house over to you George,' his father said, handing him the title deeds to The Mount.

As Adele leapt up and smothered his father's face with kisses, he protested. He intended to buy his own home and they would move out as soon a suitable property could be found. His father wouldn't hear of it. He had already begun the move to his flat in the city and would be quite happy there.

'But we could all live here together,' he insisted.

'I've made up my mind George and anyway it's better for a young couple starting out to be on their own.'

His gratitude had been tempered by a feeling of uneasiness – his father had invested so much of himself in The Mount and having barely lived in it seemed to be handing it over too readily. However, becoming busy with work and settling into married life he put his concerns aside. Adele too was occupied with ideas for the house which she threw herself into with energetic enthusiasm. In October, she began to plan a party for her twenty-first birthday, a grand affair which would allow them to throw the doors of The Mount open to society. He had been genuinely amazed at her ability – the detail of the menu, the entertainment, the guest list produced in detail – and he believed, in a deluded conceit, that she had learned from him. In the birthday week the house became mad with activity – rooms arranged and re-arranged, deliveries of food, consignments of wine, and boxes of cut flowers. In the evenings Adele paraded in front of him in the bedroom in her Paris gowns, torturing him with her inability to make a choice.

'It's all for you my darling, I want to be perfect for you' she whispered, slipping her arms around him, and asking him to help her out of her dress before she changed again.

The day before the party Adele took to her bed and refused to get up, leaving him with the embarrassing task of cancelling. Friends and guests accepted both his sincere apologies and the credible excuse which he made on his wife's behalf – that she was unfortunately prone to disabling migraine headaches. Adele stayed in bed for almost two weeks, barely eating, unresponsive and withdrawn. Eventually, against her wishes, he called the doctor.

'She's highly strung,' the doctor diagnosed, prescribing a tonic for her nerves. She recovered but the pattern of their future life together had been established.

By the end of November, concerns about his wife receded as worries about his father began to grow. He was noticeably absent from the office and rarely visited The Mount. He seemed indifferent – his energy and passion shrinking, his tailored suits hanging loose and limp like the dull grey flesh on his face. He would brook no discussion about his health, growling in irritation and swatting enquiries away with a flick of his hand.

Early on Christmas morning his father telephoned to say he would not be joining them for dinner. 'I'm out of sorts,' he said, 'I'll call you tomorrow.'

It was a bitter disappointment. He had never spent a Christmas Day without his father, and it was to have been their first together as a family in The Mount, but he had had to accept his excuses. He and Adele walked to church for the morning service, wrapped up warmly against the bite of frost in the air, and she held tightly onto his arm scared of slipping on the road. The singing of carols and the well-wishing of fellow worshippers raised his spirits and when they returned home the smell of roasting goose drifting through the house comforted him that this was what Christmas was supposed to be. They warmed themselves by the fire in the dining room and Adele made him laugh by posing under her portrait, and making him admit with her tickling hands, that she was more beautiful in the flesh.

'Aperitif,' she said, mixing them a drink. He drank it with her and then another, warm with it and with the heat from the fire. She started to pour another mixture into his glass and he refused it.

'It's Christmas George,' she begged in her little girl's voice and he let her fill it up, no longer resisting, giving himself up to the feeling of warm and happy intoxication.

'Come with me,' he took her by the hand and led her out into the vestibule.

'Oh Christmas tree, oh Christmas tree,' she sang, as he picked through the parcels under it until he found what he was looking for. They tiptoed together along the hall to the kitchen. Mrs Green turned from the range, her face red from the oven and steaming pots, and her husband jumped up from the armchair in surprise.

'Happy Christmas,' they beamed in unison, handing over the gifts and insisting they be opened. With a deal of thanks Mrs Green shooed them out of her domain and told them that dinner would be served in half an hour.

They ate in the dining room, course after course laid in front of them by the maid, and afterwards, replete and sleepy, curled up on the settee in front of the fire in the drawing room, Adele resting her head on his shoulder.

'Where's my present George?' she whispered into his ear, curling her fingers into his neck.

He moved her gently out of his arms and returned with the box, trying to hold it away from her as she darted and danced around him. She wrestled it from him and opened it on the floor, tearing at the wrappings like a child, until her hands reached the soft downy fur inside. He lifted her to her feet and held it for her, as she slipped her arms into the sleeves of the coat. She hugged it to her and then spun around opening it in a swirl, the light sheen of the silky sable caught in the glow of the fire.

'I love you George,' she said, as he caught her in an embrace, running his cheek across the exquisite softness of the rippling fur, to the softness of her neck.

On Boxing Day his father's telephone call did not come and his own calls went answered. Worried, he *drove to the flat in the afternoon and found him on the sofa, cold and struggling to breathe. At the hospital the doctors gave him little cause for hope – the cancer was advanced, they'd been treating him since May and it was only a matter of time. He visited every day, sitting quietly by the bedside, watching as the once strong face crept into a mask of death, the milky films of his eyes looking through him and beyond to some other place. He thought his father didn't recognise him but in his last words he reached out a thin waxy hand, 'You're a good boy George,' he said, 'the best son a man could have asked for.' That evening he slipped into unconsciousness, although it had taken him into the New Year to die.*

On New Year's Eve, he accompanied Adele to the annual supper dance in the Royal Hotel. He didn't want to go, concerned that the hospital might telephone, but arrangements had been made with friends and after the embarrassment of the birthday party cancellation he couldn't bring himself to disappoint. He tried to take on the festive mood but was distracted and inattentive.

Adele, dressed in her sea-blue silk Paris gown, revelled in the tide of compliments flowing around the table. He had enjoyed showing her off in it in the exotic salons of Monte Carlo but in the company of Darkhaven thought it too exposing. She brushed aside his suggestion that she cover her shoulders, squeezing his cheek and chiding him for being an old fuddy-duddy. He lifted the wrap from the back of her chair and draped it around her. She took the long ends of it in her hands, pulling it from side to side across her shoulders and slowly down the bareness of her back to her waist, her breasts pushed forward and her body shimmying like a show girl. It enraged him but he drove the anger coldly down, as the other husbands at the table watched her slyly, unable to disguise their thoughts.

Adele danced with those other husbands in turn, and then for a good part of the evening with one young man in particular, who had cut in on the dance floor. Her movements grew more provocative as they danced, until, with the floor cleared, she performed an impromptu tango with her young admirer, as the crowd offered wild encouragement. His face turned to a mask as she took her bows, whirled off the dance floor, and joined her partner at his table of young friends. As the floor filled again he watched her downing glasses of champagne, captivating her newly found companions. On the countdown to midnight he pushed through the crowd to her side.

'Five, four, three, two, one,' the bandleader called down the seconds, 'happy New Year, happy 1931.'

As the cheers went up he put his hand on her shoulder and she turned away from him, embracing the young man standing beside her, kissing him on the side of his mouth and allowing him to kiss her back. He felt that he might explode, might reach out and slap her, or punch the man who had dared to kiss his wife. He clenched his fists tightly to his side, then took her by the arm and told her they were going home.

'Don't be such a bore George,' she hissed, and turning sweetly to the table announced, 'everyone, my husband, George. Boring old George wants to take me home.'

The party protested – 'Stay, stay, stay,' they chanted, banging their glasses in time on the table as Adele conducted the raucous chorus, waving her bare arms through the air. He gripped his arm around her waist and pulled her away through the revellers, snatching up her wrap and evening bag. In the foyer he managed 'A happy New Year' to the cloakroom attendant as she handed over his hat and coat and propelled his wife out of the hotel and into the car. He drove her home in silence and followed her down the hallway into the dining room.

'Don't you think you've had enough?' he accused, as she poured herself a drink.

'Not nearly enough,' she spat, thrusting the glass at him, daring him to take it from her. He wanted to reach for it and smash it to the ground but turned from her and retreated to the door.

'Go to bed George,' she sneered, 'boring old Georgie, boring old Georgie,' she sang in a playground taunt, 'I married the wrong Montgomery, I married the wrong Montgomery.'

'What do you mean by that?' he demanded.

'Remember Monte Carlo George,' she slurred, raising the glass to her portrait, 'and you gave me those pearls and I was supposed to be so surprised, what a fool you are.'

'What?'

'Don't you see,' she laughed, 'your father had me painted in them before the honeymoon, I'd already worn them but I didn't let you know did I, I acted all surprised for poor old Georgie,' she took another drink, 'and he came to the studio every day your dear old father, to watch me being painted, he could hardly keep his hands off me.'

It was too much for him. He crossed the room in a stride and knocked the glass from her hand, his hands reaching for her throat. The stun of the slap to his face stopped him. He lifted his hand to slap her back and everything in her face – the bright laughing eyes, the upturn of the smile on her red coated mouth – had dared him to do it, willed it from him. He dropped his arm, his body trembling, and flinched as she lifted her hand again. She placed it softly on the reddening welt on his cheek.

'Poor old George,' she melted into him putting her lips on his, her mouth hot and greedy, and he allowed it, not resisting as she pulled him to the floor. After it was over she curled into his side on the rug, her breath on his neck, 'George, my George.' He lay there, shocked by what had taken place between them, unsure of the woman lying at his side, unsure of what she was.

George Montgomery stood now on the rug in front of the fireplace, where his son had been conceived, and drained the last of the whiskey from his glass. He caught a glimpse of a shadow and walked out into the hall to see Freddy disappear out of the front door. He made it out onto the step as the car accelerated away – gravel crunching under the spin of the tyres – and ran after him, but he was gone. At the gates, thunderous black clouds rumbled across the sky obscuring the sun and casting a long dark shadow along the driveway. The first drops of rain were soft, plashing gently on his shoulders. The air changed, turned cold, and hard pellets of rain smashed into him, ricocheting off the stones around his feet as he walked quickly back to the house – changeable weather. He vomited up the whiskey on the doorstep.

In the sitting room he sat shivering at his desk. His son had escaped him again but then Freddy had always escaped him – as fickle and bewildering as his mother – although Adele did not bewilder him anymore. He'd realised, devastatingly, a very long time ago that the very things which had attracted him to her had been a sign of something else altogether. Her vivacity which he had so loved, had proved to be excitability, her irrepressible spirit a rash impulsiveness and her fearlessness more akin to recklessness.

Adele's descent into darkness had slowly consumed the life of The Mount until it became the norm. There were periods of inertia, of manic activity, and moods both dark and overly bright. There were vile outbursts bordering on violence and harmful incidents which he couldn't bear to think of. Eventually he had sought help and her extended sojourns in private sanatoriums were explained away as holidays or travel. Somehow over the years they had come through it and with treatment the black periods of withdrawal lessened, but they had withdrawn from each other, living together in separation and in a studied pretence of unity in public. At least now with Adele he knew what brought it on and it was somehow easier to cope with, more understandable to him than the darkness.

The remnants of the whiskey turned over in his stomach and he felt he might be sick again. He laid his head down on his arms on top of the desk, fighting a cold wave of nausea.

'Sir, Sir.'

It woke him up.

'Are you alright Sir?'

'What?' he choked, lifting his head and trying to focus.

'You were shouting out Sir,' she said.

He cleared his throat and apologised. He had a headache.

Tess brought him a cup of tea, lifted the cold towel from over her arm and pressed it against his forehead.

'Can I get you anything else?' she asked

He put his hand up to the towel, brushing over the top of her fingers.

'You're very kind,' he said, and managed a smile up into her soft-eyed caring face.

'Bob, Bob, are you in the kitchen?' Betty McCrae shouted urgently from the living room, 'something's burning!'

There was no answer. She got up and went down the hall. The potatoes had boiled dry, their bottoms blackened and stuck to the pan. She saved the tops, scooping them out into a bowl and opened the back door to let out the charred smell. Her husband was nodding on the bench at the bottom of the garden.

'Bob,' she yelled as he started, 'you've burnt the potatoes.'

He came in as she arranged the rashers of bacon into the frying pan and put the cabbage on to boil.

'You'll have to make do with what I've saved from the potatoes,' she scolded.

He sat down at the kitchen table, contrite.

'I think Adelaide Mountjoy was bipolar,' she said, as the bacon hissed and spat in the pan.

'What on earth does that mean?' he asked.

'A manic depressive,' she informed him, 'well that's what it used to be called, but it's that other thing now.'

'Ach, everything's something else these days,' he sighed, 'but why do you think that?'

'Well according to you,' Betty stated, turning the bacon, 'Adelaide was neurotic and that fits in very well with the Adele character in the book.'

'Not that again.'

'And she drank.'

'Who?'

'Adele,' she said, turning to him, 'and I'm sure you know if Adelaide Mountjoy drank.'

He did know but chose not to tell her. He didn't need to give his wife an opportunity to go on about the drink.

'I'm convinced,' Betty continued, testing the cabbage with a knife, 'that Adele and Adelaide are one and the same.'

He held his tongue as she served up their dinner and set the plate in front of him.

'And are you sure you don't remember that Theresa O'Brien girl,' she asked, as she sat down, 'maybe that's not her real name, but reading between the lines I'm sure something happened there.'

'Pass the butter please,' the Captain said, and cutting a slab, built the cold burnt-flavoured potatoes around it.

9

Wilma was glad to be home, dropped the heavy shopping bags in the hallway, took off her coat, and plumped onto the sofa in the living room – putting everything away could wait. She opened her handbag and took out the book. It had been sold out in the Candy Box but she'd called in with Rachael on the way up the road and begged it from her. She flicked through the pages, scanning down to where she'd finished reading in The Mount.

……. *Mrs Montgomery had cut her hand*…… *'Accidents will happen,'*….. *Tess did not tell her that Mrs Montgomery drank gin in her bedroom in the afternoon.*

That was it. She pressed the book open and running her finger down the crease, continued.

'Mrs Montgomery's asking for you,' Mrs Green said, lifting the uneaten lunch plate from the tray and setting it aside for Call Me Jim to eat later.

Tess went up the stairs, working over in her mind everything that had happened the afternoon before. She hadn't done or said anything wrong, had she? She hadn't thrown the drink away, she knew she hadn't. She rapped softly on the door and went in. Adele Montgomery turned on the dressing table stool and looked at her – eyes both wary and warning. Tess held those eyes knowing there was to be no sign of judgement or reproach. It was a look she had seen from her father and knew how to hold it. Mrs Montgomery looked away and turned towards the mirror. The broken side panel, Tess noticed, had been removed.

'You're the girl from the Royal Hotel,' she said, holding out the hairbrush and flipping through the pages of her *Harper's Bazaar*.

As Tess stroked the brush through her hair, curling the dark tresses back with her fingers, Adele settled on a style from her magazine, turning her head from side to side in the mirror, as Tess combed and pinned, trying to copy the picture.

'You have a talent,' Adele said.

It was the first day of many that Tess, having been summoned, was to spend with Adele Montgomery in her bedroom. They fell easily into their afternoons with their magazines and hairstyles and Mrs Montgomery talked about the latest fashions, the fabrics and the season's colours. Once, a little while after the bottle had been brought out of the dressing table drawer, she laid her gowns out on the bed and asked Tess which one she liked best.

'You have very good taste,' she said, insisting that Tess try it on.

Tess self-consciously paraded in front of her in sea-blue silk, as Adele complimented, encouraged, and laughing sprayed perfume over her back and shoulders from the atomiser.

'A votre santé, Mademoiselle,' Adele said, raising her glass, 'a votre santé.'

Tess looked at her, confused.

'*It means cheers in French,*' she explained, making Tess repeat it after her until a guttural tone had been perfected.

As another drink was poured Tess listened, as the restaurants and nightclubs and fashion houses in Paris were excitedly described. '*That dress was bought in Paris,*' she said, running her hand down Tess' side, '*and I'll take you there, I promise I'll take you, and we'll get all dressed up and go out on the town.*' And before Tess helped Adele Montgomery into bed there was nothing surer than that they would go to Paris together.

As Adele fell asleep, Tess changed back into her uniform, put the gin bottle back into the drawer and went downstairs. Mrs Green and Call Me Jim were sitting at the kitchen table having a cup of tea.

'*I'm afraid there's a pile of dishes waiting there for you,*' Mrs Green informed her. Tess had forgotten it was baking day and turned on the tap to fill the sink, arranging the bowls and spoons and trays into order to be washed.

'*Is everything alright?*' Mrs Green asked.

'*Mrs Montgomery's sleeping,*' she replied.

'*Early today,*' Call Me Jim said, raising his eyes.

Tess finished the drying up, put everything away, and asked if there was anything else Mrs Green wanted her to do.

'*The laundry needs sorted for tomorrow,*' she instructed, '*but we've no dinner to make.*'

Mr Montgomery had telephoned to say he was eating out, she was going to get off home early, and Tess could help herself to yesterday's leftovers for her supper. Tess sorted the laundry into whites and coloureds, a pile for hand washing and one for starching, and went to her *room. She changed into her rose patterned dress, sat down at her own little dressing table and brushed out her long dark hair, the smell of Adele's Blue Grass perfume on her skin.*

'Paris,' she said to herself, 'I'm going to Paris.'

She put on her eye-shadow, coated her mouth with lipstick and walked up the corridor. The house was perfectly quiet and still. She went into the dining room and asked the pianist to play. She could sing it for him if he didn't know it – 'Take away the breath of flowers, it would surely be a sin.' She lifted a heavy crystal glass from the top of the drinks cabinet, 'A votre santé,' she said to her guests, as she mingled around the room, before inviting them to take their places for dinner. 'A votre santé,' she raised her glass to Adele Montgomery's portrait and put her hand to her neck, toying with an imaginary rope of pearls.

Tess went back to the kitchen, cut a slice of cold meat pie, buttered a piece of bread and spooned a dollop of Mrs Green's apple chutney onto her plate. The door opened and Mr Montgomery walked into the room. Tess jumped up from the chair, and trying to swallow the large bite of pie, choked out that they hadn't been expecting him home.

'Not to worry, it's entirely my fault,' he apologised, hovering at the table.

'Can I make you something Sir?' Tess asked.

'That looks rather good,' he commented, looking at her plate as she flushed. He would have it just like that and it was fine that it was cold. Tess made up the plate, cutting the crusts off the bread, made a pot of tea and took it all through to his sitting room.

'Thank you, that's perfect.'

'You're welcome Sir,' she said, putting it down on his desk.

'You look very nice tonight,' he smiled up at her, 'are you going somewhere special?'

'No,' she said having forgotten that she was all dressed up and her lipstick on, 'I mean yes,' she flustered, when she realised it, 'well not anywhere special, just a walk along the shore.'

'It's nice round there in the evenings.'

'Yes Sir.'

'I like to walk there too, at least as far as the boathouse,' he told her.

In bed that night Tess struggled to sleep, kept from dreaming by dreams of going to Paris. Turning onto her side she began to think that Mr Montgomery would not allow it, but turning onto her other side she imagined that he would. She thought of the times she'd helped Adele to get ready to go out with him to the Royal Hotel, only for her to decide against it.

'I'm not going,' she would shout out from the bedroom door.

'As you wish,' he would call back from the hallway and go out on his own.

Tess knew her father would have something to say if her mother behaved like that – letting him stand and wait for her and then not go with him. He would rant and rave, not that her mother would ever give him an excuse to. But, the Montgomerys weren't like her parents. They didn't even sleep in the same room let alone the same bed and Mr Montgomery didn't get angry with his wife. He let her do what she wanted and said nothing about it. Tess pulled the blanket around her. She knew what would happen.

'Tess and I are going to Paris,' Adele would tell him.

'As you wish,' he would say, and she fell asleep thinking how she would tell Marie about it on Monday.

The weekend passed uneventfully in a routine of chores, different only for Tess in that Adele did not ask for her.

'She's sleeping,' Mrs Green said, when she asked.

On Monday morning Tess met Marie in the Golden Dawn Café. They hadn't seen each other for weeks and Marie was full of gossip about the tourist, the girls who had come back for the season, and who was going out with whom. She and Sean were still going strong and she talked and talked about him, as Tess listened to how in love they were, and how she was just waiting for him to ask her to marry him.

'It has a ring to it doesn't it?' Marie said, 'Marie Brannigan, Mrs Marie Brannigan.'

And Marie wanted a diamond solitaire engagement ring and her dress wouldn't be bought off the peg, but made for her in Mrs Anderson's bridal salon. She would have her reception in the Royal Hotel, why shouldn't she, and a honeymoon maybe even in Dublin.

'I'm going to Paris,' Tess announced, in the midst of Marie's flow.

'What, for your honeymoon?' Marie laughed, 'you might need to find a boyfriend first.'

'I'm going with Mrs Montgomery,' she stated.

'And why would Mrs Montgomery take you to Paris?' Marie queried.

'Because she said she would,' Tess shot back, 'she's my friend and she said she's going to take me.'

'Friends is it now,' Marie said with disdain.

'Yes, and she's taking me to Paris.'

'Right,' Marie snorted, 'and your da's going to take you to Butlin's when he wins the pools.'

Tess felt the colour rise to her face and wished she could make it stop but Marie didn't seem to notice and returned to her wedding plans. She finished the last bite of her cake and said she had to go. Who does Marie think she is, Tess said to herself, as she walked down the steps onto the shore front? Theresa O'Brien's getting above herself Marie thought, as she lifted her cup and joined another table of girls on their day off from the Royal Hotel.

'You're back early,' Mrs Green commented, as Tess appeared in the kitchen, 'I thought once you girls got together you'd be out for the day.'

Tess said nothing as Mrs Green dried her hands and sat down beside her at the table. 'Oh well, get a good night's rest,' she warned, 'we've a lot to do tomorrow. We'll give Mrs Montgomery's room a good spring clean while she's away.'

'Away?' Tess asked, confused.

'A holiday,' Mrs Green informed her, 'a few weeks I suppose.'

Tess didn't need to ask where she'd gone, she knew, and Mr Montgomery hadn't said, 'As you wish,' he'd said they would go together.

'Is Mr Montgomery away too?' she trembled.

'No, no,' Mrs Green said, 'Mr Montgomery's at home, she's gone away on her own.'

'On her own,' Tess bit her lip as a long tear rolled down her cheek.

'What's all this?' Mrs Green asked, 'don't worry. She'll be all right on her own.'

Tess knew very well that she'd be alright on her own in the hotels and restaurants and shops in Paris. She had broken her promise and in bitter disappointment Tess began to cry. Mrs Green lifted up a tea towel and handed it to her to dry her eyes.

'She'll be fine,' Mrs Green comforted, patting her arm, 'don't get upset about her.'

'It's not that,' Tess sniffed, recovering herself.

'Well what on earth's the matter?' she asked.

'It's Marie, Marie upset me.'

'You young girls,' Mrs Green sighed, 'I'm sure it'll all be forgotten by tomorrow whatever it's all about.'

As Tess went to her room, Mrs Green sat down wearily in her armchair to take her forty winks. She was tired with everything that had happened today but satisfied with the way it had all worked out – Tess at least had been out of the house when Adele had been taken away and she had gone easily. It hadn't always been like that, she remembered, as she closed her eyes.

The first time, with Freddy barely a year old, she and George had persuaded her into the car and he had driven her away to the institution. He had come home scratched and bloodied and distraught, hating himself for leaving her. She had tried to comfort him and in the months that Adele was away, in peace and calm, they had retrieved their strength. And year by year their strength was tested – the doctor called to calm her rages or lift her out of despair, to bandage up her wrists or force the pills from her stomach. How many times had she had rocked Freddy in her arms, holding her hands over his ears, when his mother was strapped down and carried screaming from the house? They had gone on like that in the early days – through times of awfulness and calm – but gradually the periods when Adele was well increased and life eventually began to take *on a semblance of normality. To the outside world all was well in The Mount. Inside it, life was better, if sometimes changeable, and changeable was now driven by a different kind of weather.*

Adele Montgomery drank and they didn't try to stop her. They dealt with it and Adele now asked for help when things became too much for her. This morning, when she had taken up the tea tray, Adele had asked for George – she wanted him to come home and she wanted the doctor.

'I want to go away for a little while,' she said, 'just a little while.'

After making the necessary telephone calls Mrs Green had packed the hospital bag, helped Adele into a dressing gown and stayed with her until the men arrived. She'd gone quietly out into the car but she wouldn't have wanted Tess to have seen it, or have had to explain. They'd become too close for her liking and when Tess had started to cry she'd thought Adele might have confided something about her times away. She'd been relieved that the tears had been about some girlish argument with Marie. Perhaps someday she would talk to Tess about it all – without a doubt she already knew about the drinking although had never mentioned it – but for now some things were best left unsaid. For now, she and George would take care of Adele as they always had. They would carry on as before.

Wilma stopped reading and shivered – absorbed in the book she hadn't felt the house grow cold. She went out into the hall and turned on the heating, putting the thermostat up to full. Mrs Mountjoy wouldn't approve but now she understood a little better about her ways, for no amount of heating would take the chill out of The Mount. It was a house of ghosts and now she had a name to explain the cold chill of the bedroom. Adele had never followed her around the house the way Tess had, but she was there all the same – a tortured soul – and as unhappy in death as she'd been in life. Who had she been in life, Wilma wondered? She must have been related to Mrs Mountjoy in some way but she wouldn't find the answer there. Unlike her other elderly ladies Mrs M never talked about her family or reminisced about the past, not once in seven years.

It was half-past five and Terry would be in soon looking for his dinner. Wilma took the shopping through to the kitchen, peeled a pot of potatoes, put them on to boil, and started to fry the thick beef sausages – McMaster's butchers' best, and her husband's favourites. The front door opened as she forked the chopped scallions through the buttery pot of mash.

'I'm home.'

'I'm in the kitchen.'

'Terry, what do you know about the Mountjoys?' she asked.

'You mean Mrs Mountjoy that you work for?'

'Not her,' she tutted, 'her family, the old family, do you remember anything about them?'

'No.'

'What about old Mrs Green, she lived down the road with her sister, do you remember her?'

'Vaguely,' he conceded, 'why?'

'It doesn't matter.'

'Oh well, if it doesn't matter then,' he shrugged.

'Well you don't seem very interested.'

'Wilma, I don't know anything about anybody. I'm not interested in other people,' he said, coming up behind her at the cooker and squeezing his arms around her, 'I'm only interested in you.'

'Get off,' she pleaded, as he squeezed her tighter and rubbed his stubble into her cheek.

10

Maybelle had spent most of the morning in the garden recovering from her disturbed night's sleep and from dreaming about Teddy. The dream when it recurred, so vivid and perturbing, always left her out of sorts. She worked it off gently in the greenhouse, sewing a tray of love in a mist, and nipping the growing tips off the sweet pea. The begonias would soon be ready to plant out. She had a different spot in mind for them this year and walked down through the terraces to the bottom of the garden. She saw him then, the red-haired man standing at her gate, staring up at her house. She held her breath, unable to move and unable to take her eyes from him. When he disappeared she wasn't sure if he had been real or some ghostly extension of her dream. She walked across to the gate and tentatively looked out onto the path. He was gone, but the thin curl of smoke rising from the cigarette butt on the ground was real enough. He was no ghost. He was something else altogether.

'Anything you'd like for lunch?' Wilma had called out, distracting her, but she had no appetite and told her to finish for the day.

She had started then in the terraces, clearing away leaves and debris and digging over the damp black soil – a job she usually left for the gardener – and moved from one bed to the next, slicing through the earth with the spade, the red-haired man on her mind. She worked on until she exhausted herself and then came indoors. She sat for a while in the veranda and tried the crossword but couldn't concentrate. She went to the kitchen, took a couple of dry biscuits out of the tin and climbed the stairs, sinking gratefully between the crisp fresh sheets. Almost against her will she put on her glasses and picked up the book from the bedside table. She found her place and read on through the story of Tess O'Brien's life in the Mount, the descriptions of places and of people whom she thought she knew, not so much intriguing as disturbing. She forced herself towards the end of it, anxious as to what she might find.

Time passed for Tess, the weeks turning to months and the months to another year, the routine of the house unchanged and changeable weather more explained. Mrs Green, having decided to retire, had fully confided in Tess about Adele and although George Montgomery was reluctant to let his old housekeeper go, had been reassured that Miss O'Brien could manage the household and all that it entailed.

'And I'm not going to the ends of the earth,' Mrs Green consoled him, 'you know I'm moving in with my sister across town and you know where to find me if you need me.'

It was a wonderful opportunity for Tess – no longer a waitress or a housemaid, but Miss O'Brien, the housekeeper of The Mount. She imagined it being said in

Haveron's and Hilditch's and Foster's as she placed an order and asked for it to be delivered.

'Only the best for you Miss O'Brien,' the shopkeepers would say.

'Why that's Miss O'Brien, the housekeeper of The Mount,' their customers would whisper, as she turned on her heel and smiled graciously.

It was an opportunity she was not prepared to lose but there was, however, a problem which threatened her aspirations. She thought about it constantly. It was there when she woke in the morning, it accompanied her throughout the day, and it was there when she put her head on the pillow at night. She conjured many solutions and imagined many outcomes but none relieved her mind. Finally, in fear for her future, she took the letters from her drawer and after reading them again, went to the kitchen and asked Mrs Green if she could spare a moment. They sat down together on Tess' bed and one by one she handed the letters to Mrs Green to read. In childlike writing the facts of the matter were stated simply, though more frantically from the first letter to the last. It was quite clear something dreadful had happened and Tess was being begged to come home. Mrs Green took a handkerchief from her apron pocket, told Tess to stop crying and to stop saying she was ashamed.

'Your sister's not the first girl in the world to get herself into trouble,' she said, 'and she certainly won't be the last.'

Tess wiped at the tears in her eyes.

'What's done is done,' she comforted, 'and better to dry those tears and think about what to do now.'

Mrs Green let her talk and the months of worry were released in shifting bursts of tears, apologies, and thanks.

Of course she didn't want to leave the Mount – she couldn't let them down, especially with Mrs Green retiring, but her sister needed her. And what she'd written was true. When their father found out he'd kill her for sure, and if he didn't kill her she'd be sent to one of those places where they took your baby away and kept you locked up, sometimes for good.

'Now, now, who's ever heard of such a thing,' Mrs Green said, telling her not to take on so.

Tess was not comforted. Even if Deirdre ever got out, they'd never allow her back home and she couldn't hide it for much longer. She would have to go to her, but even if she did, what could she do to help her? On the last wipe of a tear Mrs Green told Tess what to do. She must go home for a holiday, explain that with her promotion they needed to employ a maid, and she had thought of her sister. Surely they would agree to that. She was then to bring Deirdre back to Darkhaven and they could both move into Seaview Cottage.

'Since I'm moving out I don't see why you shouldn't move in,' Mrs Green said, 'I'll speak to Mr Montgomery about it.'

'You won't say anything to him about my sister, I mean about the baby,' Tess pleaded as the promise was tearfully begged from her.

Of course she wouldn't and she would stay on at work until Tess came back – what did a few more weeks matter in a lifetime with the family. And Tess wasn't to worry, when the baby was coming she could organise for the midwife or the doctor and no one need know. For the first time in many months Tess slept easier in her bed.

Three weeks later Theresa O'Brien stepped off the bus in Darkhaven with her red-haired sister and a small but healthy nephew, and together they settled into Seaview Cottage. In the one afternoon that Mrs Green spent with her in The Mount – as the account books were handed over and again explained, and a list of instructions about how things should done was read through – nothing was mentioned about her time away. Mrs Green was just about to ask when George Montgomery took her off to his sitting room to pay her wages and explain the annual annuity which was to be settled on her for life.

In the kitchen, Tess organised a farewell tea party and a tear or two was shed as Freddy, Call Me Jim and even Adele gathered around the table and listened to George Montgomery's warm words about the woman who had been with him all his life. Freddy presented a gift from the family – a silver salver engraved with her years of service – and she shooed him off as he put his arms around her and kissed her on the cheek. At four o'clock Mrs Green handed over the keys of The Mount to Tess O'Brien, put on her hat and coat, and went out by the front door. With Mr Montgomery waiting in the car to drive her home she said goodbye to Tess on the doorstep and wished her well.

'And remember,' she said, handing her a note with her address written on it, 'when the time comes with your sister, you know where to find me.'

Tess took the note and thanked her, but unknown to Mrs Green she would not need to be found or her help needed, for the baby had already been born.

Maybelle closed the book and allowed herself a moment of relief. It hadn't been what she'd feared. Any discerning reader, of course, would see through the author's rather unsubtle inferences but nothing of the real world had been given away, not openly stated in black and white. But, what a character he had conjured up in Tess – the kind and caring Tess, the innocent and imaginative dreamer Tess, the good friend of the family, Tess. Maybelle Mountjoy, as she finally drifted into sleep, knew better.

11

Captain McCrae made a tour of the house, turned off lights and switches, locked the back and front doors, and climbed the stairs hoping that Betty was already asleep. She was not. She was resting back on the pillows, her book opened under the bedside lamp.

'Did you turn everything off?' she asked.

He had.

'Did you lock the doors?' she questioned, as he changed into his pyjamas.

He had, as he had done every night for the twenty-five years that he'd been back on dry land. He got into bed and turned to get comfortable.

'Do you mind the light?' she asked, 'I've a bit I want to finish.'

Did it matter if he minded? He closed his eyes and listened to his wife turning the pages of her book as she took in little gasps of air and let out considered hums and ha's.

For the first time in a very long time, George Montgomery was joined at the breakfast table by his son. It was a surprise. Freddy was rarely up early on a Saturday and had, as usual, been quite conscientiously avoiding him – he never seemed able to pin the boy down and his resolve to tackle him had somehow dissolved, resulting in another wasted year. He'd had other things on his mind or perhaps he had just given up on him. He looked up from his Financial Times and said good morning, but continued to read as Freddy poured a cup of tea and buttered a piece of toast.

'Anything of interest?' Freddy asked.

'Nothing that would interest you,' he replied coolly.

'I'm not so sure,' his son refuted, 'actually I've been meaning to ask you about the business.'

'What about it?' he asked raising his eyes and staring at him across the table.

'I don't know,' Freddy responded cheerfully, 'how it's all going, what's happening, you know business things.'

George Montgomery closed his newspaper, stifling the urge to mock at Freddy's vague mist of 'business things'.

'So,' his son continued, 'you must be happy about America.'

Caught off guard he talked about the company's expansion into the American market and his high hopes for their new range of products.

'Great,' Freddy enthused, 'more sales means more money, doesn't it?'

'Are you worried about your inheritance?' he asked dryly.

His son laughingly denied it and finished the remains of his toast.

'Do you have any plans for today?' Freddy asked, suggesting that they take his grandfather's old Rolls out for a spin – it could do with a run out on the road.

They had never done much together as father and son, even in their one shared passion for cars, and he agreed to the idea, finding himself cautiously pleased to have been asked. They drove up the Antrim coast road, talking about cars and relaxing into each other's company. He told Freddy how he had driven the route of the Monaco Grand Prix on his honeymoon, surprised that he had never told him before.

'I'd love to try my hand at motor racing,' Freddy said, and for a moment he thought he was about to be presented with some new venture. Instead it was suggested that they take a trip over to Silverstone sometime to watch the racing. The thought pleased him immensely.

They stopped for lunch in the Londonderry Arms Hotel and then walked across to the harbour to look at the fishing boats. He bought them both an ice cream and Freddy licked his down to the cone, bit off the end and sucked it through, the way he'd always done as a boy.

'I should have told you a long time ago,' Freddy said, crunching the last of the cone into his mouth, 'but I'm not going to build a yacht. Why would I want to give up the Elizabeth Ann, she's irreplaceable.'

'Your grandfather would have been proud to see you sail her,' he said, warmed by the admission.

As they drove on up the coast and then back through the countryside he talked about his father – his humble beginnings as a market barrow boy, the opening of his first shop, and the founding of the company.

'Nothing was handed to your grandfather on a plate. Hard work and dedication brought the rewards Freddy and always remember rewards have to be earned,' he emphasised, as Freddy pressed his foot down on the accelerator.

Just after seven o'clock they turned down into Darkhaven and he invited Freddy to dine with him in The Royal Hotel.

'I was going to go to the yacht club, why don't you come with me?' Freddy suggested. In a newly found feeling of camaraderie his father happily accepted.

The members' bar was already quite busy when they arrived – a group of Freddy's friends sitting at a corner table, and some of his own contemporaries gathered at the bar.

'To what do we owe this unexpected pleasure George?' Eric Everly blared through the cigarette smoke, 'we usually only see you here on special occasions.'

'Just out for a drink with my son,' he smiled.

'Jolly good!' Mr Pink exclaimed, shaking him firmly by the hand.

'I'll drink to that,' Captain Donaldson cheered, lifting his empty glass into the air, as George ordered drinks all round.

They drank together as rounds were bought, the company growing increasingly convivial. He listened as the men talked sailing and tides, shouting each other down just as often as they agreed, but they often deferred to Freddy, he noted, valuing his opinions.

'You should be proud of him George,' Mr Pink said quietly, putting another glass of whiskey into his hand, 'the best yachtsman in these parts by a long way.'

'I am proud of him,' he admitted, and raised his glass to his son, who smiled warmly back at him.

Freddy excused himself from the company and joined his friends. He stayed at the bar talking business with Mr Pink. There was a great burst of laughter from the corner and he turned to see a girl slapping Freddy hard

on the back. She ran her hand up onto his neck and kept
it there.

'Who's the girl over there with Freddy?' he asked,
'I'm sure I should know her.'

'One of the Dixon twins,' Mr Pink responded,
'but don't ask me which one, I can never tell them
apart.'

'Of course,' George said, turning his attention back
to business.

Eventually Freddy re-joined them at the bar and after
one more drink suggested they go home.

'Early for you Freddy,' Eric Everly roared, and
ordered another round.

'You don't have to leave on my account,' George
whispered to his son, 'if you want to stay with your
friends I'll make my own way home.'

Freddy looked across to the corner as the Dixon twin
turned and caught his eye.

'Let's go,' he said, as they quickly finished their
drink and took their leave before another could be
bought.

The night air hit him and he took Freddy's arm to
steady himself as they walked down onto the promenade
and got into the car. In minutes they were home and they
hushed each other in the vestibule, like naughty
schoolboys sneaking in. He put his hand on his son's
shoulder and thanked him for the day they'd spent
together, the first he hoped of many more to come.

'Nightcap,' Freddy suggested.

George Montgomery did not drink the generous
glass of whiskey that was poured for him in the dining
room. It turned sour and bitter not long after Freddy
started to talk.

'*I'm getting married,*' his son announced.

'*Who's the lucky girl?*' he laughed, holding up his hand to stop him speaking, '*don't tell me, I know, it's that girl from tonight, the Dixon girl.*'

'*What!*' Freddy exclaimed, '*why would you think that?*'

'*It's alright,*' he said, '*I'm not a complete fool, I saw the way she looked at you tonight and I'm not so old you know that I don't remember……*'

He wasn't given a chance to remember as he was told exactly whom his son intended to marry and why. And he wasn't given a chance to speak after his first shocked objections.

'*It's 1952 for God's sake, not the bloody dark ages,*' Freddy shouted, as he slammed out of the room, '*and you can say what like but we're getting married and that's all there is about it.*'

Sitting alone at the dining room table George Montgomery's head and heart swam in a bitter realisation. How often had a day started in just the same way with Adele, with no intimation of what was to come, although with her he had learned that it would come? An evening out, perhaps, Adele happy and attentive, talking kindly and hugging onto him and then outside in the car – 'I don't love you,' or 'I'm divorcing you.' Or an evening in around the dinner table, Adele chattering warmly to Freddy, drawing him into the intimacy of their world, and then with that little triumphant smile after his son had left the room – 'He's not yours.'

He knew Freddy was his – his eyes, his nose and hair – but there was nothing else of him in his son. He was his mother's son and he had proved it more than ever today. By the time George Montgomery went to bed he had decided how to deal with Freddy. He would reason with him just as he had reasoned with Adele in the past when she'd talked of divorce. If Freddy wanted to marry this girl he would accept it but there would be no home and no inheritance. He was confident that his son would not give everything up. He knew because he knew his mother.

He lay in bed staring up at the ceiling going over it all again in his mind. He would deal with Freddy first and then he would deal with the girl – an altogether different proposition. She had played her hand cleverly and although it had taken him by surprise it shouldn't have. He should have been prepared.

'In every transaction George,' he heard his father's voice, 'knowledge is your power.'

And there was one more thing in all of this that he needed to know. He knew who to ask, someone whom he trusted above all others, and he would call with her tomorrow.

'Bob,' she nudged him, 'who was Teddy Mountjoy involved with before he married Maybelle? Was he going to marry someone else, do you know who it was, or what happened?'

He lay still in the bed.

'Bob, are you asleep?'

He listened as she sighed, put her glasses and book on the bedside table and turned off the lamp. She fell asleep quickly in the familiar sound of little puffs of air blowing out of her lips.

Sleep didn't come so easily to him. His encounter with the stranger in the Whitecliff Inn was still on his mind. He had seen him twice now within the week –

once last Thursday and again today. Who was he, and what was he doing here? He started to drift off. At least it was Thursday again tomorrow and a morning's company with his old compatriots to look forward to. He didn't need an excuse for going out tomorrow. He fell asleep.

12

In the Deacon's House, although it was late, Dilys Bishop was very much awake. Tomorrow was art club and she was still working on the painting which she would take with her – a seascape, a yacht in full sail in the middle distance. She was pleased with the composition and particularly the sky but the white water waves were still defeating her. She scraped the paint off again with her palette knife and stopped, took her wine through to the study and turned on the computer. Nothing had been added to the book review site about 'The Montgomerys of the Mount'. She poured another glass of wine thinking she might post a comment, but then started to think about Friday's book club meeting.

Hopefully her ladies would have bought the book by now and might even have read it. She wouldn't even mind if Lillian went on and on, she would let her talk. Norma Lockhart though was a different proposition – Norma didn't like to give too much away. She'd bumped into her this morning in the Candy Box and she'd been very unforthcoming. And why should she not have asked about Edwina Mountjoy, what was wrong with that? That life so publicly played out wasn't exactly a secret in the town, but Norma had done her old Whitehaven thing, closing up and excluding her from the club.

Well, who didn't have a skeleton in their cupboard or could be sure that when the door of it was opened that the bones wouldn't fall out and rattle all around. Pleased with that thought, Dilys reached for a pen and a piece of paper and wrote it down – her interest in creative writing had begun to revive. She took another sip of wine and looked around the book lined room – the lecturer's books. No, she thought, not the lecturer's books, the lecher's books. Why hadn't she thought of that before? She laughed out loud, picked up the pen and wrote it down. Now there was a theme she could introduce on Friday night – men and their bastard children. That would fit in very well indeed with 'The Montgomerys of The Mount'. Then again, what was it that old Mrs Green had had to say about it all – 'If there were no bad women, there would be no bad men.'

Dilys reached for the book on the desk and found her way through to *Mrs Green*.

'There's a gentleman her to see you,' Maudie called out to her sister, as she opened the front door.

Mrs Green was surprised to find George Montgomery taking off his hat and coat in the hallway. She ushered him into the parlour, tidying away her knitting and ordering the cushions as he sat down on the settee, his finger rubbing under his collar, a sign to her that all was not well. She took her armchair by the fire and waited for him to broach what was on his mind. He looked tired, aged almost she thought.

He didn't quite know where to start, it was rather delicate. If he'd been the boy he'd once been to her she would have told him to spit it out, but held her tongue. It came out slowly at first, in ill-fitting pieces of a puzzle, he seemingly trying to make sense in the telling of it, as she tried to understand what she was being told. By the time he had finished he was drained, grey, and they sat silently until he could bring himself to it again.

'I know if you'd suspected anything you would have dealt with it,' he said, 'but did you even have a hint that anything was going on?'

'I did not,' she professed, 'and if I'd known she was carrying on with her betters I'd have put her out of the house and no mistake about it.'

George Montgomery shifted uncomfortably as Mrs Green tried to recover from the shock of his revelation.

'I should have seen it, but I didn't,' she sighed.

'It's not your fault,' he comforted, 'this is all Freddy's doing.'

Although hardly able to believe that Tess, a girl she'd trusted and treated like a daughter, had allowed herself to be carried away, she could not let Freddy take all of the blame.

'If there were no bad women,' she said, 'there'd be no bad men.'

George Montgomery could not excuse his son so easily and the depth of the anger that he harboured towards him crashed like a wave into the room. He railed at his carefree attitude, his inability to stick to anything, his irresponsibility, his betrayal. When it was over he slumped back on the settee, exhausted.

'I'm sorry,' he quietly apologised.

Alarmed by the outburst Mrs Green reached out and squeezed his arm. In all the years, with everything he'd had to cope with, she had never seen it before – the patience of Job, she'd often said of him.

'What I really need to know…' he choked, taking her hand.

'What is it George?' she implored.

'I need to know,' he said, raising his eyes to her, 'if the child is Freddy's.'

'What child…' she started to say, when the awful realisation came to her that this wasn't as she had thought. This wasn't some misguided dalliance – not a daft boy proposing to marry a girl who had set her sights above herself. She remembered back to an afternoon sitting with Tess O'Brien on her bed and the tears for the poor sister and the letters she'd been given to read. She thought of how she'd comforted her and offered to help, and how with all her years when nothing had got past her, she'd been taken for a fool. And then it had been her turn to rage against Tess O'Brien, and she told it all as she had known it then and as she knew it now. George Montgomery listened, his eyes lowered to the floor.

The sitting room door knocked bringing the storm to an end, and Maudie, sure that they must be ready for some tea, brought in the tray and arranged the cups and saucers and biscuits on the table, leaving the teapot to keep warm on the hearth.

'Who's to say the child is his?' Mrs Green said, as she poured, 'if she's that kind of girl anyone could be the father.'

George Montgomery twitched and fingered his collar, 'Freddy says the child is his.'

And of everything that had been said, that cut Mrs Green to the bone. If it had been admitted to then it had happened right under her nose. She didn't want to think of where they had carried on – upstairs in the house while she was there, in the bedroom she had sat in comforting Tess O'Brien, on the dark nights that Tess had left Seaview Cottage and said she wasn't afraid to walk home alone. No, she didn't want to think of that and she didn't.........

Dilys went to the kitchen, opened another bottle of wine and returned to the study.

'Here's to you Mrs Green.' she said, raising her glass, for the old housekeeper had been duped just as she had been – taken in by the innocent charm of a young girl.

Dilys had welcomed the lecturer's favoured students into her home – social evenings, long Sunday dinners, flowing academic conversation. She had particularly taken to Juliette who'd had a poor start in life, but whom her husband thought had an excellent brain. She had admired the girl, nurtured and encouraged her like a daughter. It hadn't dawned on her when they disappeared off to the study for extra tuition or walked together to the lighthouse to discuss 'poetry in poetry', that anything was amiss. She hadn't realised that Juliette's brain was not the part of her that the great lecher lecturer was interested in. What a fool she'd been taken for.

'To you Mrs Green,' Dilys said again, 'if there were no bad women, there'd be no bad men.' She finished her glass of wine, poured another and continued to read.

...... and she didn't want to think of the product of that illicit union, but the image of the child was in her mind, a child that she had not only seen but had held in her arms. She had taken a walk along the shore after church and stopped outside Seaview Cottage to admire some of Billy's roses still blooming in the

garden. It had taken her back to happy long ago memories, but also to cosy nights shared at the fireside with Tess O'Brien whom she had not seen since her retirement. As she was wondering why Tess had never called with her she heard a baby's cry and noticed the pram parked up against the garden wall. The baby's cries grew louder, squalling for attention, and when no one came she reached over the wall and lifted the choking infant out of the pram, patting its back as a tiny wet mouth turned into her neck.

The cottage door opened and a tall red-haired girl came down the path and took the child from her.

'There now Kevin,' the girl said, rocking him in her arms, 'there now.'

'He has your hair,' she said, as the girl eyed her suspiciously, 'sorry, I'm Mrs Green, I used to live here and you must be Deirdre.'

'Oh yes, my sister's told me about you.'

It had pleased her to know she was still remembered. 'Tell Tess not to be stranger,' she said, 'she knows she's welcome to call.'

'I'll tell her,' Deirdre nodded, putting the boy back into the pram and pushing it into the cottage.

She'd had no reason that day to think anything other than she'd passed a moment with a mother and her child – a child who looked well enough like the red-haired Deirdre. She knew differently now.

'I don't believe Freddy's the father,' George Montgomery stated.

'Why would he claim such a thing?' she asked.

For that he had no answer but with everything said he became the George she knew – the calm and quiet thinker, the business-headed planner. He would see

Freddy married, but not to Theresa O'Brien. And she was left in no doubt that the girl he had in mind would go along with his plan, as would his son. If Mrs Green had any misgivings these were laid to rest when Marguerite McBride walked up the aisle of May Street Presbyterian Church in Belfast, on the arm of her uncle Jack, and out onto the church steps on Freddy Montgomery's arm.

No one from Darkhaven was invited to the wedding.......

Dilys wasn't in the mood for weddings or honeymoons or descriptions of early married life. She didn't need to read it again, she'd lived it. Drinking another glass of wine she was in the mood for tragedy and several pages on she found it.

Darkhaven may have been denied a Montgomery wedding but they could not be denied a funeral and they streamed along King's Road, past the closed shop fronts and the curtain drawn windows, to the stone arched doors of the church. Inside the portico, the eminent and the ordinary sombrely accepted their orders of service from the hands of the church elders, before being directed into the body of the church and then upstairs to the balcony when it was full. They took their seats, acknowledging each other gravely, stealing glimpses around the pews, noting who was there to pay their last respects and who was not. As the organ piped mournfully up into the rafters their thoughts were with Freddy Montgomery. On this day, when no boat would sail out of Darkhaven, they remembered him as the young man he was, had been, vital with life and out on the sea. They consoled each other in whispers, withdrawing from the thought of his body in the polished oak coffin before them. They exchanged quiet remembrances of his parents and of that sad tragedy too.

As the last of the mourners took their seats the organ softened and the congregation stilled, averting their eyes as Marguerite Montgomery walked silently up the carpeted aisle – the very aisle they had been disappointed not to see her walk down as a bride. She walked up it now as a widow, stood for a moment at the coffin, and then took her seat in the Montgomery family pew. They were drawn to look at her, taking furtive glances and noting her demeanour which they would talk about afterwards. They would remark on her composure and how she had sat upright and rigid under the stained glass windows which the Montgomery family had gifted to the church – Christ with his arms outstretched suffering the little children to come unto him, Christ standing at the prow of the boat commanding the waters to still. The sad irony of it was lost on some of them but not on others. Marguerite's head remained bowed under the wide-brimmed hat which shielded her eyes from theirs. Out of those eyes, those nearest to her would assert, no tear had fallen.

The Reverend Stewart ascended the steps up into the pulpit and they raised their eyes to him as he spoke.

'The earth is the Lord's and the fullness thereof, the world and they that dwell therein. For he hath founded it upon the seas, and established it upon the floods. Who shall ascend into the hill of the Lord? Or who shall stand in his holy place?'

Let us pray.

They bowed their heads as the minister's voice, in a measured melody of solemnity, echoed around the church and they prayed with him for the soul of Frederick

George Montgomery, redeemed by the righteousness of the Lord and delivered out of earthly darkness and sin, taken up onto the hill to stand in the holy place, taken into the glory of heaven's everlasting light. Amen.

They rose together as one, opened their hymnals and lifted their voices to heaven, the men's voices deep and mournful the women's trembling above them, until they reached the end, 'Heaven's morning breaks and earth's vain shadow flees, in life in death oh Lord abide with me.' Be seated.

In the middle of the body of the church, as the minister paid tribute to Freddy, Mrs Green dabbed her eyes, her heart heavy with memories of the baby she had nursed, the scraped knees she had tended and the tears she had kissed away. She thought of the nights she had tucked him into bed, pushing his hair back out of his eyes, and counting his freckles to bring on sleep. She remembered the times she had brought him into the warmth of the kitchen to be with her when all wasn't well in the house. She had loved him like a son, just as she had loved his father. To think of George Montgomery now was almost too much to bear and the tears rolled down her soft plump cheeks, cheeks they had both turned their faces into for comfort when they were boys.

Let us pray.

'Our father who art in heaven…,' they followed him as one until the end, '….for thine is the kingdom, the power and the glory, forever and ever, amen.'

As the organ lifted them to their feet again they raised their voices in a final hymn.

'From rock and tempest fire and foe, protect them where so e'er they go. Oh hear us when we cry to thee of those in peril on the sea.'

Upstairs in the balcony Tess O'Brien steadied herself, the hymn book trembling in her hand, tears rolling off her face and dropping softly down on the congregation below. She watched as the young men Freddy had sailed with moved forward to the coffin, raised him up on their arm linked shoulders, and slowly bore him away. Coming down from the balcony Tess' red-rimmed eyes met those of Mrs Green across the porch. In the space that separated them lay a hurt – not only of another loved one lost, but for Mrs Green the deep pain of a betrayal. She kept her eyes on Tess', searching them for something of the girl she had known, but saw nothing of her in the boldness of the look that held her eye. As bold as brass she was, standing there in Adele Montgomery's velvet-trimmed Sunday coat and hat and comfortable enough, by the look of her, in a dead woman's clothes. Theresa O'Brien looked away, swivelled on her heel and disappeared out into the crowd. That girl, Mrs Green thought to herself, has forgotten the tin she was baked in.

The hearse moved slowly away and behind it Freddy Montgomery was carried on a black shouldered sea, men moving forward to take their lift. The procession halted in sight of The Mount, stopping in a moment of respect for the home he had come out of, and in an unrehearsed gesture they turned him to the sea, before the coffin was placed into the hearse and driven away for burial in Islandmagee. The men followed on to the graveside as the women made their way quietly home. There had been no invitation to The Mount and no arrangement made for the people of Darkhaven to come together to share their memories of the life of one of their own. In the circumstances they could forgive the grieving young widow, left with a child barely a week old, left alone with all the Montgomerys now so tragically gone. They would give her time before they came to offer their condolences in person, before they helped her through, and brought her into the fold.

Mrs Green made her way home, made a pot of tea and carried it through to the parlour, sinking down wearily in her armchair waiting for it to brew. She hadn't read the leaves for a while – not since George – not since she'd foreseen his own tragedy. Could it really only have been six short months ago? He'd called with her at Christmas and brought her a magnificent hamper sent all the way from Fortnum and Mason's in London. She'd chided him for his extravagance but had been delighted with it, picking through the exotic contents and expressing her pleasure, which had pleased him. And she'd been pleased to find him a changed man since the last time he had visited in his distress. As he drank his tea he appeared relaxed and happy – Freddy was married, Marguerite was expecting and Adele was well. In the New Year he was going to London on business but intended to make a holiday out of it and had persuaded Adele to accompany him. He hoped she wouldn't change her mind at the last minute but he'd promised her shopping and shows it would do them both good. It would be good for the newly-weds too, to have some time alone.

'We'll take the Larne ferry over to Stranraer and motor down from Scotland,' he said.

Mrs Green was relieved to hear they would take the boat – she distrusted this new-fangled idea of flying.

'Perhaps when we get back you'll come and visit,' he invited, 'we miss you at the house.'

'And I hope the house is being well looked after,' she posed, 'I believe that Tess is still....'

'No one could look after us like you did,' he deflected and rose to his feet.

She had presented him with an opportunity to tell her why Tess O'Brien was still working at The Mount but he hadn't risen to it. She held back, not wanting to dampen his spirits or remind him of unpleasant matters but for the life of her she couldn't understand it, not when there was a child involved in it all, and especially when Freddy and his wife were living there too. No doubt George Montgomery had his reasons but it was quite beyond her.

On the doorstep he wished her a happy Christmas, leant forward and embraced her in a rigid hug – an awkward outward display of a deeply held and mutual affection. She stood and waved after him as the car drove off in a first light fall of snow. As she closed the door against the cold and retreated into the warmth of the parlour she hadn't known that she would never see him again.

Having returned to the Mount George Montgomery sat down at his desk in the sitting room and, pen in hand, regarded the blank sheets of writing paper in front of him. He hadn't allowed Mrs Green to ask him why Tess O'Brien was still in his employ but it was an unasked question which sometime, in some distant future, might need an answer. As the nib of his pen scraped across the paper he unburdened himself to the one person who deserved to know.

As a confession was being written Mrs Green turned George Montgomery's teacup over onto the saucer. She hadn't tried to read his cup when he was with her – he *would have laughed it off as nonsense – but she couldn't resist searching the pattern for the bright and happy life ahead of him, the life that he deserved. She'd found only death in the desperate hands reaching up out of a black sea of leaves, stretching and grasping to be saved. She wished she had never looked into that cup and that she had left it alone, for the tea leaves didn't lie.*

It had stayed with her over Christmas, playing on her mind and affecting her spirits. She'd cooked the Christmas dinner and Maudie had eaten heartily but her own appetite had been dulled. As she'd listened to the new young Queen's broadcast on the radio – asking them all to pray for her and for all the days of her life and service – she'd thought of another whom she would pray for, and for all the days of the life that were left to him. Coming into the New Year she'd thought of going to George Montgomery, to try to persuade him not to go away and to stay safely at home, but hadn't. She had waited in silence for the tragedy to come and it had come as surely as the sea comes to the shore.

Mrs Green took the order of service out of her handbag and brought her scrapbook out from the sideboard, looking through it to find a place for Freddy. There were so many pictures of the Coronation waiting to be pasted and the other newspaper clippings which she hadn't been able to bring herself to look at again. The headline was in front of her now, black and stark – Larne Steamer Abandoned in Gale – Water strewn with wreckage as passengers' wave for help.

'Why George,' she asked herself, 'why did you try to come home on that ferry in such a storm?'

And it had been a storm like no other they had ever seen, biblical in its strength and fury, as it raged across the Irish Sea on the last day of January in 1953. She had felt its rage herself, almost blown off her feet when she'd opened the door to go out, and it had taken her and Maudie all of their strength to close it again against the gale.

'I told you not to go the shop,' Maudie gave off, picking up the letters and ornaments blown from the hallstand.

They dampened down the fire in the parlour, extinguishing the flames being sucked up the chimney, and retreated to the back room. Maudie switched on the wireless, turning the knobs as it whistled and whirred through the frequencies, trying to find a weather forecast. They caught the tail end of the news with reports of severe storm damage all over the British Isles and the announcer returned to the lead story – the loss of the Princess Victoria somewhere out towards the Copeland Islands. They looked at each other in disbelief, and then in horror, as it was reported that the ferry had sunk in the storm and that the situation regarding survivors was not as yet fully known – some it was believed had been picked up from life rafts, but many had been lost. As they listened they prayed for those poor souls out there somewhere in that raging sea. Mrs Green tried not to think the unthinkable but she already knew, and in the early hours alone in an armchair by the wireless, she wept.

The next morning she walked down to the promenade, hills of seaweed ripped from the seabed and thrown over the twisted railings onto the road.

'I've never seen anything like it,' Mr Everly told her, shovelling sand and stones and debris from his doorway, 'we thought the waves were going to put the windows in, even up there on the third floor.'

She stood with him for a moment, looking out towards the Copeland Islands – the sea now eerily calm – and they talked quietly and sadly of the dreadful news about the Princess Victoria, unable to take it in. She bought a newspaper and returning home spread it out on the parlour table and relayed the reports of the tragedy to her sister.

'Oh Maudie, those poor people,' she sighed, 'it says they were all gathered together in the lounge at the top of the ship, they knew they were being looked for and didn't believe they would sink.'

'Oh dear Lord,' Maudie choked, wringing her handkerchief in her fingers.

'And they stayed calm but didn't know that no one could find the ferry because the waves were like mountains,' Mrs Green continued tearfully.

Maudie shuddered at the thought.

'They handed out life jackets at midday but the ship was listing at forty five degrees,' Mrs Green carried on, running her finger along the line of newsprint.

'Like this,' Maudie said, holding her arm out across the table, 'she was going over on her side.'

'Yes, it says the walls had become the floor as they made their way up to the life rafts and that the crew and the male passengers helped the woman and children in.'

'Oh no, not children,' Maudie sniffled, and put her face into the handkerchief.

'It gets worse,' Mrs Green read on, 'one raft was smashed against the side of the ship and another containing eight women and a child was swamped and sank. As the ship was being abandoned many passengers were simply washed into the sea. When her position was finally pinpointed, the Donaghadee and

Portpatrick Lifeboat worked tirelessly in the dreadful conditions, along with the other vessels in the area, and succeeded in rescuing thirty three people.'

'Thank God at least for that,' Maudie cried.

'Captain James Ferguson went down with his ship,' she continued, 'as did the radio operator David Broadfoot who stayed at his post still sending messages for assistance as the Princess Victoria finally sank.'

Mrs Green took off her glasses and put her hands over face. She could read no more of it. Maudie reached for the newspaper.

'The Northern Ireland Prime Minister, Lord Brookeborough paid tribute,' she read out, 'the waves that yesterday were mountainous are relatively calm again but they've become the tomb of one hundred and thirty of our fellow citizens. Under this cruel stroke of fate, many families are sorrowing today. They have the heartfelt sympathy of us all.'

As Maudie continued to read the reports for herself Mrs Green climbed up the stairs to lie down for a while. In the darkened room she prayed for the lost and she prayed too that what she thought she already knew was an old woman's nonsense. The following day when Freddy Montgomery walked up her front steps her old woman's nonsense was confirmed. Freddy, shaken and pale, had felt she should hear the news from him and she appreciated that he had thought of her in his time of trouble.

'Why?' she questioned, 'why would your father board a ferry in a gale when he was scared of the sea. He could have waited, why didn't they wait?'

'I don't know,' Freddy shook his head, 'but it seems conditions weren't so bad when they left Stranraer, it was

only when they got out into open sea that the storm really hit.'

Freddy talked about it then – the attempt to turn back to port as a huge wave breached the doors of the car deck disabling the ship and how she had drifted away, for six long hours she had drifted and couldn't be found. Mrs Green couldn't bear to think of those hours, not for any of those poor souls and not for George and Adele.

'Is there no hope they might be found?' she asked, although she knew.

'They're not amongst the survivors,' he said, biting down on his lip as she put her arms around him.

Mrs Green put the newspaper clippings back into her scrapbook and closed it. She would never hold Freddy in her arms again but at least, unlike his parents whose bodies had never been found, she would have his grave to visit. There was no mystery as to where Freddy lay, only a mystery as to how he had lost his life. Only the good Lord above would ever really know the truth of that, but there was, she knew, one other truth – the sea was remorseless and unprejudiced in its power. It had claimed the life of George who feared it and of Freddy who loved it.

'Go to bed,' Dilys said to herself, 'go to bed.' Oh well, not long to the end of the chapter and still some wine left. She carried on.

Saddened and pained by her memories of the dead Mrs Green's thoughts turned to the living. There was a practical matter which needed to be discussed and with George and Freddy gone it needed to be discussed with Marguerite Montgomery. She didn't know much about her, other than the little which George had confided as he'd laid out his plan for Freddy to marry a seriously-minded, trustworthy young woman. She had no reason to doubt his judgement but would give it enough time to be respectful.

Two days after the funeral, Doreen Everly, with less consideration and with a different intent, strode purposefully through the gates of The Mount. She had heard rumours of those who had called to pay their respects being turned away, which she could quite understand – bereavement could bring out the best and the worst of Darkhaven. The worst, other than the downright nosey, were those with little or no connection to the family, who under the guise of condolence saw an opportunity to ingratiate themselves and befriend. They had obviously been seen for what they were. Doreen had decided it was time that the town showed the best of itself and that old Darkhaven rallied round – the past was past and Marguerite should be taken into their bosom. Clutching a bunch of cut flowers she rapped on the heavy brass doorknocker and waited. When the door finally opened she smiled sympathetically and started to introduce herself.

'Mrs Montgomery's not receiving any callers,' she was curtly informed.

She understood, of course, that not just anyone was being received and requested that the girl inform the lady of the house that Mrs Everly was here to see her.

'As I've already said she's not receiving callers,' she was told again.

Obviously the girl did not know who she was, which was forgivable, but her offhand, upstart manner was not.

'And who might you be?' Doreen demanded, drawing herself up imperiously.

'Theresa O'Brien, the housekeeper,' she replied, looking Doreen up and down.

It was only at her utter insistence that the insolent girl retreated up the hallway bearing her request, but not before the door had been closed in her face. She waited on the doorstep shocked to have been treated in such a manner. There were clearly staffing problems at the Mount and she would offer her advice about it. Poor Marguerite had so much to learn.

And she had come today not only to offer her sympathies but her support, for Marguerite would now undoubtedly need someone to lean on and who better than she? She had been her neighbour on the promenade and had watched her grow up. For years she had listened to Ella's frustrations about the girl and she didn't want to think-ill of the dead, but even if Ella McBride had lived, she would not have been able to instruct Marguerite on the finer points of living in society. That Ella had died shortly after the wedding, she couldn't help but think, had been a blessing in disguise.

For Doreen, the wedding had been and remained something of a mystery. She had not been invited – knew of no one from the town who had been – but deciding to set an example of graciousness had called to the Brides' door with a wedding gift. Expecting to be invited in to view the presents she had braced herself for the inevitable crowing about the match and grandiose descriptions of the impending nuptials. To her surprise Ella had kept her on the doorstep and had been unusually unforthcoming. She had gleaned only that it was to be a quiet family affair with the ceremony to be held not in Darkhaven but in Belfast.

'Who can understand young people today,' Ella said, 'they have their own ideas and it's what they want.'

Doreen had found it peculiar that the Montgomerys, with their close affiliation to the church, would not want their son to be married in Darkhaven but Ella wouldn't be drawn. And although she had prompted her with the names of some of the best city hotels Ella seemed unable to remember where the reception was to be held. There had been no talk of the wedding dress, bridesmaids or the honeymoon, and never in all her years as a neighbour had she been so quickly released from Ella McBride's company. It dawned on her when she sat down in her own parlour that the Montgomerys were being gracious in consideration of their future in-laws – to the point of allowing their only son to marry in a cheap, affordable little commoner garden do. Well, of course the well-bred Montgomerys would set such an example, just as she had with the wedding gift, for which she had barely been thanked.

On the morning of the wedding Doreen Everly positioned herself at her bedroom window hoping to at least catch a glimpse of the bride. At ten o'clock George Montgomery's Bentley drew up on the promenade and she leant out in anticipation. A dark-suited Jack McBride came down the steps followed by an utterly extraordinary vision in floating primrose yellow, a white-gloved hand holding on to the brim of a large white ribbon-trimmed hat. As the chauffeur stepped out and opened the back door of the car Ella tipped herself in, like a great wobbling blancmange. Doreen was unable to stifle a laugh as the Bentley drove sedately away and she waited for another car to come for Marguerite, hoping against hope that Ella had had no *influence on the choosing of the bridal gown. Eventually she gave it up. Wherever Marguerite had spent the eve of her wedding it hadn't been on the promenade and the details of the wedding day Doreen Everly could only speculate about, with those who cared to listen.*

The door of The Mount opened.

'Mrs Montgomery is not receiving any callers,' Theresa O'Brien stated, and closed the door again in her face.

Well, obviously her request had not been delivered, why else would she not have been admitted? She thought to knock again and demand an explanation but decided against it. Perhaps it was a bad time to call – Marguerite may very well be indisposed, or attending to the baby. That was all the wretched girl had had to say. She really would have to advise Marguerite about the hiring of good staff and at the first opportunity.

Doreen stepped out onto the driveway, still holding the flowers which in the effrontery of the exchange she had forgotten to present. She walked down the path and, although still very much put out, stopped to admire the magnificent display of delphiniums and dahlias. At least, she conceded, the gardener was doing his job. She heard voices, and curiosity getting the better of her, stepped gingerly over the flower bed and walked across the neatly manicured lawn. As she neared the hedge the voices turned into laughter and she pushed up onto her toes to look over into the back garden. And there as large as life, sitting in the sun on the patio, was Marguerite McBride, neither indisposed nor occupied.

Doreen watched as the housekeeper poured from a teapot, straining to catch their conversation, trying to hear what could possibly be causing such amusement in a house of bereavement. Her eye was drawn to a movement across the garden. A young red-haired girl was hanging washing on the line, a small red-haired child pulling at her apron. The girl grabbed at him and he ran away unsteadily up the garden pulling himself up the patio steps on his hands and knees.

'And who might you be?' Marguerite asked, coaxing him with a biscuit, as she and the housekeeper laughed.

'And who might you be?' Theresa O'Brien said, drawing herself up in a pose as she caught the boy and tickled him.

Doreen Everly retreated across the lawn and through the flower beds leaving a clump of broken stemmed dahlias in her wake and a bunch of cut flowers in the driveway. She had still not composed herself when she crossed the road to the Recreation Grounds. The lady bowlers were still on the green and she took a seat in the pavilion veranda, her anger still trembling, as she waited for the last ends to be played. Then she would tell her friends all about the merry young widow sunning herself in the garden and laughing aloud with the staff. They would hardly be surprised at Marguerite McBride's lack of dignity or decorum. The girl had no breeding and was unfit to bear the Montgomery name. Even Ella must be turning in her grave at such behaviour, not that her supposed niece would care. She hadn't even returned from honeymoon for the funeral, not so much as a word, she'd heard, when Jack McBride had found his wife lying dead of a brain haemorrhage in the kitchen. Doreen lit a cigarette and watched as the first rink toed their bowls away from the jack, and packed them away into their bowling bags. She was ready and waiting to share her thoughts on the sad state of affairs at The Mount and the consequences of a son being allowed to marry beneath himself.

Two weeks after Doreen Everly had been turned away Mrs Green walked to the telephone box at the end of the road, placed a call, and asked to speak to Theresa O'Brien. The maid informed her that Monday was Miss O'Brien's day off. With what she had hoped for confirmed, she replaced the receiver, and fifteen minutes later knocked on the front door of The Mount and enquired if Mrs Montgomery would see her. As she waited she thought about the matters which she had come to discuss. Her annuity had been promised to her and she wanted to be assured that that promise would be kept. The other matter which she had not yet decided if she would broach was more delicate and difficult, a burden she had carried since George Montgomery had told her of it. The maid returned and brought her through to the drawing room where Marguerite Montgomery, pale but composed, rose and shook the hand of the only person who had been admitted to the house since the funeral.

'Mr Montgomery and Freddy often spoke of you,' Marguerite said, inviting her sit.

Over tea and cake Mrs Green reminisced about her years with the Montgomerys, sharing stories of George and Freddy as boys, and they warmed to each other, consoled a little in their loss.

'They thought of you as family,' Marguerite told her.

Comforted, she asked about her annuity and was assured that the family's wishes would be carried through. She expressed her gratitude to the new Mrs Montgomery, impressed by her quiet dignity.

'Would you like to see the baby?' Marguerite asked.

She hadn't expected that and held back her tears as the nurse brought in a little bundle and placed it in her arms.

'This is Frederica,' Marguerite smiled.

'Frederica,' Mrs Green cooed, and stroked the tiny cheek with the back of her finger. The baby opened her eyes and looked up at her – those eyes had looked up at her before, George's eyes, Freddy's eyes. She brushed away a tear and smoothed her hand across the little downy red-haired head.

'She's a Montgomery sure enough,' Mrs Green said, as Frederica grasped her fist around her finger, and she brought it to her lips and kissed it.

Half an hour later, Mrs Green walked down the driveway and out through the gates of The Mount for the last time, with her annuity secured and relieved of her burden. Whether it had been right or wrong to tell only God above would ever know, but as she'd held Frederica in her arms she'd known that the child was all that was legitimately left of the family and that nothing, or no one, must come between her and her rightful place. She had acted not out of revenge but out of loyalty and love.

Dilys closed the book and finished the last mouthful of wine. She wished she'd had a friend like Mrs Green – an honourable woman who put family first. No one had told her about Juliette's child, she'd been left to find it out for herself. If she'd known earlier she might have been able to keep her family together. Mrs Green had been right to tell.

Dilys climbed the stairs to bed, changed into her nightdress and slipped onto the cold sheet under the duvet – she still, after all these years, slept on her side of the bed. At a time she would have reached out in the darkness hoping to find him there, but not anymore. Juliette was welcome to him. She could look after her ageing Romeo with his aches and pains and replaced hips. The thought of it – Juliette and old rumpled Romeo – made her laugh out loud and she wondered why she'd never thought of it before. She hoped she would remember it in the morning to write it down. Anyway, she had more to think about than them. Tomorrow was art club, her painting was as ready as it could be, and she could have a small lie in.

13

Charles Livermore was the last of the Thursday morning club to arrive in the Whitecliff Inn, having been delayed by his wife's insistence that he read a chapter in her latest book. He was entirely uninterested in her endless supply of romance novels, although constantly grateful that they diverted her attention from him. Humouring her he turned to the ear marked page. When he finally raised his eyes she was regarding him intently with one of her, 'I told you so looks'.

'I've been telling you about it all week,' she scolded.

Perhaps she had, but after fifty years of marriage he was practised at appearing to listen when he was not. He had had to agree with her, however, that something very strange indeed was going on. She had reluctantly allowed him to borrow her book, under strict instructions that he was to bring it home and not lend it to anyone.

Driving down the avenue Charles Livermore was in an exceptionally good mood, not only looking forward to male company and whiskey, but for once to being able to contribute something. The others always had some chosen topic to expound on, or brought in some article of interest to be discussed, but he had never really been one for putting anything forward – too many years of enforced listening to Lillian to offer up much in the way of conversation. Beside him on the car seat though was something which he was sure would hold their attention.

The other gentlemen were already seated at the window when he arrived and, having ordered his drink, he surprised the gathering by announcing that he had something to read to them. It was a little long but if they would bear with him he was sure they would find it quite remarkable.

'What's it about?' Norman Erskine asked, rather unenthusiastically.

It was, he explained, a fictional account of an incident which he thought most of them would remember. There were names which would be very familiar to them and others which they could make up their own minds about.

'Just get on with it Charlie,' Captain McCrae intervened, unusually testily.

Charles Livermore swallowed a mouthful of whiskey, cleared his throat, and began to read.

As Dr Dunbar stated at the inquest he remembered nothing unusual in Mr Montgomery's demeanour in his newly found circumstance of fatherhood. Having been assured that a healthy baby had been delivered, Freddy, Mr Montgomery, invited him to stay for breakfast and he accompanied him to the kitchen. Despite some coaxing from Theresa O'Brien, the housekeeper, he had stayed only for a cup of tea as he was anxious to get on the road. Freddy had then shown him to the front door and that was the last time he had seen him.

'Dr Dunbar, you say,' Leslie Garfield interrupted, wrinkling his nose and sniffing his whiskey, 'now there's a name from the past.'

'He delivered my two,' Norman Erskine said.

'And my son,' Charles Livermore offered.

'And most of mine,' Mr Garfield added, 'and God help you if it interfered with the horse racing.'

The men laughed and raised their glasses to Doctor Dunbar, remembering the great doctor he'd been and the enjoyment of his home visits when you could hardly get a doctor out now. Diverted, they complained about trying to make an appointment at the clinic these days with being placed on hold and suffering the endless jangling music.

'Gentlemen,' Captain McCrae boomed, tapping his glass on the table, 'he delivered one of mine too, but let's give Charlie a chance and no more interruptions please.'

Grateful for the intervention Charles Livermore continued, and his friends, quietened by the reprimand, settled down to hear him out.

Nurse Diamond relayed that in her long experience as an attending midwife nothing untoward had occurred. Mr Montgomery entered the bedroom, shook hands with the Doctor, smiled at his wife and looked at the child in the crib. He then accompanied the Doctor out of the room. Sometime after that she closed the bedroom windows and saw Mr Montgomery walking down the back garden and out through the gate – it must have been around eight o' clock. She hadn't found it in the slightest bit unusual. There was nothing for him to do in the house and perhaps he wanted to take advantage of the good weather. Miss O'Brien then called her downstairs for some breakfast and having been up half the night she gratefully accepted. With nothing more for her to do, she left the house at around half-past eight. She could add nothing more.

Captain Robert McCrae, home on leave and walking his dog along the shore front, saw Freddy Montgomery at the bottom of the yacht club slipway.

'Fine morning for a sail,' he shouted out to him or something to that effect, as a breeze was getting up.

'A fine morning indeed,' Freddy shouted back.

Captain McCrae remembered quite clearly that Freddy was smoking a rather large cigar, which was maybe unusual so early in the morning, but he had not known then that he had just become a father. He was also holding what appeared to be a bottle of whiskey which was early even for Freddy – he didn't mean Freddy in particular of course.

'Is that you they're talking about Bob?' Norman Erskine interrupted, quite taken aback.

'Of course it is,' Mr Garfield jumped in, 'who else would it be, there's only one Captain Robert McCrae.'

'Well I don't know you can be sure about that,' Norman retorted.

'Who also walks his dog along the shore!' Mr Garfield exclaimed contemptuously, 'of course it's Bob.'

'Gentlemen, please,' the Captain called them to order, as Charles Livermore continued.

Captain McCrae watched Freddy row out to the Elizabeth Ann and then saw him under sail. It was low tide and the tip of the Hailcock Rock was visible. Freddy cleared it and appeared to be charting a course out towards the Copeland Islands. He had seen nothing unusual in the handling of the yacht, or its course, as it made out to sea. It must have been around nine o'clock. He continued his walk up to the lighthouse, came back along the top cliff path, and made his way home through the town. He had not seen the yacht return towards the shore and had only heard later in the day what had happened. He could only say that in his short exchange with Freddy he had seemed cheerful enough and could attest, with both expertise and certainty, that the Elizabeth Ann was totally seaworthy – he had sailed on her with Freddy only the week before and she had handled beautifully.

Doreen Everly stated that she opened her bedroom windows at eleven o'clock to air the room – she'd already been up for hours of course. There was a nice sea breeze but it certainly wasn't windy. Captain Donaldson, she noticed, was manoeuvring a punt down the slipway at the yacht club and young John Frackelton was following behind him with a pair of oars. She was sure it was John because the Captain had no time for young people but seemed to have taken to the boy because of his love of the sea. She then saw Freddy Montgomery's yacht sailing back towards the shore. She had no idea how many knots he was doing, but he appeared to be clipping along at a fair speed. She couldn't say if the tip of the Hailcock Rock had been visible – she'd had no reason to consider it – but was unlikely to forget the scraping, splintering crunch when he hit it. From her second floor bedroom window she undoubtedly, and most unfortunately, had had the best view of the whole dreadful situation and could say with certainty there had been no last minute attempt to veer away – the yacht, as she had watched it sail in, had held its course. It was already sinking when she ran downstairs to telephone the local constabulary and raise the alarm.

Captain Donaldson testified that he had not seen the Elizabeth Ann strike the Hailcock Rock. At the time he and young John Frackelton had been putting a punt into the water off the slipway. On hearing the crash they rowed out towards the stricken vessel but by the time they reached the rock the yacht had already gone under. There had been no immediate sign of anyone in the water. They continued looking even after the coast guard arrived but he had already formed the opinion that Freddy must have gone down with the yacht. He could offer no logical explanation for what had occurred. Freddy Montgomery was a first class sailor, he knew the waters like the back of his hand, and was well aware of any hidden dangers. He must have sailed around the Hailcock Rock on hundreds of occasions and why he had struck it on that particular day, in those conditions, remained a mystery to him.

Constable McCullough stated that four hours after the incident Freddy Montgomery's body was spotted by a group of tourists from the Royal Hotel who had been enjoying an afternoon stroll towards the lighthouse. The current had dragged the body under and carried it across the bay to the Port Davey quay where it was seen floating in shallow water just out beyond the Wren's Eggs. Once alerted, he led a group of local men along the shorefront and taking charge, directed two of the company to wade out and retrieve the body which was carried across the sand and laid lifeless on the footpath. He had dispatched Norman Erskine back to the promenade to fetch his car – it was better to get the body moved back into the town and away from the gaze of the gathering crowd.

'Now that's more like it,' Norman Erskine shouted delightedly, 'it wouldn't have been right if I wasn't named, because I was there that day.'

'But it was my car,' Lesley Garfield insisted 'I went back to get the car. You didn't have a car then Norman if you remember. Teddy Mountjoy was put in my car.'

'Who was put in the car?' Mr Livingstone, a newcomer to the group asked confused, 'I thought it was this Freddy Montgomery chap.'

Captain McCrae tried to explain that although the incident in Charlie's story was real enough some of the names had been changed.

'They certainly have,' Mr Garfield bristled, 'because I drove Teddy Mountjoy's body back to the police station. It was me, not you Norman.'

'But it was me who waded out and brought Teddy's body out of the water,' Norman Erskine insisted, 'if you remember, it was me and Captain Donaldson. And that wasn't easy you know, dead weight and slippery with the water.'

'I know it wasn't. I was there watching you trying to bring him out,' Mr Garfield sniffed, but I don't know how this writer fellow has managed to get your name and not mine, even though he's got it wrong.'

'So what was the outcome?' Mr Livingstone asked.

'Outcome of what,' Norman Erskine snarled.

'Well, I thought we were listening to an account of an inquest,' Mr Livingstone countered, 'is it not reasonable to ask about the outcome?'

'Accidental death,' the group chorused to the newcomer, as they broke away to replenish their drinks.

At the bar counter, as Noreen refilled their glasses, they pondered long forgotten questions of their own about the outcome of the inquest still unable to understand how Teddy Mountjoy had managed to hit the Hailcock Rock and some of them still unconvinced by the verdict.

'If I may be so bold,' Mr Livingstone said, returning from the bar, 'let's raise our glasses to Charles for a most interesting morning.'

Charles Livermore beamed with delight and took a long drink of whiskey, his mouth dry from reading.

'Really quite fascinating Charles,' Mr Livingstone congratulated, as the others turned to each other in conversation, 'and when may I ask did all of this happen?'

'It was a long time ago,' Charles shook his head, 'but we could never forget the year you see because it was the same year that.... the same year as the other awful.....'

'The same year as the Princess Victoria,' Captain McCrae, overhearing the conversation, gently prompted.

'Yes,' Charles let out a long sigh.

'The 31st of January 1953,' the Captain continued, 'Teddy's parents were lost with the Princess Victoria and then Teddy died in June.'

'That's right,' Charles sadly agreed, as the Captain reached out and squeezed his shoulder, 'that's right.'

The Thursday morning club finished their drinks and departed for home, asking Charles on the way out where they could buy a copy of the book. Captain McCrae retired to his stool at the bar and ordered a whiskey.

'Noreen, can I borrow your book for a minute?' he asked.

'I didn't think you were interested Captain,' she said, handing it over the counter.

He flicked through the pages to find the part about the inquest and read it for himself. He had not seen Teddy – or Freddy for that matter – smoking a large cigar in celebration of his daughter's birth. Even he could recognise that as an author's cliché. But he had given evidence at the inquest, as had the others named.

'I think you're more interested than you're letting on Captain,' Noreen bantered, asking if he wanted a refill. He closed the book and handed it back to her.

'Nothing to write home about,' he shrugged, and accepted another whiskey, now that he'd been persuaded.

14

As Captain McCrae was accepting another whiskey at the bar counter of the Whitecliff Inn, his wife covered the chicken salad and put it in the fridge. Betty didn't expect him to be home on time for lunch on Thursdays, not that she would admit that to him, but hoped he would get back before she went out to art club. She took her tea through to the living room, opened her book and re-read the chapter about the inquest – just to be sure. No, there was no doubt that the Captain Robert McCrae referred to was her husband and she could hardly wait to tell him. Bob of course might not be pleased. He'd been prickly about the book and quite evasive when she'd questioned him about the Mountjoys and the Theresa O'Brien character. She was sure he knew more than he was prepared to admit but whatever was at the bottom of it all she was delighted to have found his name in it. And why would he not be in book about Whitehaven with him being born and bred?

It was a quarter-to two. She wanted to get to art club and get seated at her table before Dilys Bishop arrived. If she was caught in the car park there would be yet another invitation to join her book club. Betty had nothing against shared interests in books but Dilys was too pushy, always trying to organize them into a feeling of community spirit. That had existed amongst them long before Dilys Bishop had blown in. She still had time to avoid her, time for another chapter.

Freddy Montgomery's unexpected and tragic demise was to prove the catalyst for an unexpected transformation which occurred in the year after his death at the Darkhaven regatta. On the announcement of the winner of the 'Frederick Montgomery Memorial Trophy', Marguerite Montgomery stepped forward to present the prize – an exquisitely engraved silver cup. Little had been seen or heard of Marguerite since the funeral. Callers to The Mount had continued to be turned away.

One of those callers, who had bitterly recalled her rebuff at every given opportunity throughout the year, sat now at her table in the yacht club with her gin and tonic, cigarette in hand, and a red glossed sneer on her mouth. Doreen Everly had made it her business to turn any sympathy for the so called Mrs Montgomery to disapproval and disdain. Marguerite remained unworthy, the cuckoo in the nest of their hopes, the cuckoo who had stolen the prize, and who now had her hands on the Montgomery fortune.

As quiet was called for, Doreen brought her drink to her lips and raised her eyes to her friends in anticipation of the disaster to come, for it would undoubtedly be just that. How could Marguerite McBride possibly hold the attention of a company of her betters? She would shrink into insignificance in front of them, in a mumbling embarrassment, and be seen for what she was. The seated circle around Marguerite hushed, as they scrutinized her, and as Doreen sensed blood.

'As you know, my husband started to sail here as a very young boy, the start of his devoted affiliation to the yacht club,' Marguerite stated unfalteringly, ' following in the footsteps of his grandfather, a founder member.'

'And what would she know about that,' Doreen Everly sneered across her table.

'It is an honour to gift this trophy in his name and also to assure the members that the Montgomery family patronage of the past will unquestionably continue into the future.'

A deeply voiced 'Here, here' emanated from the back of the room.

'In recognition of my husband's passion for sailing,' Marguerite continued, 'it is my intention to set up a fund to enable the club to encourage more young people to learn to sail. I know that Freddy, although he lost his life to the sea too young, would wholeheartedly approve and it is only fitting that others be given the opportunity to be part of something which was so much part of him.'

Another 'here, here' built into a chorus of approval, accompanied by a ripple, and then a wave of applause as Marguerite bowed her head and humbly accepted the rising ovation. She then lifted the silver cup from the table and presented the memorial trophy to the rather awestruck recipient. Her words had been perfectly judged and perfectly judged too was her appearance. Gone was the limp dangling hair, now cut in short-layered locks in the fashionable Italian style. The face, once unremarkable, was noted for its complexion, the dark grey eyes above the high cheekbones accentuated by a trace of eye shadow, the coral coated lips full and smiling. No one in the room could deny that Marguerite

189

Montgomery was indeed a handsome woman. And she displayed a certain elegance that the women both admired and envied, and some envied more than others.

'Well of course we could all be dressed like that if we had the Montgomery money to pay for it,' Doreen Everly hissed around her table, dismissing her companions admiration of Marguerite's ensemble. Montgomery money may have paid for the pique-trimmed, saxe-blue Dior suit, but it was her tall slim figure which carried it off. And she carried herself with a confidence and poise they had not seen in her before.

Marguerite stayed for the remainder of the afternoon, talking with the yacht club officers and being introduced to their wives, her white-gloved hand occasionally toying with the strand of south sea pearls at her neck, as she sipped her martini. She received several invitations for afternoon tea and to dine, some of which she accepted and some which she did not.

On leaving, Doreen Everly made a point of following her to the door.

'My dear Marguerite,' she simpered, 'how lovely to see you, it really has been too long.'

'Mrs Everly.'

'Oh Doreen please, first names between old friends and neighbours, not that we're neighbours now of course,' she laughed.

'Indeed'

'You really must come to tea, shall we say Tuesday?' Doreen invited.

'That's not convenient.'

'Of course, what am I thinking of, I mean with your little girl and everything,' Doreen realised, 'perhaps it would easier if I call on you.'

'I don't think so,' Marguerite said coolly, and turning away, walked out through the door of the yacht club.

On returning to The Mount she went upstairs to the nursery. The nanny put her finger to her lips as she came through the door – Frederica was asleep. Relieved, Marguerite went downstairs. Motherhood was not coming naturally to her. She had felt no rush of love towards her daughter when she'd been born and the child sleeping upstairs perplexed her. Frederica tended to squirm and cry when she picked her up and embarrassed by her own shortcomings she mostly left her in the nanny's care. Perhaps when Frederica was older it would get easier. Marguerite mixed a weak martini, took it through to the sitting room, and sat down at George Montgomery's desk.

'You're a Montgomery now Marguerite,' he'd said, in evenings spent in this very room, as he'd talked at length about business and about it should be conducted. And she had conducted herself well this afternoon. She hadn't let herself down in front of Darkhaven's prying and judgemental eyes but had prepared herself well, just as he had taught her. And today she felt that Darkhaven had accepted her as a Montgomery too. She had seen it as those critical eyes around her had melted into smiles. She had felt it in the warm applause and in the respect which had been shown. She had finally taken on the mantle although she had started to wrap herself in it the year before, each decision which she had made, bringing the cloak ever closer to the clasp.

Her first decision had been taken in the weeks after Freddy's funeral when Mrs Green had called on her. She hadn't had the heart to turn the old housekeeper away and without knowing if she had the right to, assured her *that her annuity would continue to be paid. The second decision, made on that same day in June 1953, had been a direct consequence of Mrs Green's visit. Haunted by the shadows and half-truths of the past, which had been exposed so painfully but well-meaningfully during the afternoon, she had been unable to sleep. Pacing the bedroom there had been only one comforting thought.*

'She's a Montgomery sure enough,' Mrs Green had said as she'd nursed Frederica, who hadn't squirmed or cried, and on that thought Marguerite had decided what to do.

Betty McCrae got up and looked out of the window. Up the hill she could see that Dilys' car was still in the driveway of the Deacon's House. Not quite sure if that was now an advantage or a disadvantage she sat back down and continued her chapter.

As the sun began to rise beyond the Copeland Islands Marguerite bathed and went to the dressing room, the closets still full of Adele Montgomery's clothes. Freddy hadn't cared about them and she'd kept the furs, which fitted her, and the gowns which didn't, but too exquisite to be disposed of. In a generosity of spirit she had given some of the things she didn't want to a delighted Tess, understanding that a girl in her position would never be able to afford such clothes. During her sleepless night, kept awake by Mrs Green's revelation, she had truly considered Theresa O'Brien's position.

At half-past seven Marguerite brushed out her long limp hair, clasped the Montgomery pearls around her neck, smoothed the fitted jacket of her tweed suit down over her the top of her skirt, and took a final look in the mirror. She went downstairs to the sitting room, opened the safe, and making a quick calculation counted out the banknotes and placed them into an envelope. In the hallway she told the maid that she wanted to speak to Miss O'Brien as soon as she came in.

'I'll see her in the dining room,' she instructed.

Theresa O'Brien was late for work that morning – she hadn't felt the need to rush, she could make her own time. She walked slowly along the shorefront from Seaview Cottage, thinking of everything that had happened and of the consequences to her. George and Adele were dead, Freddy was dead, and she mourned them but grief had to be overcome, she had to think of her future. She wasn't unduly worried. She'd had the running of the house to herself for long enough and Marguerite would have to rely on her even more than ever now.

'Marguerite,' she blew the name scathingly out of her mouth.

How she and Adele had laughed about her – the little mouse that Freddy had been forced to marry, the little mouse who didn't know how to dress, who didn't know how to hold herself. How Adele had railed against the marriage and that she wasn't good enough for Freddy. It had brought on an episode of changeable weather but even that had not swayed George Montgomery. He had had his way about it as he had about everything. If he hadn't how different things might have been? It was too late for all of that now.

Tess turned the black velvet collar of Adele Montgomery's coat up around her neck in the chill of the morning sea mist. Who did Marguerite think she was, expecting gratitude from her for the gift of a dead woman's clothes? And the mouse had kept the best of *everything for herself. How ridiculous she would look in Adele's Paris gowns – much too tall to wear them, and without the class to carry them off. Tess knew she would look better in them, hadn't she worn them, hadn't the real Mrs Montgomery complimented her on her taste? Adele had been her friend and had she not died they would have gone to Paris. The mouse didn't know about that. The mouse didn't know anything and was no threat, no threat whatsoever to Theresa O'Brien.*

'Mrs Montgomery's been asking for you,' the maid flustered, as Tess came through the kitchen door, 'you're to go to the dining room.'

'Who?' she dismissed.

'Mrs Montgomery,' the girl repeated.

'What Mrs Montgomery would that be,' Tess snapped, taking off her coat, 'I'll go when I'm ready,' and told the girl to make her a cup of tea.

'I'm just telling you what I was told,' she said, pouring a cup from the pot.

When Theresa O'Brien finished her tea she walked along the corridor and knocked on the dining room door. Marguerite drew herself up in front of Adele Montgomery's portrait and fixed her eyes on the clock on the mantelpiece as Tess O'Brien walked into the room. It was twenty-five to nine but no explanation or apology for tardiness was offered. She handed the envelope to Tess and told her to open it.

'Really there's no need,' Tess exclaimed, her eyes opening wide as she thumbed through the notes of her unexpected bonus.

'There's every need,' Marguerite said coldly, 'consider this your severance pay, your month's wages and a month in lieu of notice.'

Tess didn't understand, unable to take in the words or the implication behind them.

'You are dismissed from your position Miss O'Brien and I think you'll find that I have been more than generous with the monies which I believe are owed to you.'

'I don't understand,' Tess' voice cracked.

'Oh, I think you do Miss O'Brien, I think you understand very well.'

Their eyes met, searching in the shadows of the past.

'You will leave my house today,' Marguerite commanded, 'leave your keys and the account books in the kitchen before you go.'

'But what about Seaview......'

'You will vacate the cottage within seven days and take your relations, all of your relations,' she emphasised, 'with you.'

Pushed into a corner and gathering her defences Tess prepared to deliver the blow.

'I don't think you understand about my relations,' Tess countered, 'about one of them.'

'Oh I think I do,' Marguerite hit back.

'Well I don't think George or Freddy would be happy about him being put out of his home,' she said defiantly, 'neither of them would want......'

'Mr Montgomery, to you,' she corrected.

'Mr Montgomery,' Tess clenched her teeth, 'wouldn't stand for this.'

'Mr Montgomery is dead,' Marguerite declared stonily, 'and it is my wish that you leave my house immediately.'

In the first week of July, Theresa O'Brien and her clan vacated Seaview Cottage, and at the end of the month

Marguerite received a letter, informing her that the board of the Montgomery Ulster Linen Company would be meeting to discuss matters extraordinaire. She was not expected to attend in person – the board, wholly sympathetic of her recent loss, understood that she needed time to grieve and would also now want to devote her life to motherhood. She would be informed of the outcomes concerning the future of the company. As she read the letter she wished that Uncle Jack was here to advise her – there was little about the workings of the company that he didn't know – but he wasn't here now that she needed him and she hadn't been there when he needed her.

Not wishing to interrupt her honeymoon he had not informed her of Aunt Ella's death – had she known she would have come home. She visited on her return, awkwardly trying to comfort him, neither of them knowing quite what to say. She meant to visit again but discovered she was expecting and became busy with preparations for the baby. She should have invited him for Christmas, her first in The Mount, but the Montgomerys hadn't suggested it and she hadn't known how to ask. Two days after Boxing Day she called to the promenade with a gift – an expensive Omega Seamaster watch.

'Very nice,' he muttered, opening the box and setting it aside on the kitchen table.

'I suppose you know Mr Montgomery's sending me to the New York office on business,' he said. She hadn't known but pretended that she did.

He complained about the length of the boat journey, and travelling in winter, and if the trains in New York were likely to run on time. He cheered a little as he talked about the business and the sales figures from America. Eventually he tugged on his watch chain and pulled the timepiece out of his waistcoat pocket.

'She's never missed a second,' he said, standing up from the table.

'I'll come and see you before you leave,' she offered.

'No need,' he replied.

'Well have a safe journey then.'

'Look after yourself,' he said, his hand resting just briefly on her arm as he guided her out.

Two weeks after Jack McBride sailed safely past the Statue of Liberty into New York Harbour, on a cold grey January morning, George and Adele Montgomery perished in the Irish Sea off the Copeland Islands. The company requested that he stay on in the New York office until matters were resolved. In March, Marguerite received a letter telling her of his intention to retire – without George Montgomery at the helm he didn't want to carry on. At the end of that letter, almost in a post script, he mentioned a widow woman in the New York office whom it seemed he intended to marry. It surprised her, but in her advanced pregnancy and in trying to comfort Freddy in the loss of his parents, the thought of Uncle Jack bringing a new wife home to Darkhaven was not at the forefront of her concerns. They'd all had their grief and must find comfort in their own way.

And then grief had come again in June when Freddy had also been taken by the sea. Uncle Jack wrote, offering condolences in her loss and hoping she might find comfort in the birth of her daughter. She learned he had already married and would now make his home in America. Not wishing to burden her he had employed an agent to sell the house on the promenade and had arranged for the contents to be auctioned, but if there was anything she wanted it was hers to take. She hadn't wanted anything from the house but in the first week of August, as she'd drafted a reply to the Montgomery board's letter and requested an agenda for the meeting, she had made a decision about what was hers to take.

Had they really in the Montgomery offices, in such a short time, forgotten quiet little Marguerite McBride who had sent her figures up to them neatly tallied? Had it been inconceivable to them that George Montgomery had recognised her worth, not only in marrying his son, but as an eager student of the company business? Marguerite attended the board meeting to discuss matters extraordinaire, accompanied by the family solicitor, Andrew McNair. The dark-suited men around the table huffed and puffed, answering her questions with condescension, until they had had to grudgingly concede to her and to her place.

'Young Freddy was an easier proposition,' she heard one of them whisper, as they all regarded the prospect of a woman invading their male domain with horror, their faces set in disappointment that their take-over plan, so carefully formulated, was in tatters.

On the steps outside, where George Montgomery had once taken her hand and told her he was pleased she had joined them, Andrew McNair now took her hand in his.

'Welcome to the board Marguerite,' he said, 'and remember, you hold the majority share, they can't make a decision without you.'

She had known that before the meeting but the letter which he handed to her on the doorstep of The Mount, after he had driven her home, had come as a surprise. The manila envelope was addressed to her in George

Montgomery's familiar hand – 'To Mrs Marguerite Montgomery, to be opened in the event of my death.'

'But he's been dead for months,' she looked questioningly at the solicitor, 'why are you only giving this to me now?'

Marguerite finished her Martini, opened the safe and took out the manila envelope. It was a year since Andrew McNair had entrusted it to her and then awaited her instruction. She unfolded the letter and read it again.

My dear Marguerite,

My solicitors have been instructed to deliver this letter to you in the event of my death, or at a time thereafter which they deem appropriate. If your and Freddy's marriage proves successful, which I hope for, there may never be cause for you to receive this letter. If, however, at some future time any unexpected claims are made upon the Montgomery estate or name, and I am not here to protect the family, the contents are yours to use as you see fit.

I once confided to you that Freddy had become involved with someone. My feelings of concern over this and the actions which I took (and those you know), I hope you can believe were the genuine concerns of a father for his son. Although I did not disclose it to you at the time, and nor have I since, the young woman in question is known to you. At the time of writing this letter she still works in this house. The person in question is Theresa O'Brien.

In the circumstances you have every right to feel aggrieved that I have allowed her to continue to work in The Mount and now I need to offer you an explanation as to why. It is a difficult admission, but the fact is that there was a child. That child is....

Marguerite replaced the letter in the envelope and locked it away in the safe. She didn't need to finish it – she knew that part by heart and she'd known about the child, from Mrs Green, before George Montgomery had seen fit to reveal it from the grave. His concern about a future claim, however, had proved prophetic. According to the claimant, promises had been regarding the child's upkeep. Although Andrew McNair had advised her that no such provision had been made in writing and that it would be impossible to prove, she had made her decision. The solicitor was instructed to make a payment – a very generous amount, with a binding proviso that no further money would be paid.

But, that was all in the past. Within a year of bereavement and birth she had triumphed over the board of directors and over Theresa O'Brien and, today, over Darkhaven. She was Mrs Marguerite Montgomery, the mother of Frederica, a legitimate red-haired Montgomery child and one who could never be denied. She had truly assumed the Montgomery mantle and she wore it well.

Betty McCrae slipped the marker between the pages of her book, lifted her bag and went out to the car, hoping, although running late, to get to art club before Dilys Bishop arrived. Captain McCrae left the Whitecliff Inn with Skipper and walked slowly up the road hoping that his wife had left before he arrived home. There was something he wanted to do without raising her suspicions. His own suspicions had been raised the previous day during his conversation with the stranger in the Whitecliff Inn and this morning Charlie Livermore's piece, and the spectre of Teddy Mountjoy, had started him thinking again. He had almost reached his gate when a car drove down the hill and pulled up on the kerb.

'The famous Captain McCrae,' Dilys Bishop hooted, winding down the window and bringing him to a halt. He never did quite know what that woman was talking about and it registered on his face.

'The book,' she shouted, 'don't tell me you don't know you're in the book?'

'What book?' he responded, dismissively.

'Now Captain, I think you're having a little joke with me,' she screeched.

He should have walked on, but didn't, and listened as she expounded her theory.

'You see, it's very clear to me,' she finally concluded, 'that the Montgomery family and our very own Mountjoys are one and the same.'

'I wouldn't know, I haven't read it,' he informed her.

'But you must have known them all way back then,' she fished, 'you must have known Maybelle and Teddy when they were young. I'm sure you know what Teddy Mountjoy got up to,' she winked at him.

'I have no idea what you're talking about,' he said coldly.

'Now Captain,' she chided, 'I'm sure you know all the town's little secrets.'

He had just been about to tell her off for insinuating that he was interested in gossip when she drove away in a grinding of gears, 'Must go, late for art club,' she blared out of the window.

He saw the note on the kitchen table, 'SALAD IN THE FRIDGE!' He was in trouble but he always was on Thursday. He opened a can of dog food, knocking the tin against the bowl until the contents slid out in a wobbling jellied lump, and leaving Skipper to his lunch, climbed the three flights of stairs to the top of the house.

He couldn't remember the last time he'd been in the box room but everything was in order – familiar pieces of discarded furniture arranged against the walls, a succession of neatly stacked boxes, their contents clearly labelled in Betty's hand. He brought the decks of photograph albums out of the cupboard, lifted out the shirt box, and leafed through the pile of old loose pictures. He found it – a group photograph – six young men in their sailing whites staring out at the camera. He turned the picture over and held it up to the light, just able to make out the faded pencil inscription on the back – Regatta Day, Whitehaven Yacht Club, 1950. And there was Teddy Mountjoy standing in the middle of the front row. He brought the photograph up closer and studied Teddy's face, but the peak of his cap had cast a shadow partly obscuring his features. It wouldn't do.

There was another photograph he was sure, he and Teddy together at the helm of the Elizabeth Ann. He remembered it had been published in the local newspaper, for some reason, and Betty had obtained several copies. It was, she had said, her Stewart Granger photograph of him, and she had had it framed, cutting Teddy out of it. In their early married life it had sat on top of the piano in the drawing room. He didn't know where the framed version was now.

He found an original un-cut copy at the bottom of the box, wistfully regarded his own much younger countenance, and then studied Teddy's face. There was no mistaking the aquiline Mountjoy nose and the small cleft of the chin. It was a black and white image but he remembered the colour of Teddy's hair, the deep auburn stranded with red gold. He hadn't seen Teddy Mountjoy for fifty years but was now in no doubt that he had seen his face yesterday in the Whitecliff Inn, or at least a very good likeness of it. He put the picture into his pocket and carefully replaced the box and the albums. No one would ever know they'd been disturbed. He went back down to the kitchen, took his salad out of the fridge, and sat down at the table. Cutting through the slices of cold chicken he began to think about what to do. By the time he'd finished his lunch he had decided to pay a call.

15

Marie Devlin pulled the chair across the bedroom floor to the built-in wardrobe and steadied it against the door frame. Her youngest daughter, still living at home, had been giving off to her lately about climbing up on chairs to wash the windows or clear out the cupboards. It irritated her. She might be well into in her seventies, but was still fit for it. She didn't want to be thought of as an old woman and didn't think it of herself. Geraldine should be grateful that she was still active and able.

Marie had just returned home from her afternoon art club. She enjoyed painting and had become quite good at it. In the last exhibition she had sold a water colour – a spray of summer flowers in delicate pinks and purples and blues. She looked forward to club but hadn't enjoyed this afternoon's session. She had joined her usual table but Miss Dixon had started on about her arthritis, and not to be outdone Mrs Hanley senior had given a detailed description of a recent hip replacement, which had led to a general bemoaning of aches and pains and failing health. Looking at her wrinkled companions she had become irritated – not at the vagaries of health problems in older age – but that her company enjoyed talking about it, and worse in a mode of one-upmanship. Only a raised eye from Betty McCrae had led her to believe that she wasn't alone in her annoyance and when Dilys Bishop had clattered through the door, apologising loudly for being late, she had at first been pleased with the distraction.

Dilys didn't normally sit with them but her usual seat had been taken. It hadn't taken the latecomer long, once she'd organized her paints and brushes, to turn the conversation to an entirely different subject – 'The Montgomerys of the Mount'. Dilys had enquired if they knew about the book and if any of them were reading it. Apart from Miss Dixon, most had replied that they were, but she had regaled them anyhow with a potted version of the plot, proceeding to talk over anyone who offered an opinion. The characters were drawn from real Whitehaven people, Dilys had professed, and the stories told about them were true to life.

'And one of them is actually here amongst us, at least by association,' she hooted.

Marie had grown distinctly uncomfortable, waiting for what was coming, as Dilys charged on.

'I'm sure you know Bob's in the book Betty,' Dilys said, 'our very own Captain McCrae, the famous Captain.'

'And why wouldn't he be in a book about Whitehaven?' Betty retorted, 'he's Whitehaven born and bred.'

'There is that,' Dilys responded unenthusiastically, 'but then he's not exactly a character in it,' she sniffed, before suggesting they could all work it out for themselves – about who was really who – and they were not to forget that she had been the one to put them on the scent.

Marie had felt her temper begin to rise. Who did Dilys Bishop think she was sitting there pronouncing to them about their town in her English accent? How long had that woman been here? Not anything like as long as she'd been in Whitehaven, even if not born and bred. There had been a day when she would have shamed her impertinence, and she'd thought about it, but a look from Betty had persuaded her against it. She'd also heard her husband's voice.

'Rise above it Marie,' she'd heard him say, 'rise above it.' And she had, remembering too how he used to laughingly warn their sons never to marry a red-haired woman.

Annoyed though, she'd packed her art materials away, made her excuses and left. Her friends, hardly noticing her departure, had started to ask Dilys Bishop to share more of her ideas. Driving home she had thought about the damned book that had stirred up the town, and along with it, memories of her own.

The shoe box was wedged in the far corner on the top shelf of the wardrobe. She managed to wiggle it free, climbed down from the chair, and brought it over to the bed. She picked through her long unlooked at trove of photographs – her steps and stairs of children captured on a black and white beach on a summer holiday in Portrush – the two oldest boys buried up to their necks in sand, the youngest children building a sandcastle with their buckets and spades, and one of her posing unashamedly in a swimsuit. And one of Pat standing outside the caravan, all dressed up in a suit and tie, waiting to take her dancing. She remembered that holiday – all seven of them crammed into the caravan, and her sons screaming their heads off on the rollercoaster with their father, she watching with the girls, all of them too scared to go on. It had been a week of ice-cream and candy floss and dispensing halfpennies and pennies for the amusement arcade. Good days. She set the photographs on the bed with the little pile of children's drawings and cards to mummy and daddy, and opened some of the trinket boxes with their collection of rings and necklaces and beads.

She found what she was looking for at the bottom of the shoe box and pressed the clip of the faded velvet case. The lid popped open, exposing the star burst brooch, as bright and glittering as the day that Sean had given it to her – the brooch that had been lost and found one night long ago on the dance floor of the Rinkha ballroom. She had forgotten all about it until the book had brought it back to her, along with memories of people she had known and of the young life she had lived. Dilys Bishop, the blow-in, might think she knew who everyone was or had been, but she knew nothing about her. And Dilys would hardly be interested in a girl who had worked in the Royal Hotel or had once been in love with Sean Brady, the Sean Brannigan of the book.

When she saw Sean now at mass with his purple-cheeked drinker's face, or saw him shuffling bald headed down into the town, she wondered what she had ever seen in him. But then he had been a catch, the leader of their little pack, the one who shone bright above all the others in his shadow – her first love. And she had been madly in love with him. Even now she could recall the memory of the feeling, but not the feeling of it. The years had long since taken care of that.

But all those years ago when he'd broken up with her she'd been in despair. She'd cried her heart out to her best friend, Tess O'Brien, and together they'd planned how to win him back. She'd bought the new dress and Tess had restyled her hair and fixed her make-up. She'd forced herself out and nursed her heart as Sean went through the girls in the town, dancing them round the floor of the Rinkha ballroom, and sliding his arm around them in the back row of the picture house. She had even persuaded Tess to ask Mrs Green to read her cup – there was man in the leaves, she'd been told, a man she already knew and he would come to her, but she must wait until he was ready. And she had waited and waited, until she could wait no longer. She had begged Tess to go to Sean, tell him that she wanted to get back together with him, and to meet her in the Rinkha. It was the first time she had ever really fallen out with Tess.

The dance floor was packed when she arrived after her Saturday night shift in the Royal Hotel but she saw Sean immediately – tall above the crowd, his unmistakable thick blond hair – and in his arms Tess O'Brien. She watched them dancing together, Sean's hand in the small of her back, holding her close, too close, Tess smiling up into his face, all eyes at him. She wanted to trail her off the floor by the hair of her head but waited until the song ended. As she caught Tess' eye, her best friend jumped back just a little too quickly out of Sean's arms. She confronted her in the powder room and Tess professed her innocence.

'I was only doing what you asked me to do,' she said, 'I couldn't help it that he pulled me onto the dance floor.'

'So did you talk to him then?' Marie interrogated.

'I tried,' Tess pleaded, 'but he couldn't hear me over the music. Do you want me to try again now?'

Marie did not and told Tess O'Brien in no uncertain terms that she knew exactly what she was up to, 'Keep your hands off my man,' she screamed at her.

'But he's not yours is he?' Tess retorted.

She flew at her, pushed her across the room and pinned her to the wall, warning her again to stay away from Sean.

'Find a man of your own,' Marie hissed into her face.

And then in a sob Tess told her that she could never be interested in Sean because she did have a man of her own.

'Who,' Marie wanted to know, 'who?' she asked again and again. Theresa O'Brien would not give up a name.

They'd made it up with each other by the end of the night but their friendship had never been quite the same. She'd remained suspicious of Tess, no longer confiding in her about Sean, and Tess had remained wary of her. They had continued to see each other, but not as often as before, and then her life had taken a different turn.

Pat had come along – in fact he'd been waiting there all the time – one of the crowd but more than that Sean's best friend. She had turned to Pat Devlin, let him take her out, and she had to admit, used him to try to make Sean jealous. She could laugh about it now and Pat had laughed about it too, keeping her going in the early years that she had taken it all a step too far by marrying him before it was too late. She'd hated it when he'd said that, as if he felt he was second best, because it wasn't true. She'd married Pat because she had come to love him – not in that mad passionate first love way – but in a better way, a lasting way.

Tess O'Brien, although invited, had not come to their wedding – too busy then, she'd assumed, with her new duties as housekeeper of The Mount, or perhaps too grand by then for the likes of her and Pat.

'Rise above it Marie,' Pat had advised, as she'd given out in anger and disappointment at her friend, 'and anyway,' he said, 'I'm glad she didn't come.'

She'd had forty seven good years with Pat and she missed him. Marie caught her reflection in the dressing table mirror – her red hair lightly streaked with grey but thick and healthy. She had kept her figure, if a little fuller, and her skin was still good, still firm under her fingers as she ran them down her face from her cheekbones to her neck. She wondered what Tess O'Brien looked like now if she was still alive. It must be fifty years since she'd seen her but she still remembered the last occasion.

A few months after their marriage, she and Pat had moved out of his mother's house into their first own home and had been busy settling in. She'd loved living in that horseshoe of war built prefabs – a little community of friendly neighbours and proudly tended gardens. She had also been pregnant with their first child which they were thrilled about. When the door knocked that day she'd been expecting to see her mother-in-law who had taken to calling daily, dispensing advice as she sat in their living room knitting bootees and baby cardigans. But there on the doorstep was Tess. She invited her in and proudly showed her around her new home, noticing, as she went to make a cup of tea, how Tess brushed her hand over the seat of the old second hand sofa before she sat down and perched on the edge of it. Tess stirred her tea with the shared teaspoon and then held it out to her, dangling it between her finger and thumb.

'I didn't bother about saucers,' Marie apologised, following Tess' eyes around the room, over her uncarpeted floor, the one curtained window and partly papered walls. She saw the scornful look on her face, but held her tongue. She and Pat might not have much, but they had each other and a home of their own and she was proud of that.

As Tess sipped her tea – her little finger held out from her cup like a lady – she announced that she had handed in her notice at The Mount. She'd been very happy with the Mountjoys, she said, but everything had changed.

'It must have been a terrible shock,' Marie sympathised, 'I mean with Teddy Mountjoy drowning, especially after what happened to his parents.'

Tess missed them all of course, they'd been like a family to her, but really it was the new Mrs Mountjoy who was the problem. She couldn't work for her – the woman had no idea about how to run a grand house, no style, no class. It was impossible for her to continue and she wouldn't stay even if she was begged.

'I was wondering,' Tess asked, 'if there are any jobs going at the hotel?'

'There will be,' Marie replied, 'they'll be looking for someone for my job.'

'Are you leaving?'

'I suppose in a few months anyway,' she smiled, patting her stomach, 'I'm expecting.'

She thought that Tess would jump up and hug her with delight but she didn't move from the sofa.

'That's too long to wait,' Tess said matter-of-factly, 'is there nothing going now?'

'I know they're short of chambermaids,' Marie informed her, 'but you'd hardly want to go back to that.'

'Not for me,' Tess' eyes fluttered in disbelief, 'for my sister,' she said, 'a position for my sister.'

Listening to her Marie discovered that a job in the Royal Hotel, or any job in any hotel in the country for that matter, was no longer good enough for Theresa O'Brien. She was off to London to work in a high-class establishment where people in the society columns and even the Royal Family dined. She was merely trying to find a place for Deirdre before she left. Marie offered to put in a good word with Mr McAllister. She showed Tess to the door and with barely a thank you and with no gesture of affection, she clipped off down the road, nose in the air and without a backward glance. She had never seen or heard of Theresa O'Brien again. Deirdre had not come to work in the Royal Hotel but she knew she'd stayed on in Whitehaven for a few years with her little boy. Eventually, they too had disappeared.

Marie put the brooch away, tidied everything back into the shoe box, and lay down on the bed. She was tired and might even have a nap before Geraldine got home from work. She closed her eyes but couldn't sleep – too many questions going around in her head. How had her name ended up in this book and who could have written it? It wasn't a secret that she'd worked in The Royal Hotel but who would remember or care about that now? Anyone could have guessed that she'd danced at the Rinkha – they all had in those days – and a few people might remember that a lifetime ago she'd gone out with Sean Brady. But who could have known about that brooch? Tess knew, Sean knew, but he wouldn't remember what day of the week it was. Somebody had their facts to hand but something in the book had annoyed her, something that wasn't true at all. Her Pat had never been sweet on Theresa O'Brien – he wouldn't have lowered himself – and had never bought her a china donkey or anything else in his life.

Marie got up and climbed back on the chair, pushing the shoe box back into the wardrobe. She pulled it out again, lifted out the velvet box and went downstairs. In the kitchen she took the stew out of the fridge, scooped it into a saucepan, and left it on the cooker. She went out into the hall, opened the cupboard door under the stairs and lifted out the plastic charity bag. She pushed Sean Brady's brooch down in amongst her donations of other second hand goods, to be left out in the morning.

16

Before the Thursday morning club had gathered in the Whitecliff Inn and before Wilma arrived, Maybelle Mountjoy lay back on her chair in the veranda, closed her eyes and pushed her book in under the cushion. She didn't need to be reminded of the exquisite silver cup that Marguerite Montgomery had presented at the regatta – she had presented it herself every year since Teddy's death, but there was one particular occasion which she was unlikely to forget.

It had been the sixteenth year on which she had been called upon to do the honours and the year of Edwina's seventeenth birthday. She remembered that David Livermore, Charles and Lillian's strapping teenage son, had been the recipient that year and had presented her with a large bouquet, kissing her on the check as he handed it over. In the far corner of the room she'd noticed Edwina, ensconced with a group of young sailors, giggling and nudging her companions. Her daughter's performance during the presentation had annoyed her and her irritation only increased when Doreen Everly approached and invited her to her table. Fortuitously the club Commodore, Captain Donaldson, had appeared at her side and rescued her, although she would have declined. Happy with whiskey the Captain talked about the day's sailing and then began to talk about Teddy, about his prowess as a sailor and the mischief he'd got up to.

'Tried to sell my yacht you know,' he blustered, 'put a damned for-sale sign up on her.'

Maybelle had heard the story many times before but laughed along with him.

'We'll never see the likes of Teddy again,' the Captain sighed, 'but young David has it in him to be a very fine yachtsman.'

'So I believe,' Maybelle agreed.

'And I think he's got an eye for Edwina,' he said, winking.

That Maybelle did not know – her daughter did not confide in her – but unusually she found herself confiding in the Captain that she hoped Edwina would go to University before she thought of anything else.

'Better she find herself a good husband,' the Captain advised, 'and she could do a lot worse than young David.'

Maybelle smiled – Captain Donaldson's attitudes had obviously bypassed the liberation of the 1960s and remained unshakeable in 1970. Leaving him to his convictions she decided to go home and walked along the corridor to the ladies' cloakroom to retrieve her bouquet. The inner door was slightly ajar and someone uttered a long 'shush' as Doreen Everly's unmistakable wheezy tones dropped to a whisper.

'Well I'm just saying if I was David Livermore's mother I'd soon knock some sense into him.'

'What do you mean?'

'You know what I mean,' Doreen intoned, 'mooning around after a girl like that. He has no idea, doesn't know the half of it.'

'I had heard something about it.'

'How could you not?' Doreen continued, 'it's the talk of the town. Lock up your sons, lock up your husbands, that's what I say, it's anything in trouser where Edwina Mountjoy's concerned.'

'Surely not.'

'It surely is,' Doreen rolled on, 'I have it on very good authority that the latest is Sean Brady, can you believe it, Sean Brady of all people, he's old enough to be her father and apart from the fact that he's a married man, well,' she paused whispering it, 'well, he's a catholic.'

'Is that so bad?'

'Oh my dear, you're English, you don't understand about these things,' Doreen said, 'it makes it worse again.'

'Poor Mrs Mountjoy.'

Doreen Everly let out a loud contemptuous snort.

'Poor nothing, walking about with her nose stuck in the air, looking down on us all, refusing to sit with us. I don't know who she thinks she is. Believe me I could tell you a thing or two about Maybelle McBraid.'

'Do you think she knows about Edwina?'

'Well, she'll know soon enough, if what I've heard is anything to go by, and then we'll see about her airs and graces,' she spat, 'but will we ever know who the father is, that's the question. Sean Brady's certainly not the first one to have been there and mark my words he won't be the last.'

'Don't say that Doreen.'

'Dilys, you aren't fully acquainted with small town life yet, when you've lived here as long as I have you won't be so naïve. I don't like to say it, but I can only repeat the name my husband used for the girl last week, and he's not one to use such language, but in his opinion, and I can't disagree with him, she's nothing more than a common little whore. Well, now I've said it, and I would never use such a word myself as you know, I'm only repeating what my husband said. Everyone's saying it, or if they're not saying it they're thinking it. Anyway, what would you expect? Like mother, like daughter.'

'Surely you don't mean Mrs Mountjoy was....'

'Not in that way,' Doreen cut her off, 'what man would have looked at her, and it's still a mystery as to how she caught Teddy Mountjoy, or maybe not if you know what I mean, but she was quite unsuitable, low, and as they say, blood will out.'

Maybelle heard them making ready to return to the bar and retreated down the corridor and out of the club, a cold sweat rising from the small of her back. She made it to the car, before the nausea settled deep in her stomach, and somehow home and into the house before she was sick. Rage turned to tears before the rage came again. She walked the rooms in the house and then found herself at the bottom of the garden. She went to Edwina's room, with the thought of throwing her belongings out of the house. She got into the car, to drive back to the club to find her daughter, and got back out. She paced the house again until she had exhausted herself.

She sat for a long time at the dining room table – her world turned around and dragged down into a bitter place. She hadn't needed the vile and vicious Doreen Everly to remind her of what they had all said about her

– that she wasn't good enough, that Teddy had married down, and that no good would come of it. But she had proved them wrong. She had earned her place and her right to it by the way she had lived her life. And she had lived it graciously. All through the years she had preserved the great Mountjoy name, kept all their little secrets and protected their fortune. She deserved to bear the name more than some of them ever had. She looked up at Adelaide Mountjoy's portrait above the fireplace. There was more of Adelaide in Edwina than there was any part of her – blood will out.

She pushed her emotions away, went to the sitting room, and sat down at George Mountjoy's desk.

'Everything is in the plan Maybelle,' she could almost hear him say, 'Plan, take charge, and carry it through.' And he had been the consummate planner. He had made his plan, taken charge of Teddy's life, had brought her into it, and that part at least he had seen through. The rest of it had been left in her hands and she'd done what she'd had to do. She knew what she had to do now.

It had grown dark when she heard the front door open. Edwina bounced past the sitting room carrying her long forgotten bouquet. She called out to her and she came to the doorway, reluctant to come in – she was going out, her friends were waiting for her. Maybelle informed her daughter that she was not going anywhere and told her to sit down. Edwina sighed and threw herself down on a chair, the alcohol on her breath drifting across the desk, her face flushed and mouth tight and resentful. She wanted to draw her hand across that face but restrained herself and informed her daughter coldly of the turn that her life was about to take. And

Edwina's life had taken a turn, but in the end not the one that she had planned or wanted for her.

'Good morning Mrs Mountjoy,' Wilma greeted, stepping into the veranda and handing over the post.

'Oh, good morning Wilma,' she started, 'I didn't hear you come in.'

Maybelle discarded the pile of unsolicited flyers and asked her to dispose of them.

'I think you might want to keep this,' Wilma said, studying the stamps on the airmail letter, 'it's from America.'

'Yes indeed,' she took it and slipped it into her pocket.

'I'll make a start with the laundry then,' Wilma informed her, 'and no lunch and afternoon tea as usual?'

'Perfect,' Maybelle replied and went upstairs, as Wilma set off for the laundry room, wondering who it was who wrote so regularly from America.

In the bedroom Maybelle sat down on the bed and opened her letter – it would be a comfort to read it compared to the reading she had done of late. Helen was an excellent correspondent, her letters a mixture of erudite insight about her work and interspersed with family news and life in Ithaca. They'd been writing to each other for nearly thirty years and telephoned occasionally, but it was the letters which they both enjoyed. Maybelle had received the first letter shortly after her Uncle Jack had died. She had known about Helen, the child of her uncle's late middle age – an unexpected arrival to him and the younger American widow whom he'd married – but when he wrote he rarely mentioned his daughter. And it hadn't meant much to her then, she'd been busy and involved in her own life.

When he died, Helen had written tentatively and thoughtfully, introducing herself as her half-sister. It hadn't really come as a revelation – deep down she'd always suspected that Uncle Jack was indeed her own father. She had replied with acceptance of the fact that they were sisters, asked that the past be left alone, but had expressed a desire to keep in touch. Helen had respected her wishes and they had begun their correspondence. It had come as a delight to them both early on that they shared an interest in literature. She had proudly followed her sister's academic career from graduation to doctorate to professorship – a life that she had once imagined for herself. Over the years they had planned to visit each other but so far had never managed it. Maybelle lay down on the bed and re-read Helen's letter thinking that she might actually accept the invitation to attend her nephew's wedding. Looking at the enclosed photograph of the handsome dark-haired young man, posing beside his intended, she could see Uncle Jack in him. She started to draft a reply in her head and fell asleep.

Just as Wilma was arranging the cake stand for afternoon tea the doorbell rang. She wasn't aware that anyone was expected – she would have been informed – but no matter, she knew how to deal with unwelcome callers. She opened the front door to find Captain McCrae on the doorstep and asked politely if Mrs Mountjoy was expecting him. She was not, but if it was convenient he would like to see her, it was a matter of some urgency. Unsure about bringing him in but reluctant to leave him on the doorstep, Wilma took him around the side of the house to the patio. She ran across the garden and brought in the washing – Mrs M wouldn't approve of it being on the line when there was company.

'I was just coming to look for you,' Wilma said, finding Maybelle coming down the stairs, 'Captain McCrae's here, I hope you don't mind but I took him round to the patio.'

'How lovely to see you Bob,' Maybelle said, taking his hand.

'And you Maybelle, it's been too long,' he replied.

Wilma went back to the kitchen wondering how long he would stay – she could just about get the washing back out and finished off if he didn't delay. She put the kettle on, brought the cake stand out of the cupboard, and arranged a good selection of pastries on the doilies. Deciding that the everyday tea service wouldn't do she searched out the better china and organised the tray.

On the patio the Captain didn't quite know where to start, 'Maybelle,' he said, 'we've known each other for very long time and you know I would never interfere in your business but there's something going on that I think you need to know about.'

'My goodness, this sounds rather serious,' she met the concerned look.

'Well, maybe or maybe not, but it's about this book that's been written, have you heard about it?'

She had, and he was glad that that was at least something he wouldn't have to explain. The rest of it though would be difficult. Maybelle was certainly not a naïve woman but he didn't know if she was aware of the age-old rumoured indiscretion which he would have to broach or how she would react to it. She might deny all knowledge of it, or tell him to mind his own business, or worse, send him away with a flea in his ear. It wasn't easy when the family linen was being washed in public. But then he wasn't responsible for that, it was all because of this damned book. As he was thinking about how to proceed Wilma appeared with the tea tray and he maintained a discreet silence as she went back to the kitchen and returned with the cake stand. After Maybelle had poured and persuaded him to have a macaroon, he took the photograph out of his pocket.

'My heavens Bob,' she declared, holding the picture out and then drawing it into focus, 'I think I've seen this before, or something very like it, but of Teddy, I don't remember you being in it.'

'It's Teddy I want to talk to you about,' the Captain said, as Maybelle raised her eyes and looked at him, just, he thought, a little warily.

And then, apologising for any offence he might be about to cause, he described his encounter with the stranger in the Whitecliff Inn and told her as plainly and delicately as he could of his suspicions about him, hoping that he would be forgiven. Maybelle listened and said nothing, keeping her eyes fixed on some distant point beyond the shoreline until he had finished.

'I appreciate you coming to me Bob,' she finally said, standing up from the table and extending her hand, an indication that it was time for him to leave.

'What do you think this fellow's up to?' the Captain asked as she walked him around to the front of the house.

'I'm sure it's nothing to worry about,' she brushed it aside, 'and Bob, I'm sure I can rely on you keep this between ourselves.'

The Captain left her in no doubt of that and walked out through the gates of The Mount, relieved, but unsure if what he had confided in Maybelle had already been known to her. Maybelle returned to the patio as Wilma was clearing away the tea service.

'Is that Captain McCrae?' she asked, lifting the photograph from the table.

'It is.'

'He was very handsome,' Wilma said, and curiosity getting the better of her asked, 'who's the other man?'

'My husband,' Maybelle replied.

It was the first time Wilma had seen a picture of Teddy Mountjoy. It had always struck her as odd that there were no family photographs on display in The Mount. Most of her elderly ladies had a clutter of frames on their sideboards and mantelpieces but not Mrs M.

'He was very handsome too,' Wilma commented, unable to take her eyes off the image.

'Yes, I suppose he was.'

'It's a lovely photograph,' Wilma said, as Maybelle retrieved it from her, 'it would look nice in a frame.'

Maybelle went to the sitting room, opened the bottom drawer of the desk and felt into the back of it, her hand searching for the paper bag. She brought it out carefully and lifted out the picture frame from the shards of broken glass. And there was Teddy, the very same image that had been brought to her today, although someone had cut Bob out of it when it had been framed. It had been a long time since she'd looked at Teddy's face in a photograph and over fifty years since she'd seen it in life. No, that wasn't true. She had seen his face yesterday at the garden gate.

17

Norma Lockhart placed the last of the groceries into the cupboards, folded the plastic bags into the drawer, and made a cup of tea. She sat down at the kitchen table, took the shopping receipt out of her handbag, and started to tot it up. It wouldn't total, out by a pound and several pence. She tried again and then threw the pen down in disgust. Either the supermarket till was wrong or she was repeating her own mistake. It was probably her. She hadn't been able to concentrate all morning or, in fact, since Dilys Bishop had cornered her in the Candy Box the previous day and tried to draw her into some ridiculous theory about Edwina Mountjoy.

Since then Edwina had been constantly on her mind. She remembered her as a little red-haired girl, playing in the garden and around the house with her own daughter, Sonya. They'd been inseparable childhood friends – Edwina a little giggler and always up to mischief and begging hugs. The girls had attended the same primary and secondary school until that last year when Edwina had mysteriously been removed and sent off to some Swiss finishing school. Maybelle had made it known that that had always been the plan, but few had been convinced. She had asked Sonya about it but her daughter had been unforthcoming.

'We're not friends anymore mum and I don't know anything about it,' she'd bristled, 'one week Edwina was there at school, the next she wasn't, and that's it.'

And Norma remembered she'd been glad their friendship had cooled in the teenage years. Once, waiting for Sonya at the High School gates, she'd seen Edwina heading off down the lane towards the shore front, a cigarette in her mouth and the skirt of her uniform hitched up to her thighs. A group of local boys were following after her, making grabs at her tie as she swirled it through the air, and making grabs at her. It wasn't her place to judge but she wouldn't have liked Sonya to have been behaving like that. The town, however, had been quick enough to judge Edwina Mountjoy's sudden disappearance. There had been talk of boys, even men, and rumours of a pregnancy.

In the summer of 1972 Edwina returned from finishing school and called in, all full of news and chatter, and Norma had been happy to see her.

'This is Jan,' she said excitedly, introducing the young German man on her arm as her fiancée. Hand in hand they talked about their wedding plans, where they were going to live, and what they were going to do with their lives.

An engagement party was held in The Mount – a sign of Maybelle's approval – and invitations were both gratefully accepted and jealously sought. The doors of the house had not been opened to them for some time and they felt honoured to have been asked – their place in old Whitehaven society recognised – but also curious to see the Mountjoys at home together. The guests mingled freely and easily, the bright happy mood reflected in the polished splendour of the house. They accepted a vol-au-vent, a salmon mousse or cream cheese topped cracker, from the bow-tied waiters' silver platters, and the more adventurous dipped into the guacamole or tried an olive. Large glasses of fruity sangria were dispensed from crystal punch bowls and a well-stocked bar catered to more traditional tastes. Maybelle, welcoming and gracious, mingled around the chattering groups, introducing her future son-in-law with pride – some had rather snidely suggested with relief.

At the centre of attention, though, was Edwina. All eyes were on her, taking in every detail. She had inherited none of her grandmother's remarkable beauty and would never be the Elizabeth Taylor of Whitehaven. She was more her father's daughter – the aquiline Mountjoy nose dominating her face, the dark scattering of freckles attempting to hide under a layer of foundation. The rich auburn Mountjoy hair had eluded her, leaving her a brighter redder tinge, but she had inherited Teddy's eyes and they danced hazel green and bright with excitement.

Flitting from group to group Edwina held out her hand as the guests admired her engagement ring – the emerald, she sweetly disclosed, chosen by her fiancée because of the Emerald Isle. Her green silk off-the-shoulder dress perfectly matched the colour of the diamond set stone, and she revealed to several ladies who enquired that it was from Chanel in Paris. As their eyes followed Edwina around the rooms they easily excused her giddiness in the celebratory atmosphere, and in the flow of expensive champagne. Most believed, and it was commented upon, that Switzerland had worked.

The less convinced, however, studied the tall slim figure and whispered about the past, wondering – although there was no sign beneath the fall of the dress from the waist to the floor – about the closeness of the date of the impending marriage. And somehow all of them that night, the generous and the ungenerous, watched and waited for a slip, a lapse, some awful moment to validate the past. Norma had already gone home when the awful moment came. She would hear about it the next morning but before that they had danced.

The younger guests had set up a record player in the veranda and spilled out onto the patio dancing about to the latest hits. Norma and Bert and Charles and Lillian Livermore retreated down the steps to the tables around the lawn. It wasn't their music and they watched, increasingly amused by the jiggling, gyrating dancers on the patio above. She and Lillian opened a bottle of champagne but their husbands turned their noses up at it, and went in search of whiskey. The tempo on the impromptu dance floor increased and as the music grew louder young David Livermore came strutting and pouting across the flagstones, his shirt unbuttoned, shoulders snapping, and singing loudly into a beer bottle. Lillian shook her head and peeked through her fingers, mortified, but the cheering crowd around him appreciated it and even Norma recognised the Mick Jagger impression.

After David had brought the house down the music stopped and she caught sight of Bert and Maybelle in the veranda, flipping through a box of records. The youngsters protested as they commandeered the player and Norma clenched her teeth as the arm screeched across the vinyl and jumped and hissed as they found the song.

'Do do do do do dup rip da do,' she recognized the familiar strains immediately, 'do do do do do dup rip da do.' Bert soft-shoe shuffled down the patio steps, reached for her hand and pulled onto the lawn, as a melody of voices soared into the air.

'Let's show them how it's done,' he whispered into her ear, whisking her into a turn, ' take away the breath of flowers it would surely be a sin,' he sang, moving her around the lawn as she stayed up on her toes, keeping her high heels from sinking into the grass. It had been a long time since they'd danced but she followed his lead familiarly and easily, to their song.

'Is it a sin to love you so, to hold you close,' the Four Aces harmonised, as Bert pulled her closer to him in a dramatic jerk, 'and know you are leaving,' he spun her out and away.

Lillian and Charles joined them, following not so much in a foxtrot as a waltz, and then much to their amazement Jan lead Maybelle down the patio steps and swept her onto the lawn. They moved aside, surprised that a young man could actually dance and astonished at Maybelle who glided around in his hold. Norma, in all the years she'd known her, had never seen her dance before. As the song reached its final crescendo Jan bowed and kissed Maybelle's hand, and as they all smiled delightedly, the young ones retrieved control of the record player. She and Bert had left soon after that, seeking out Maybelle to thank her for such a memorable evening, and had walked home down the avenue in the moonlight, Bert still humming their song as the music and laughter from the party drifted out across the bay in the cool night air. There had been no portent of what was to come.

It was as the last few guests were leaving that it was realized that Edwina could not be found. Maybelle looked for her in the house but she wasn't there. Jan searched the garden and then went out the gate onto the top cliff path. Lillian sent David after him, worried that even on a clear moonlit night a stranger might get lost, or worse, near the cliffs. The two young men walked along the path calling for Edwina, and then cut down the Golden Stairs onto the shore. Jan thought they might find her there, it would be just like Edwina to go paddling or swimming in the moonlight – she was fearless and it was what he loved about her. She was not there, and deciding that she was probably safely home in bed, they started back along the shore. Rounding the bend at Port Davey they noticed a light in the boathouse. Jan opened the doors and as David Livermore told his parents when he got home they had found Edwina inside.

'What on earth was she doing there?' Lillian quizzed.

David squirmed, trying to think of a way to put it, 'She was at it,' he said.

'At what?' Lillian's eyebrows knitted together in incomprehension.

'In the act,' he ventured, looking to his father for help, 'she was having it off,' he blurted when no help was forthcoming.

'With whom?' his mother asked.

He didn't know – he hadn't exactly got a good look at his face had he. His father laughed sending them both into a fit. When he brought the giggles under control he was able to say it was a local lad – Seamus something maybe.

'Oh my God,' his mother shuddered, and continued asking questions which David couldn't answer.

He didn't know how Edwina had met up with him, he didn't think he'd been at the party and he didn't know what had happened. When he'd left the boathouse Jan was shouting and Edwina and, whatever his name was, were putting their clothes back on. At that, his father choked back a laugh sending them into another fit.

'You made a lucky escape with that one,' Charles laughed, hugging onto his son.

'What do you mean?'

'I thought you were sweet on Edwina at one time,' he said.

'You must be joking,' David denied, as his giggles turned into hiccups, and going to the kitchen for a glass of water he slipped away to bed.

Over breakfast Lillian drew the story from David again, piece by appalling piece, and overnight he had remembered the boy's name – Seamus Brady.

'You don't mean Sean Brady's son?' she gasped, looking across the table at her husband.

As Charles forked the last mouthful of soda bread and bacon into his mouth, he couldn't stop her blurting it out.

'But Charles wasn't it because of Sean Brady that Edwina was sent away, wasn't he … ..'

'Seamus Brady's father, that's right,' Charles choked and started to cough, drowning her out, as the end bite of his breakfast went down the wrong way.

His son slapped him hard on the back as he spluttered and wheezed for breath, tears rolling down his reddening cheeks. Having saved his father from choking to death and having hardly touched his fry, David Livermore left the house and half an hour later the more lurid details of what he had witness in the boathouse, which he could never have divulged to his parents, were graphically described to his friends.

It hadn't taken long for Norma Lockhart to hear of the dreadful events of the previous evening. Within fifteen minutes of David going out Lillian had called and related the whole sorry tale. Unusually her neighbour had not delayed. She'd watched her walk down the avenue into the Hanley's driveway – the gossip was about to be spread. Shortly afterwards Norma had heard, unsurprisingly, that the wedding had been called off. In the next few months she saw Maybelle at church and occasionally at the yacht club, although Edwina was never mentioned in her presence. Outside of her company, however, the town continued to talk. Varying views were put forward as to whether Edwina had been thrown out of The Mount or whether she had left of her own accord. According to some Maybelle had changed her will and had cut Edwina off from the Mountjoy fortune, although the armchair lawyers amongst them theorised about the trust fund set up by her grandfather and if it could be legally withheld. Edwina's whereabouts were conjectured upon. Some swore that she had moved away, some had seen her only yesterday and it was had on good authority that she was living with Seamus Brady. And then, after a while, the memory of the unfortunate events of the engagement party faded and so too did conjecture about Edwina, as Whitehaven's attention turned, as it so often did, to the misfortunes of others.

18

Sitting in the veranda, Maybelle heard the hum of the dryer starting up in the laundry room.

'It just needs a quick a blast,' Wilma apologised, coming through the door, 'I didn't want to put it back out with the Captain being here.'

'Quite right,' Maybelle agreed and opening her handbag handed Wilma her wages envelop.

'Thank you Mrs Mountjoy and I'll come and sort it out tomorrow.'

'No need for that Wilma, I can see to it, and I'll see you as usual on Sunday.'

As Wilma left, Maybelle felt down behind her cushion for the book. Bob McCrae had not told her anything that she didn't already know – she knew her family's secrets – but had given nothing away to him. He'd meant well though, and she had appreciated that, and that the old bonds of loyalty amongst old Whitehaven still counted for something. Those bonds didn't matter to someone else and she needed to get to the end of that person's story. She put on her glasses and started to read.

Marguerite sat at the breakfast table, pushing the congealing scrambled eggs around her plate, glancing occasionally at the ashen faced Jan. They had barely exchanged a word and his grim demeanour showed little sign of forgiveness. Against all reason she hoped it could be retrieved but, with what she'd overheard the night before, it was unlikely. She'd waited up when he'd gone out to look for Frederica, more angry than worried that her daughter had slipped away from her own engagement party. Eventually she'd heard them come in, arguing, and had stepped unseen into the sitting room. During the heated exchange her daughter's sordid little tryst had been all too painfully exposed.

Sipping her tea, Marguerite was thinking of a way to broach the subject, when Frederica appeared – eyes smudged with mascara, hair un-brushed, her dressing gown untied. She sat down and buttered a piece of toast, complaining that the tea was cold.

'I don't know why we can't have coffee,' she whined, 'in Switzerland everyone drinks coffee.'

'Is that all you have to say for yourself,' Marguerite shouted, bringing her hands down sharply on the table as Frederica shrugged her shoulders and rolled her eyes, her lips pursed in disregard.

'If you'll please excuse me Mrs Montgomery,' Jan stood up from the table, 'I need to talk to Frederica.'

Sighing, her daughter took the time to butter another piece of toast, and gnawing on it followed him to the sitting room. Later, when Jan found her in the veranda and asked her to order him a taxi to the airport she tried to persuade him to stay, but he was adamant.

'I will remember our dance,' he shouted out of the window, as the taxi pulled away.

And so will I Marguerite thought as she waved after him, and standing on the doorstep, overwhelmed by his good grace, she wept.

She found Frederica back in bed and told her to get up. They rowed, stung each other with hurts which could never be taken back, and at the end of it she delivered an ultimatum.

'I won't have our good name dragged through the mud,' she asserted, 'if you want to live in my house you'll live by rules or you'll get out.'

'Your house,' Frederica screamed, 'your house. That's all you've ever cared about. Well keep your precious house. You've always cared more about it and your precious name than you've ever cared about me.'

Later, she heard the front door slam and watched from the window as Frederica struggled down the driveway with a suitcase. A blond-haired boy stepped out from behind the gates and took it from her. So, Frederica had made her choice – a not uncommon dramatic gesture – but she was sure that her daughter would return in a day or two when she had calmed down. The days turned into weeks and Marguerite assumed an air of normality in the round of shopping, church and social events. The looks and whispers didn't escape her but nothing was mentioned in front of her, apart from the one enquiry which interrupted her Friday night's drinks table in the yacht club.

'I believe Frederica's away from home,' Doreen Everly said snidely, 'gone back to Switzerland with that handsome fiancée of hers, has she?'

Marguerite didn't dignify that with an answer. She knew Frederica wasn't in Switzerland and although she didn't know her exact whereabouts, sensed that she wasn't too far away. Two months later she was proved right. Regatta day had come around again and, dressed and ready to go, she got up from the dressing table to close the bedroom windows. Looking out over the bay she saw the yachts making for the starting line for the first race of the day and a movement on the top path caught her eye. Edwina and the blond-haired boy ducked in behind the hedge outside the garden gate.

Unable to quell a feeling of uneasiness Marguerite didn't delay in the yacht club and immediately after presenting the Memorial Trophy, returned home. The wardrobes and drawers in Edwina's bedroom had been emptied – only a few unwanted pieces left scattered on the floor. How childish, she thought, that her daughter couldn't have called to arrange to take her things, preferring to sneak in like a thief. On that thought she went downstairs to the sitting room. The wooden panel in front of the safe had been opened and not properly closed. She felt in the desk drawer for the safe key – it was there, but not where it should have been. No doubt they had tried, but been defeated by the combination. She walked through to the dining room. The display of silver in the cabinets had not been touched and none of the valuable porcelain was missing. She went upstairs to her bedroom and checked through her boxes of jewellery. Nothing had been taken. She sat for a while at the window, watching the last of the visiting yachts sailing out of the bay back to their home ports. When she could sit no longer she moved her diamonds, better gems and the Montgomery pearls, to a place where her daughter had not brought them out from to play with as a child. On the Monday morning she telephoned the locksmith to come and change the locks on all of the outer doors of The Mount. Wherever her daughter was she neither knew nor cared. She was disowned. She was dead to her.

Maybelle closed the book and closed her eyes as it all came back. And it came, not in the raging torrent of the past but in a flood, not crashing through the sea wall but rising unstoppably over her defences, as fiction ebbed and flowed into fact. She had given Edwina an ultimatum after an engagement party. There had been the most terrible row and they'd also hurt each other with accusations which could never be taken back.

'You sent me away, sent me away without a care, because you've never cared about me,' Edwina had bitterly accused.

It wasn't true. She'd sent her to Switzerland precisely because she did care. She'd wanted to protect her daughter and her reputation and had told her so.

'Your reputation you mean,' Edwina screamed, 'it's all about you and your great Mountjoy name. You've always cared more about that than you've ever cared about me – your name and your money and your property.'

'It's all been for you,' she reasoned with her daughter, 'and I've given you everything.'

'Except love.'

Those were the deeply wounding words which Edwina had left her with. She might have had the locks changed when she suspected that Edwina had been in the house, but she had never locked her heart against her daughter or disowned her. And she'd always cared and known where Edwina was, even if she'd had to learn it in the unguarded gossip mongering of the town – 'Just imagine Maybelle Mountjoy's daughter living in a bedsit with young Seamus Brady, how are the mighty fallen!'

And that had only been the beginning of it. When that relationship ended her suspicions about her daughter's whereabouts had been confirmed, by chance, one summer's afternoon in 1974.

'Hello Mrs Mountjoy,' a girl's voice had called out from the avenue.

She hadn't seen Sonya Lockhart since she'd gone off to University and unable to avoid a conversation had walked across from the flower bed to the gate. They chatted for a while, Sonya telling her all about her economics course at Cambridge and of her life there.

'I've just been talking to Edwina around the shore,' Sonya finally said, 'and I'm going to see her paintings next week. It's that artists' community, that old farmhouse up on the hill out on the other side of town, isn't it? I suppose you've already seen her work.'

Maybelle smiled and said that of course she was happy Edwina had found an interest.

'She's certainly looking well on it,' Sonya said.

'Yes indeed,' Maybelle agreed, and saying goodbye brought the encounter to an end.

She had already heard a rumour that Edwina was living in this farmhouse but had never heard it described as an artists' community – in her circle it was referred to as a hippy hang out, a drink and drugs den. She wasn't particularly comforted by the news that Edwina was supposedly painting, and although Sonya had said she looked well, her concerns about her daughter ran deeper than her whereabouts or interests or even health.

Three weeks previously Edwina had turned twenty-one and Maybelle had met with the family lawyers in an attempt to prevent her trust fund from being released. Bar having her child declared incompetent or insane there was no other legal recourse and she had had to accept that a very substantial amount of money was about to be signed over. She'd asked the lawyers to try to persuade her daughter to invest the capital and accept a monthly allowance. Edwina had refused and the inheritance was paid in full.

'I should have stepped in then,' Maybelle said to herself, eyes opening and then closing again, 'I should have found you then.'

But, as Edwina was dispensing money to support her farmhouse friends' habits, and her own, Maybelle had had her own financial concerns. The textile industry was in crisis, struggling against cheaper production and workforces elsewhere in the world, and following exhaustive rounds of meetings she had finally decided, with deep regret, to sell the company. She had got out in time – the family money, investments and The Mount secured – but although she had protected her own future she had been unable to protect her daughter.

When Edwina's experiment with communal living came to an end – as most of them drifted away to other places or back into the mainstream – she had moved in with a new boyfriend who was an entirely different proposition to her erstwhile 'artistic' companions. Rinty Skelton was well known around Whitehaven – a rogue and not a loveable one. He had lived for most of his life on the wrong side of the law and was now rumoured to be the leader of a local paramilitary organizations. Maybelle had seen him strutting around the town in his long black leather coat and sunglasses – the unofficial uniform of the self-appointed godfather. He was too smart to be caught, relying on his wily animal wits and sending out the little lesser boys to do his bidding.

Once she had driven over King's Bridge and seen Edwina on his arm – her skirt too short, tottering on heels too high, her red hair turned peroxide blond. She had hardly recognised her daughter, in her gangster's moll disguise, or could believe that she had fallen for the hard man charm that ridiculously captivated ridiculous women. The sight had provoked her into trying to contact Edwina and she'd managed to obtain a telephone number. A man's voice answered the call and she explained who she was. He surprised her by introducing himself as Richard, told her how pleased he was that she had phoned, and chatted amiably.

I'd like to speak to my daughter,' she interrupted.

'Hold on a minute,' he replied.

There was a long pause and she waited nervously, rehearsed words dissolving away, but there would be no admonishments or recriminations from her, she just wanted to ask Edwina if they could meet. She could hear voices talking in the background and knew Edwina was there.

'I'm sorry Mrs Mountjoy,' Rinty Skelton said down the line, 'I thought she was upstairs but she must have nipped out to the shop. I'll get her call you when she gets back.'

Edwina did not call and, rejected, Maybelle did not attempt to call her again. Still, she had lived in hope that it would as usual fizzle out. In the spring of 1978, enjoying a Friday night drink in the yacht club, she learned that it had not.

'I wasn't expecting to see you here tonight Maybelle,' Doreen Everly said, through her lizard smile, 'I mean with the wedding tomorrow I thought you'd be much too busy.'

Maybelle met her eyes and said nothing.

'It's at the registry office in Carrickfergus I believe,' Doreen continued, 'oh well I suppose church weddings aren't the thing these days. I hope you're not too disappointed?'

'Not at all.'

'Do give my best to Edwina and to her intended,' Doreen said, 'now what is his name again, Skelton isn't it, Rinty Skelton, oh dear how could I have forgotten that name,' she smirked.

Maybelle stayed at her table just long enough to give vague but reasonable responses to her friends' questions about the wedding. As she got up to leave, Doreen turned whispering to her circle. She knew what she was saying – she was telling all who cared to listen that Maybelle Mountjoy knew nothing about the wedding at all. A few days later she sent a card wishing Edwina well and hoping that she would get in touch. Edwina did not reply.

Their estrangement continued throughout the eight or nine years of Edwina's marriage – a union which she knew to have been drink-fuelled and violent. She had seen Edwina occasionally in the town over those years, cowed and broken, looking old before her time. By some miracle Rinty Skelton hadn't killed her – he'd thrown her out when he'd finally tired of her and, she'd always suspected, when what was left of Edwina's money was eventually gone. She should have stepped in then. She should have put away her fear of rejection and brought her home but had stayed away as Edwina moved in and out with a succession of men, her life in a downward spiral of private pain and public scandal. She couldn't bring herself to think of that.

Maybelle got up and walked over to the veranda windows, looking out across the bay and out to sea. It was a glorious evening, the calm pane of sea reflecting back the sun. How often had she looked out of these windows to nights like this, and on just as many nights to raging storms? She ran her hand along the window sill sweeping the dead geranium petals onto the floor. She would sweep them up tomorrow. Everything would be swept up tomorrow.

19

Norma Lockhart plumped the pillows up behind her back and waited for her Thursday night telephone call from Sonya – a ritual established many years ago when her daughter had made the move to London. It had been a career choice which of course she and Bert had accepted, even if they'd never understood exactly what she did in her high-powered banking job in the city. She'd been in London now for nearly thirty years and, although there were frequent visits back and forth, she still missed her, and especially since Bert had passed away – four years already. Bert had been so proud of Sonya but had never been able to resist goading her.

'Not courting yet then?' he always enquired, and more persistently as she approached her forties, upsetting many a visit.

Then, in her fortieth year, Sonya had taken them completely by surprise by announcing that she had found mister right, had married, and produced their only grandchild, a beloved boy that neither of them had ever expected to come into their lives. Ben was eleven now, and Sonya was the same age as Edwina Mountjoy would have been had she lived. Poor Edwina.

'You must know if Edwina and Frederica are one and the same,' Dilys Bishops' words came back to her.

Waiting for the phone to ring Norma lifted the book from the bedside table and continued, reluctantly, with *Frederica*.

'*Get your friggin hands off me,*' *Frederica screamed, and kicked, knocking the young constable's cap off his head as he tried to get her into the back of the police car. As he bent to retrieve it Frederica made off across the waste ground behind the bakery towards the railway lines.*

'*Jesus*', *his sergeant shouted, struggling to get out from behind the wheel, 'get after her.*'

The constable brought her down on the embankment as his superior puffed up after him.

'*I'm not sure who to arrest,*' *he laughed, as the young officer disentangled himself from Frederica's raised skirt.*

They brought her back to the car and the sergeant started to caution her, '*Frederica Skelton, I'm arresting you for......*'

'*For what?*' *she spat, as he turned his face away from the stale alcohol on her breath 'what have I done?*'

'*Frederica,*' *he pacified, 'it's not like this is the first time, but in broad daylight, in the middle of the day for pity's sake come on, it's an indecency charge, people phoned, they saw it.*'

'*I didn't do anything,*' *she maintained.*

'*Look, there were witnesses, I have to take you in, just get into the car,*' *he said.*

'*So you got here in time to arrest me,*' *she shouted, 'but not the fella that walked up the road past you, why don't you go after him?*'

'*Would you like to give us a name,*' *the constable asked, taking out his notebook.*

'*Yeah, maybe I will, and you can charge him with not paying.*'

'*That's enough now, you don't want to get charged with more than you have to,*' *the sergeant shut her up, and told the constable to put his notebook away, as he finished his formal caution.*

Norma stopped, closed the book and pushed it into the back of the bedside cabinet. She'd had enough and didn't need to be reminded of that incident, although the reportage in the local newspaper at the time had been more prosaic – Edwina Skelton, fined and placed on probation for an act of gross indecency in a public place at three o'clock in the afternoon with a person or persons unknown. The vultures in the town had already stripped bare the bones of Edwina's life and they didn't need to be picked over again – neither in fact nor in fiction. Poor Maybelle, she thought, to have to suffer all of this being dragged up again. Sonya would take her mind off it. Sonya would cheer her up.

The phone rang and she reached for it eagerly, waiting for news about Ben, and ready to tell her daughter about what she'd been doing all week.

'Mum,' Sonya said excitedly, 'I've just come across this book, 'The Montgomerys of the Mount' and you'll never believe it, but I'm sure it's set in Whitehaven. Have you heard about it?'

'Yes,' Norma sighed, her heart sinking as she admitted she was reading it.

'Well fame at last mum!'

'What do you mean?'

'That bit about you finding a brooch in the Rinkha and returning to its owner,' she explained.

'What brooch?' Norma asked, 'I don't know what you're talking about.'

Sonya asked her to hold on a minute and then came back on the line.

'Here it is,' she said, and began to read.

.......a girl held out her hand, the brooch cradled in her palm. Marie ran to her, hugging and thanking her, unwilling to let her go.

'I'm just glad I found it,' the girl said, trying to extract herself from Marie's embrace, 'I have to get back, my boyfriend's waiting for me.'

'What's your name,' Marie called after her, as she went out through the door.

'Norma,' she shouted back, 'Norma Mercer.'

'Well, that's you isn't it,' Sonya insisted, 'you were Norma Mercer to your own name and I don't think there was another one around.'

Norma didn't answer.

'So, who was the boyfriend then,' Sonya laughed, 'was it dad or someone I don't know about?'

'Oh don't be so silly,' her mother scolded, 'and I don't know what that's about, I haven't read that bit.'

'Well I've read it from cover to cover,' Sonya told her, 'and believe me when you do you'll recognise a lot of people, and Edwina Mountjoy for one.'

'That poor girl,' Norma sighed, as Sonya began to relate how she'd bumped into Edwina over the years.

The first time had been on her last summer home from University. She'd gone for a walk along her much missed shore and had met her coming back from the lighthouse. Edwina, although she now went by Deena, had been glowing and flowing, dreamy and carefree in her maxi skirt and gypsy blouse and love beads. She was living in some kind of commune and devoting her life to painting. Edwina had invited her to come and see her work, and she'd promised that she would, but hadn't.

'You've never told me that before,' Norma said.

'Have I not?' Sonya replied.

And she had never told her mother about the next time she'd encountered Edwina and she would not tell her now. It was in the summer of 1992 and she, her husband and baby Ben, had come home for her parents' ruby wedding anniversary. At their request it was to be a small house party, a gathering of family and old friends. The evening before the party she'd gone to the local off-licence to buy some champagne and there had been an altercation at the counter. An old dishevelled woman was being refused service and in a stream of bad language and threats was eventually guided out of the door.

'It's a pity of her,' the assistant said, as she paid for the champagne, 'but she's barred. I mean we know she gets people to come in and buy drink for her, and there's not much we can do about that, but we don't serve her. She knows that.'

The woman was still there on the forecourt when she went outside – long greying hair hanging down around her in matted clumps, fingers scrabbing constantly at the sores around her mouth. A group of teenage boys, drinking cans of beer at the side of the shop, started to taunt her. One of them was pushed forward out of the huddle and strutted towards her with a five pound note.

'He'll shag you for it,' the others chanted, as he waved it at her.

'Shag dirty Deena,' he brayed, 'I'd pay a fiver not to friggin shag her.'

His friends roared in approval, their laughter spurring him on. The woman lunged at the five pound note as he danced around her, holding it up out of her reach. She caught hold of his jacket, pulling him hard towards her, and he tore away retreating back to the pack. She ran at them screaming and swearing and the boys ran off towards the promenade, shouting and hooting. One of them turned and threw a beer can. It landed at the woman's feet, the froth exploding out onto the pavement, and she picked it up and put it to her mouth, draining what was left.

It had been such a pitifully sad and cruel scene and even before she'd realised that Deena was Edwina she'd thought to intervene. She hadn't. She sat in the car for a while and watched until Edwina dragged herself slowly away across the railway lines. It was the last time she'd ever seen her.

'It's a shame Edwina didn't carry on with her painting,' Norma sighed, 'maybe if she'd persisted things would have turned out differently.'

'Oh really mum,' Sonya dismissed, 'Edwina was never going to put her mind anything. She always had too many issues.'

'Like what?' Norma asked.

'Well, I suppose it was a mother thing.'

'What does that mean?'

'I don't know,' Sonya diffused, 'I just remember she always hated her mother, seemed to blame her for everything.'

'Why is it always about mothers, why do they always get the blame?' Norma countered, 'I mean I know Teddy wasn't there for her but.......'

'Actually, now that you mention him, I did want to ask you about Mr Mountjoy,' Sonya interrupted, 'I know he died when Edwina was born but she never talked about him, so I just wondered what he was like, I mean was he like the Freddy character in the book.'

Norma sighed on the other end of the phone and wearily told her daughter that she'd been listening to this sort of thing all week and didn't really have an opinion on who was who between it all. Sonya sensed her mother's reluctance but coaxed it out of her. Teddy had been full of fun and mischief and very popular. He'd been a Mountjoy of course and a catch – what girl wouldn't have been impressed with his yacht and his Aston Martin and his money?

'And he was a good dancer,' her mother said, 'I remember him dancing at the Rinkha.'

'I suppose that's where Mrs Mountjoy met him then,' Sonya posed, 'isn't that where everyone met in those days?'

'Oh yes,' Norma confirmed, 'that's where I met your father and where Charles and Lillian met and I'm sure Bob and Betty and..........'

'........and Mr and Mrs Mountjoy,' Sonya diverted her from a trip down memory lane.

'Come to think of it,' Norma mused, 'I don't ever remember Maybelle dancing at the Rinkha.'

'So how did they meet then?'

'I'm really not sure.'

'Perhaps through work,' Sonya suggested, 'maybe like Marguerite, Maybelle married the boss' son?'

'Oh, I see where you're going with this,' Norma replied a little testily.

'I'm sorry, but it's just that I found that part of the book a little contrived,' Sonya explained, 'I mean it was virtually an arranged marriage. George Montgomery pushes Freddy into it and Marguerite goes along with it.'

'And what's your point?'

'That surely things like that didn't happen in the fifties and wouldn't have where Mr and Mrs Mountjoy were concerned.'

'Honestly Sonya, I'm surprised at you,' Norma sighed, 'I think you're confusing fiction with fact.'

'So the Mountjoys were a love match then?'

'I really have no idea.'

'But you must at least have been at their wedding,' Sonya persisted, 'everyone must have been, it must have been the Whitehaven wedding of the year.'

'Well thanks,' her mother said, 'your father and I got married that year too.'

'Ok, but a Mountjoy wedding, it must have been something. You must remember it.'

'I wasn't invited,' Norma stated, 'no one was. And it wasn't in Whitehaven it might have been in Belfast or somewhere.'

'Ah ha, I see.'

'See what?

'Well it's just that it fits with the book.'

'Does it?' Norma queried, 'because I wouldn't know. I didn't really get to know Maybelle until after Teddy's death.'

'I wanted to ask you about that, if he..........'

'Enough!'

'Sorry mum, just one last thing, I promise,' Sonya conceded, 'did Edwina and Mrs Mountjoy ever make it up.'

'Not that I know of,' her mother replied sadly.

To Norma's relief her grandson came onto the phone, the sweetness of his child's voice easing her irritation. He'd been picked for the school swimming team and was full of talk about it. She promised the next time he came to visit she would watch him swim in the sea.

'Can we go to Granny's next week?' she heard him ask, as Sonya came back on the line.

They said goodnight and as usual Norma advised her daughter to get to bed early. She still worried that she worked too hard.

'I'll try, she responded, 'but I've a feeling I'll be reading for a while. I've started it again.'

'Honestly Sonya,' her mother chided, 'I don't know why you would want to read that again.'

Norma hung up and lay back into the pillows. Sonya had not taken her mind off all of this and had not cheered her up at all – quite the contrary.

20

As Norma Lockhart and her daughter were talking on the phone Maybelle Mountjoy made a telephone call from her sitting room. He hadn't been difficult to find. There were few guesthouses left in the town and she'd supposed that a visitor might want a sea view from the promenade. The landlady confirmed that the gentleman whom she'd described was indeed a guest, although was presently out. She left her number for him to return her call and waited alone with her thoughts.

'What do you think this fellow's up to?' Bob McCrae had asked her, after he'd divulged his supposed origins.

She hadn't needed Bob to tell her who he was, but what he was up to, that she needed to know. For many years he had cast an uneasy shadow and she'd always half expected him to appear from somewhere out of the blue beyond, drawn by the belief of a fortune to be had. But why now? And according to Bob he'd already been here for a week – why hadn't he tried to contact her? They were questions that only he could answer but if he was seeking to make some claim on the Mountjoy estate, she had her answer for him. Whatever he wanted – his book, and she was sure he had written it – had rattled the skeletons around her and she had decided to finally lay the bones to rest.

Maybelle opened the safe and brought out an old manila envelope – 'To Mrs Maybelle Mountjoy, to be opened in the event of my death.' She had once known the letter by heart, but not for a long time now. She put on her glasses and read it again.

My dear Maybelle,

My solicitors have been instructed to deliver this letter to you in the event of my death, or at a time thereafter which they deem appropriate.

She scanned quickly through the first paragraphs of George Mountjoy's letter until she came to it.

...... the fact is there was a child.

The telephone rang. With an arrangement made, she opened a notepad and did what George would have told her to do – she made a plan. When she'd finished, a neat chronology of dates and places and events filled several pages. She read through it again and took the notepad and manila envelope through to the lounge, placing them on the small table beside her armchair. They might never need to be shown, that would depend on what transpired in the morning, but they were there, and she was ready.

Maybelle filled a hot water bottle, climbed the stairs, and walking along the landing opened the door of Edwina's old bedroom. She'd rarely been in the room since the last time her daughter had been home. It smelt musty. She opened the window to let in the night air and looked out across the town – an amphitheatre of house lights hugged around the bay. Ten years ago she'd found Edwina in one of those houses – the one run-down property in the neat row, let out by social services to the down and outs. She had found her the day after the Lockharts' ruby wedding anniversary, prompted to find her by something that had been said at the party.

It had been a quite pleasant evening. The expected old Whitehaven friends had been there and Sonya whom she hadn't seen for years had been an excellent hostess. She'd had a long and interesting conversation with Sonya's husband, a stockbroker, and he had generously given her some very good advice. During supper, Captains Donaldson and McCrae had reminisced, trying to outdo each other with their old sea stories, and afterwards she'd found herself in the lounge with the ladies. The conversation amongst the women had inevitably turned to children and family. Lillian Livermore had gone on rather too long about Doctor David, and not to be outdone the others had babbled on about their own children's success – lawyer this, engineer that, manager so and so. Rather bored, she had joined most of the husbands in the kitchen where the conversation had been slightly more stimulating. Making ready to go home she had thanked Bert and said it was lovely to see Sonya again.

'You know Maybelle,' he said, 'for all her success I'm happier that she's made a family for herself. I'd hate to think of her ending up alone and I'm glad she hasn't left it too late.'

His words had strangely stayed with her and had spurred her, in a mixture of emotions, to reach out to her own daughter. Edwina had been surprised to see her at her door but hadn't closed it in her face and she'd followed her into a cold, barely furnished room. After an awkward attempt at conversation she had said what she should have said many years before.

'Come home Edwina.'

As silent tears built into a sob and then a shuddering of weeping she'd gathered what was left of her daughter into her arms, nursing her and smoothing the last red strands of hair away from her face. She took Edwina home to The Mount that night – tried to feed her and helped her into bed. She lay down beside her and listened to her laboured breathing, moving with her as she twitched and turned. It wasn't too late. She would care for her and restore her with her own strength.

In the morning Edwina managed some breakfast, wandered around a little and then joined her in the veranda.

'This photograph,' she said, holding up a silver framed picture of her father at the helm of the Elizabeth Ann, 'it was on the desk in the sitting room, can I have it?'

'Of course, why don't you put it in your room?'

'What was he like?' she asked.

'Oh Edwina, it's such a long time ago,' Maybelle sighed, 'but your father was a gentleman, such a nice man and everyone loved him.'

'Did you love each other?'

'I've never really been sure what people mean by that, but we somehow suited each other, we were happy enough and then we had you.'

Edwina started to shiver – she wanted to go and despite her mother's protests, she insisted. Sitting in the car outside the run-down house Maybelle put her hand on her daughter's arm.

'I want you to come home for good,' she said.

'I just need today to get ready, come for me tomorrow.'

The next morning, as Maybelle got into the car to bring her daughter home, the window cleaner appeared in the driveway. Counting his money out of her purse she realised that two twenty pound notes were missing. Edwina must have taken them and it annoyed her that she hadn't just asked, but she wasn't going to let it upset the day.

She drove to the house and knocked on the door. There was no answer. She pushed her way between the bush and the front window, rubbing her hand over the grimy glass, trying to see in through the half pulled rags of curtains. She could see Edwina sitting up on the settee. She rapped loudly and rapped again but Edwina didn't move. She must be in a deep sleep, or maybe unconscious. Mind racing Maybelle went to the house next door for help – there was no one at home. She saw a man across the road on his doorstep and ran over to him, trying to explain that something was wrong. He brought her inside, trying to calm her, and asked her start again.

'I'll go and take a look,' he said, 'you stay here with my wife.'

Maybelle watched from their living room window and it wasn't long before she saw him coming back down the road.

'Marie,' he called his wife out into the hall.

'What's wrong Pat?'

'I think we better phone the police.'

It wasn't long after the police arrived that she learned, whilst being comforted on a stranger's settee, that her daughter was dead. And she learned later that Edwina had been found with an empty vodka bottle on the settee beside her and another opened and spilled on the floor. Chronic alcoholism had been given as the major contributing factor on the death certificate and she knew the money Edwina had stolen from her had been the last nail in the coffin of her daughter's thirty nine years.

A month after she buried Edwina, Maybelle opened the door to find a tall, strawberry-blond-haired woman, on the doorstep of The Mount.

'Mrs Mountjoy?'

'Yes.'

'Sorry to bother you, I'm Marie, Marie Devlin, I..... we met...'

'Of course,' Maybelle said recognising her, 'I'm sorry, I've been meaning to get in touch to thank you, please come in.'

'No, my husband's waiting for me in the car,' Marie politely refused, 'it's just that the Housing Executive have been clearing your daughter's house and Pat found this in the skip. We thought it was a personal thing that you should have.'

'That's very kind of you,' Maybelle smiled, as she was handed a small paper bag.

'Just be careful,' Marie warned her, 'I'm afraid the glass is broken.'

'Thank you,' Maybelle said, 'and also for your kindness before, both of you.'

'We're very sorry about your daughter.'

'Thank you.'

Maybelle went through to the sitting room and opened the bag – the photograph of Teddy which Edwina had asked for, glass shattered in the frame. She closed the bag around it again, opened the bottom drawer of the desk and put it away inside. She sat for a moment and then gathered the collection of family photographs from the desk top – George and Adelaide Mountjoy, George's father and mother, childhood portraits of Edwina – and placed them in the drawer with Teddy. Four generations of Mountjoys and all of them dead, nearly all of them dead.

As they drove down the driveway of The Mount, Marie turned and looked back up at the house.

'This is where Tess used to work,' she said.

'Who?' Pat asked.

'Tess, Tess O'Brien.'

'Now there's a blast from the past,' he raised his eyes, and turned the car out onto the road.

'She didn't think much of her you know,' she continued.

'Who?'

'For God's sake Pat,' she scolded, 'Tess didn't think much of Mrs Mountjoy, she told me about her once.'

'Aye well, I'm sure Mrs Mountjoy didn't think much of her,' he said.

'She seems like a very nice lady to me,' Marie went on, 'and don't say who, I mean Mrs Mountjoy.'

'Aye and God help her,' he sighed.

'I know, it's hard to believe that Edwina Skelton was her daughter,' Marie sighed too.

'She didn't have her sorrows to seek there, that's for sure,' he said.

21

He returned to the guest house in the evening to find the landlady waiting for him.

'There was a phone call for you, a local woman, and you're to phone her back,' Mrs Rogan said, handing him a piece of paper.

'Are you sure it was for me?' he queried. He hadn't given anyone a contact address.

'Well, I've only one red-haired Englishman staying with me and that would be you wouldn't it. Seems she doesn't know your name though?'

He caught a withering landlady look as Mrs Rogan folded her arms across a rather large expanse of bosom and barricaded the stairs in defence of her realm. He didn't need to be told that she ran a proper establishment and was more than up to the task of repelling any invader shenanigans. Dryly, she invited him to use the telephone on the hall stand and stayed firmly encamped.

'Thanks, but I'll call from my mobile,' he muttered, and squeezed past her up the stairs.

'You're leaving tomorrow aren't you?' she called up after him.

He turned and confirmed that he was.

'I'll make your bill up in the morning,' she shouted, as he rounded the bannister onto the second flight, 'and out by ten o'clock.'

In his room he sat down by the window and punched the unknown number into his mobile.

'Good evening,' a woman's voice said down the line, 'how kind of you to return my call. This is Maybelle Mountjoy speaking. I wonder if it would be convenient for you to call with me tomorrow morning.'

Taken aback he stuttered that would be fine.

'Shall we say ten o'clock then,' she invited, 'I believe you know where to find me.'

'Can I ask what it's.......?'

'Until tomorrow then,' she cut him off, and the line went dead.

He had not expected this. He took the half bottle of whiskey out of his pocket, poured a large measure into a tea cup, and opened the window before he lit his first cigarette. Why did she want to meet him and how did she know he was in town? Why had she assumed that he knew where she lived? Did she know who he was? He drank another whiskey, pondering his own questions, but whatever the answers he would not forgo the opportunity to meet Maybelle Mountjoy. By the time he finished the bottle he had decided on an approach. He would tread carefully, respectful of her vulnerability in old age, and try not to upset her as he gently unwound the thread of her memory, back to the beginnings of his life. He put the last dribble of whiskey from the bottle to his head. He thought about going to the off licence to buy another but realised he was too late. He could still make last orders in the pub but decided against it – no doubt Mrs Rogan would be keeping an eye on his comings and goings, watching out for him trying to slip the mystery woman into his room on his last night, bless her. Besides, he shouldn't have any more to drink, better to keep a fairly clear head for tomorrow. He went to bed thinking of the conversation to come and how he would guide Maybelle Mountjoy carefully through it.

True to her word Mrs Rogan presented him with the bill along with his breakfast. The fry had diminished – a sausage and rasher less – which amused him, but was more than adequate. He didn't really have an appetite, thinking of the visit to come and more nervously of the favour he would have to ask of his landlady. As Mrs Rogan cleared the table he asked if he could leave his bags with her and collect them later.

'There's someone I have to see this morning,' he told her.

'No doubt,' her nose wrinkled, but she agreed to his request.

At half-past nine, with his baggage stored behind the reception desk, he walked along the promenade, turned up Marine Parade and along to the Recreation grounds. He stopped and smoked a cigarette and then another, before starting up the avenue. At five to ten he walked through the gates of The Mount and up the driveway. He rang the doorbell and waited.

She wasn't quite the little old lady he'd imagined. Elderly, yes, but tall and straight and trim – the creases of her grey twill trousers immaculately pressed, the white silk blouse buttoned down the front with little squares of mother of pearl and pearls around her neck. The snow white hair was styled short around her ears but softly waved. The face, under the highly defined cheek bones was lined with age but the dark grey eyes, when she looked at him, were bright and clear.

'Good morning,' she greeted, 'do come in.'

He followed her through the cool marble vestibule, past the sweep of the staircase, and into the lounge.

'It's such a lovely morning I thought we might take tea on the patio,' she said, leading him out through the veranda and into the garden.

The table had already been laid – Royal Worcester cups, saucers and side plates, and a cake stand filled with pastries. Maybelle Mountjoy lifted the teapot and poured.

'Thank you for inviting me,' he said, 'I wasn't sure that you would want to ....'

'Milk?' she asked, and poured some into his cup as he nodded.

'I realise,' he continued, 'that this might be difficult for......'

'Sugar?' she asked, lifting a cube from the bowl with a little pair of silver tongs. He declined as she milked her own cup.

'Now do tell me, have you been enjoying your time in Whitehaven?' she enquired.

Sipping his tea he realised it was better to do it this way – give her time, start with the pleasantries and lead gently in. He told her about his walks along the shore and how he'd enjoyed them.

'It is quite remarkable,' she commented, 'the Victorians built the Blackhead path and walked it, and visitors to the town can still enjoy it today.'

'I was wondering,' he ventured, 'if you might remember the O'Brien family. I believe they worked here at one time?'

'Please do help yourself,' she invited, gesturing towards the cake stand, 'the macaroons are wonderful, an old family favourite.'

He lifted a macaroon and put it on his plate.

'Now, let me think, O'Brien,' Maybelle pondered, 'and they worked in Whitehaven?'

'Well yes, but actually here in this house.'

'I'm not sure,' she said, taking a macaroon from the stand, 'so many people have come and gone over the years.'

'There was Deirdre O'Brien,' he prompted, 'red-haired and quite tall.'

'No, I'm afraid that doesn't ring any immediate bells,' she replied, biting into the meringue and wiping a trace of cream from her mouth with a linen napkin, 'but I presume you know her?'

'My mother,' he stated.

'I see.'

'There was also my aunt Theresa,' he persisted, 'Tess, Tess O'Brien, I understand she was the housekeeper here at one time.'

'Oh dear, age is a terrible thing,' she paused, 'the memory isn't what it was, but Tess O'Brien, I think I do remember her.'

He had guided her towards it and would take her forward.

'Let me top up your tea,' Maybelle said, re-filling his cup, 'so now Tess, your aunt didn't you say, what ever became of her?'

Having been asked he could only respond. Aunt Theresa had left Whitehaven in the early fifties to work in Claridge's Hotel in London. A few years later he and his mother had also moved to London but he hadn't known her then. Growing up her name had never been mention to him or to his half-brothers and sisters. It was only in his aunt's widowhood that they'd found each other and formed a relationship.

'So she married?'

'Yes, but well into her forties,' he told her, 'a rich businessman who had dealings with the hotel.'

'I presume there were no children, I mean with your aunt having married later in life?'

'Only me,' he replied, meeting her unflinching eyes, 'actually I was her.....

......favourite,' Maybelle cut in, 'she favoured you above the others and you got to know her.'

'Yes,' he agreed, checking himself. He was being too hasty. It was too soon to present her with a stark reality and he would learn more if he allowed it to come from her.

He talked instead of visits to his aunt's riverside house in Henley-on-Thames and how she'd entertained him with her stories about the grand people she'd met at Claridge's – the Royal family, the film stars and the American magnates.

'She could tell a story,' he confided.

'Indeed.'

She'd also talked of her time at the Royal Hotel and in The Mount, of living in Seaview Cottage, and of the people she'd known in Whitehaven.

'That was towards the end though,' he divulged, 'she passed away three years ago.'

'Oh.'

'I was hoping you might be able to tell me more about her life in.......'

'It's getting a little chilly,' Maybelle shivered, rubbing her hands up the sleeves of her blouse as a bank of cloud drifted across the sun, 'shall we go inside Mr O'Brien.'

'Actually, my name's not O'Brien, its Callahan,' he explained, 'Kevin Callahan. I took my step-father's name.'

'Well, let's go in.'

He followed her through the veranda and into lounge, 'If you'll excuse me for a moment,' she said, returning with a tray, carefully balancing a bottle of Blackbush whiskey, glasses and an ashtray.

'The sun is over the yard arm somewhere in the world I do believe,' she smiled, setting it down on the coffee table, 'would you like to do the honours?'

He poured for them and brought the heavy crystal tumbler to his mouth, the whiskey warm and smooth.

'Please smoke if you want to,' she offered, setting the ashtray in front of him.

He thanked her and brought a packet of cigarettes out of his pocket.

'As I was saying, I'd be very interested to hear about my aunt's life here, just to fill in the gaps.'

'And I'd be very interested,' Maybelle said, settling into her armchair, 'to hear all about this book of yours.'

'I've been caught on then,' he sucked in his breath, and drained the whiskey from his glass.

'Indeed you have Mr O'Brien, sorry, Mr Callahan, oh dear, and then you write under a different name again, I can't quite keep up.'

'Please just call me Kevin, it's less complicated.'

Maybelle poured him another whiskey as he lit a cigarette.

'Now, of course you couldn't possibly know that I have an interest in literature,' she confided, 'so do tell me about your book, tell me how you came to write it?'

He'd always wanted to write but it had taken him a long time to find his way to it, just with the demands of work and the distractions of life in general. Then, about five years ago, Aunt Tess had unexpectedly contacted him. When she died, to his utter surprise, she left him everything – the house, a portfolio of shares, investments and capital.

'Which I presume she inherited from her husband?'

'Well yes, but I believe she also at some time had money of her own.'

The unexpected windfall had allowed him to retire and pursue his dream of writing a book.

'And you have achieved it,' Maybelle congratulated, pouring him another whiskey, 'but I'm interested to know where you start creatively, where does the idea come from?'

Tess' recollections of her young life in Whitehaven, he revealed, had inspired him – he'd felt there was a story in it and it had started to flow from there. And he'd also had his own childhood memories to work from.

'I was seven when I left Whitehaven,' he said, 'so I remember playing on the shore and the sweet shop and some other places in the town.'

'Good childhood memories,' Maybelle smiled.

'Yes,' he nodded, 'but I wish I remember living in Seaview Cottage. I was too young but Tess described it to me. Do you remember me living there?' he asked.

'I don't.'

'I asked my mother about it, about why we left there to live in a boarding house before we moved away, but she never wanted talk about anything to do with here.'

'And your mother, is she still.......?'

'Oh yes, Deirdre's still in the land of the living, still in the same house on the same awful council estate. I have more than the means to help her but she won't let me.'

'Why on earth not?'

'That's a good question,' he sighed, revealing how he'd told her of his inheritance and of his willingness to provide for her.

'I won't take a penny piece of her money or anything else,' Deirdre had spat at him when he'd offered to move her to a better place or bring her to live with him in Henley-on-Thames. 'She might have left it all to you now Kevin, in her guilt,' she'd said, 'but better she'd acknowledged you in this life and not stolen away what was provided for you.' He hadn't understood what she'd meant and had pushed her and pushed her until it had all come out in a long sour tale. That's when he'd learned that Tess, not Deirdre, was his mother and whoever his father was, money had been provided for his future but Tess has used it for herself.

'My goodness,' Maybelle said, 'an extraordinary story, but in a way the beginnings of your book.'

'True,' he agreed, 'and I suppose writing it has been quite catar.. cahar....'

'Cathartic,' she said, and laughed.

'Yes, cathartic,' he got his tongue around it, and laughed with her, taking a mouthful of whiskey and lighting another cigarette, 'but there's always still the one question, who was my father? He must have cared about me if he provided money for me.'

'If you'll just excuse me for one moment,' Maybelle apologised, lifting the ashtray from the coffee table and going out of the lounge door.

He put his hand into his jacket pocket and brought out an old newspaper clipping – a picture of a young man at the helm of a yacht. When she came back he would show it to her and ask – somehow he would just ask was this man, Teddy Mountjoy, my father? He drained the whiskey and steeling himself, poured another.

In the kitchen, Maybelle emptied the ashtray into the bin. She'd learned what she needed to know. Even without the future proceeds of his unimaginative little upstairs-downstairs novel, he was a man of quite considerable means. He was not here to make some financial claim on the Mountjoy estate and anyhow she'd legally attended to that prospect long ago when everything had been left in her hands. Theresa O'Brien had been paid a very generous lump sum for her child, whatever she chose to do with it. The world of course had changed – gratefully accepted payments of the past no longer enough to deny in law the biological molecules of a claim to heritage. And as he'd talked she'd realised that's what he was – a soul in search of a father and a legitimate name, a name which he hoped to find in her house.

'Mrs Mountjoy,' he said, fiddling with his collar, as she came back into the lounge, 'I have a photograph here from an old newspaper. I found it when I was going through Tess' papers.'

'It's a task isn't it,' she sympathised 'I've recently been going through a lot of old family papers myself and it's quite amazing what's accumulated over a lifetime.'

'It is,' he agreed, handing her the clipping.

'My goodness,' she said, putting on her glasses and studying it, 'that's my husband, Teddy.'

'I thought so,' he said, his head swimming as he glanced at her, 'Tess talked about him and about his parents, about of all of you really.'

'Did she?'

'And it's just when I found the picture, I'm sorry, but I thought I looked like him, I just wondered if........'

'I'm afraid I can't see any great likeness,' she stopped him, 'but I've never been particularly good with faces.'

'Mrs Mountjoy,' he said, unable took at her, 'I would hate to upset you but I have to ask if the man in this picture was my father?'

'Is that what Tess O'Brien told you?'

'No,' he said, trying to meet her eyes, 'it's just the way she talked about him and about the family, she seemed to feel connected in some way and then the photograph, I suppose I........'

'...... put two and two together,' she interjected.

'Maybe I did and I'm sorry if this is unpleasant.'

'Well, it's not a question that anyone would welcome,' she stated calmly, 'but I might be able to help.'

'Can you?' he asked, his eyes starting to mist.

'Now tell me when you were born.'

'1951, August 1951.'

'Let me see,' she said, lifting the notepad from the table, 'because as I said I've recently been going over some old papers, working on a family history to tell you the truth, not that it would ever be published, just a small project to keep me occupied, just charting events and travels and such.'

Maybelle flipped through the pages of her notepad.

'Ah, here it is, there's quite a lot, but the relevant date would be September the 5th 1950.'

'Sorry?' he tried to focus.

'You see, according to my notes,' she continued, 'on that date Teddy left for England, and then went on to travel in France and Italy. He didn't return home until the summer of 1951.'

'Again I'm sorry but what does that mean?'

'It means, if you'll excuse me for being indelicate, that at the time you were conceived my husband was not in the country.'

He drew in a breath, 'So he couldn't have been my father.'

'No,' she shook her head, 'and not I suppose the ending you were hoping for.'

'No,' he agreed, wiping his hand across his eyes.

'But just think what has come out of it all. You've written your book, something you've always wanted to do, and it's been a success.'

'Yes, but.....'

'No buts, Mr O'Brien, you have a talent, an enviable talent for make-believe.'

'Thank you,' he managed, as his lungs began to rasp and cough.

'Is that the time already,' Maybelle stood up, looking at the clock, 'I'm terribly sorry but I have an appointment.'

He got up from the chair too quickly, his head light as he followed her out into the vestibule.

'I hope I haven't upset you in any way,' he said on the doorstep.

'There was nothing you could have upset me about,' she replied.

'Perhaps we could keep in touch?' he asked, stumbling down the steps onto the driveway.

'Perhaps,' she said, closing the door of The Mount.

Maybelle Mountjoy returned to the lounge, retrieved the notepad and manila envelope, and went through to the dining room. She tore the written pages out of the pad and threw them into the fireplace. She may have miscopied some of the dates from the family papers but they had served her purpose in convincing him that Teddy Mountjoy was not his father. She took the letter out of the manila envelope, reached for the box of matches behind the coal scuttle and lit the corner of the first page of George Mountjoy's letter, reading it for the last time as the paragraphs burned away.

.......there was a child. The child is mine. As I hope you know, I am not a man who has ever indulged in affairs and can make no excuse, other than it was a lonely man's ill-judged folly. In some small defence I was fond of her but made her no promises and I realised only too late that she did have expectations and indeed ambitions. She had set her sights on marriage and I will spare you the details of how she thought Adelaide could be put away. When I tried to bring things to an end, suffice it say, she caught me out. I arranged for her to go away and have the baby and brought them back here, the boy supposedly her sister's. It might have been the wrong thing to do but I couldn't abandon all responsibility.

Maybelle dropped the page into the fireplace and lit the corner of the next.

.......it was the greatest shock when Teddy expressed his intention to marry her. Perhaps now you can

understand that I could never have allowed it. But it's worked out for the best hasn't it? You and Teddy are happy enough together aren't you?

Now that you are expecting my grandchild I find I must express the truth and I will resolve the fact that Miss O'Brien is still in my employ. That would be only fair to you. I hope that you will never be put in a position to have to use any of what I have confided in you.

Forgive me Maybelle and if you do ever receive this letter, I rest assured that I have left everything and the future of the family in the safest and most trusted of hands.

Yours respectfully and affectionately,
George Mountjoy.

Maybelle let the page fall from her hand and watched as the letter burnt away to a ribbon of ash. George Mountjoy's confession, when she'd received it all those ago, had come as a shock – she'd believed that Teddy was the boy's father for Mrs Green had told her so. It would have made no difference to her decision to dismiss Theresa O'Brien. In fact, it would have strengthened her resolve. She could not have allowed George's son, although illegitimate, to take any kind of precedence over Edwina. It had all been left in her hands, she had dealt with it then and she had dealt with it today. Had she been wrong not to tell him who his father was? She didn't believe so and she had not lied to him. He had asked about Teddy but about no other. Besides, she owed him nothing. He had chosen to wash the dirty family linen in public and that was unforgivable.

Maybelle Mountjoy scrapped the remnants of ash down through the grate with the poker and went through to the veranda. The sun had come out again from behind the clouds, bathing the bay in light. She sat down in her chair and folded the newspaper to the cryptic crossword. The rest of her afternoon was taken care of.

Epilogue

Maybelle Mountjoy died on Thursday the 14th of April 2005, two years after she had invited Kevin O'Brien to visit her in The Mount. Wilma, having taken afternoon tea through to the veranda, discovered that she had slipped peacefully away. She looked just like herself, eyes closed and face turned out towards the sea and the Copeland Islands. Beside her on the table, the Daily Telegraph cryptic crossword had been completed.

Maybelle was buried from the Presbyterian Church, the funeral attended by her old Whitehaven contemporaries – Norma Lockhart, the McCraes and the Livermores amongst others. Wilma found herself sitting beside Dilys Bishop and gave no explanation, when asked, if she had also been a friend of the family. The older weaker voices amongst them sang 'Abide with Me', as they had for her husband over fifty year before, and they strained through 'Oh God Our Help in Ages Past', the organ as usual pitched too high for them. Maybelle's coffin was not borne out of the church or carried on their shoulders over King's Bridge – they were too old to carry her. She was wheeled respectfully down the aisle and out into the hearse and some of them drove after it to the cemetery, to see her laid to rest with Teddy and Edwina. They talked of her that afternoon when they returned home – of what they remembered of her, of her joys and sorrows in life, and of the woman she had been.

In accordance with her will Wilma received a bequest of nine thousand pounds, each year of her dedicated service acknowledged, and the choice of any household goods that she wished to take. The remainder of the very substantial Mountjoy estate, including The Mount, was bequeathed to Professor Helen Guildersleeve, of Ithaca, New York State.

The Mount surprised Helen when she and her husband drove up the driveway in their hire car on their first visit to Northern Ireland. She had romantically imagined a small Irish cottage, not the imposing edifice which loomed in front of them – Maybelle had been exceedingly humble in her correspondence. By arrangement, Wilma met them on the doorstep, settled them in, and left her phone number in case they needed help with anything.

On her first morning Helen walked through the grand old rooms and down through the grounds. She recognised some of the features of the garden which Maybelle had described in her letters, and sat down under the apple tree trying to take it all in.

'Breakfast,' Paul shouted from the patio, 'it'll have to be tea. I can't find coffee in this house.'

Over tea they again discussed the previous plans for her inheritance – a holiday home for them, for their sons and their families, and possibly rentals in between. Now it didn't seem feasible. It was a property which would require considerable maintenance and upkeep which would be difficult to do from a distance. In the afternoon they took a walk along the top cliff path to the lighthouse, spiralled down the steps, along past the caves, and onto the shore. Maybelle had written about it, had described it quite poetically, but the outstanding natural beauty of the scenery almost took Helen's breath away. They walked on along towards the town and onto the promenade and she tried to pick out her father's house in the row, trying to imagine a life that Jack McBraid had rarely talked about, a life before she'd known him. They called into the Whitecliff Inn for a drink and the teenage barmaid asked if she was from America.

'I thought so,' the girl said, 'by your accent.'

She told her she was related to the Mountjoy family.

'Never heard of them,' the girl shrugged.

As they fell into bed that night, under the crisp linen sheets, she told Paul that she wanted to keep the house.

'How can we give this up,' she said, 'such a place, in such a magnificent place?'

When she woke, she'd come around to what he'd said on the pillow before she'd fallen asleep – that she was being sentimental and would think better of it in the morning. After breakfast she telephoned Wilma who gave them directions to the local realtor's office and also kindly agreed to meet them in The Mount in the afternoon. She was grateful when Wilma arrived and took charge, and together they started to clear drawers and closets sorting piles to be kept and piles for donations and recycling.

'I'm not sure where to put these,' Helen said, coming out of Maybelle's dressing room and dropping an armful of silk gowns and fur coats onto the bed.

'Perfect for the local theatre group,' Wilma told her, 'they're always looking for costumes for the Christmas pantomime.'

Three weeks of sorting and clearing ensued, with Wilma when she could spare the time, and with a professional company having been called in to box up the furniture and items which Helen wanted shipped to America. Amongst the items was the portrait of Adelaide Mountjoy which had hung above the mantelpiece since it was painted in 1930. The Mountjoy pearls and the other pieces of good jewellery were carried safely aboard the departing aircraft at Belfast International Airport, in Helen's hand luggage. Her letters to Maybelle, over their thirty years of correspondence, were lovingly stowed in her suitcase in the hold. The day before the Guildersleeves flew home they took Wilma out for lunch and afterwards visited the cemetery. As Helen respectfully laid her flowers on Maybelle's grave Wilma's eye was caught by a weathered granite headstone not to too far away. In Loving Memory of William Green, it read, and below that Susanna Green – 1887 to 1969. Wilma wished she had had flowers to put on it.

Three months after Helen's visit The Mount was sold to a young outsider professional couple, with interests in property development. Their application to have the house demolished and exclusive apartments built on the site is currently with the planning division of the local council. Wilma has seen the application and the objections from old Whitehaven. She is not worried. She knows the ghosts who walk The Mount and she knows that now, they also have Mrs M to contend with.

One month after Maybelle's death, Kevin O'Brien published his second novel – 'Darkhaven'. He hopes that Mrs Mountjoy got around to reading the advanced copy which he posted to her. As in his professional life, his personal life has also become more fulfilling. He has married and recently celebrated the birth of his first child, a son. He has abandoned the search for his own biological father, content, that when he looks into Freddy's bright hazel eyes, that they will know each other. When Freddy is older he intends to bring him to Whitehaven on holiday, play with him in the rock pools on the shore, and maybe help the little King of his castle to climb the Wren's Eggs.

Captain Robert McCrae still walks along the shore, if not so often – it's not quite the same since old Skipper had to be put down. They had their walks and kept their company and their secrets. He still keeps company with the Thursday Club in the Whitecliff Inn but it too has suffered its losses, a couple of his old friends having died and others not in good health. Betty still gets annoyed when he's 'delayed' and late home for lunch, but he doesn't delay so much anymore. Betty continues to go to art club and still enjoys reading. She has just started 'Darkhaven' and although she isn't finding it such a page turner as 'The Montgomerys of The Mount', is struggling on with it. She has yet to join the book club, although Dilys continues to invite.

Dilys Bishop has finally come into her prime in Whitehaven, appointed to president of various clubs and associations, as other old residents have lost interest or died. She still believes she has a book to write but is currently much too busy with other things. The other things take her mind off her daughter, the fond after-thought, currently undergoing treatment for alcohol addiction in a rehab clinic in England. She blames the lecturer for it, for breaking up the home, for depriving her daughter of stable foundations and for bringing them to this. Juliette, she has recently learned, has left the lecturer for a younger man but he has a carer who comes in to assist with feeding and toiletry functions. Dilys, all things considered, feels that she has made a lucky escape.

Norma Lockhart is looking forward to her grandson visiting in the summer, the first time he will come on his own. Ben has asked to be entered into the annual long distance swim, from the yacht club to the Hailcock Rock, and is confident he will win. She shudders a little at the thought of it but has to accept that the young are fearless, undaunted and unaffected by age. She had to take Lillian home again this morning when she found her wandering in the avenue. Poor Charlie, the way Lillian screams when he opens the door and she begs not to be left with that strange man. It comforts her that Wilma now goes to them a couple of times a week and at least takes care of the house.

Marie Devlin still goes to her weekly art club, contributes to the annual exhibition, and has sold several more pieces of her work. She finds herself thinking more and more often of the old days in the Royal Hotel and nights spent dancing with Pat in the Rinkha ballroom. She remembers those times with fondness and sometimes even talks to Geraldine about the good times she had with her old friend Tess O'Brien when they were young. She has, as Pat would have told her do, risen above it.

Old Whitehaven grows older and year by year memories of the old town and of things past disappear with them into the grave, another chapter closed. The Blackhead Path, however, remains open and the local council under increasing pressure has invested some money, if not enough, towards its upkeep. It is walked daily by a new generation of residents and visitors –and they are free, in all of its glory, to forge memories of their own.

Lightning Source UK Ltd.
Milton Keynes UK
UKOW02f1930080515

251189UK00003B/146/P